LATIN COURSE FOR SCHOOLS

Part III

LATIN COURSE FOR SCHOOLS

Part III

by
L. A. WILDING, M.A.

Senior Classical Master, Dragon School, Oxford
Late Assistant Master, St. Edward's School
Formerly Scholar of Oriel College, Oxford

DUCKWORTH

This impression 2001
First Duckworth edition 1996
First published by
Faber & Faber Ltd. in 1953

Gerald Duckworth & Co. Ltd.
61 Frith Street, London W1D 3JL
Tel: 020 7434 4242
Fax: 020 7434 4420
Email: inquiries@duckworth-publishers.co.uk
www.ducknet.co.uk

A catalogue record for this book is available
from the British Library

ISBN 0 7156 2676 0

Preface

The aim of Part III has been to cover all the remaining common constructions not dealt with in Parts I and II; to set out sentences and passages, mainly in original Latin, which will illustrate the use of these constructions, and to provide exercises upon them for practice in composition. Vocabularies have been provided, but there is no summary of grammar; it is assumed that by this stage most teachers will prefer that their pupils should use, when necessary, a separate Latin Grammar.

The number of sentences is purposely large; a good supply of them is helpful in oral class-work and also for revision purposes. Their subject-matter is generally related to that of continuous passages that have already occurred in the course; this gives them, it is hoped, more meaning and point than is sometimes found in isolated sentences; furthermore, vocabulary and syntax, through repetition, become rooted in the mind more easily.

No verse is included; to have embarked upon this would have made the book very large; the constructions to be found in Latin poetry are generally simpler than those in Latin prose, and a start with Ovid and Virgil may well be made before the end of Part III is reached.

The chief problem has been to find continuous passages of classical Latin which provided examples of the constructions covered by each successive chapter and yet did not contain other unfamiliar constructions; at the same time the matter of the passages had to be sufficiently interesting to warrant their inclusion; prolonged search brought to light representative passages from Cicero, Caesar, Livy, and Pliny, which seem to fulfil these conditions. There has been very little alteration of the original Latin text, except by way of omission, occasionally to avoid a still unfamiliar construction, but more often for the sake of the unity of a passage.

The exercises in Latin Prose composition are again founded on the principle of re-translation, but a little more latitude is

7

Preface

taken in the English form, so that the pupil may have more exercise in thought as well as in Latin; in this way the 'proses' may be said to point the way to the writing of harder Latin Prose; on this art good manuals have been published which still hold their own.

A study of the Contents indicates the scope of the book. It is written primarily for the teaching of Latin, rather than as a guide for the passing of particular examinations; however, to anticipate questions on this point, it may be claimed that the book should be of considerable use to candidates for the Ordinary and Advanced levels of the General Certificate Examination, Public School scholarships, and University and College entrance examinations.

For the information of those who have not used this course before, it should be added that the ground covered by Part II includes the main uses of the Participles, Indirect Statement, simple uses of the Independent Subjunctive, Consecutive Clauses, Final Clauses, Indirect Commands and Petitions, and Indirect Questions.

I am again most grateful to Mr. J. B. Poynton, of Winchester College, and to Mr. R. St. J. Yates, of the Dragon School, both for their constructive suggestions and for their corrections, and once more to Mr. Poynton for his help with the proofs; and I thank both Messrs. Faber and Faber and a number of schools for encouraging me to complete this course.

Oxford, 1953

Long quantities in the main text are occasionally marked for the purpose of immediate guidance; they are marked more fully in the vocabularies.

It is felt that the explanation of variant grammatical forms, e.g. **curasse** *for* **curavisse,** *should at this stage be left to the teacher.*

Contents

10   *Contents*

Contents

MAPS

Chapter 1
Relatives and Correlatives

---

(1) Ei qui in dextro cornu instructi erant, hostes exspectabant.
Those on the right wing were waiting for the enemy.

Literally, it is *those who had been drawn up on the right wing*, etc., but we may translate it quite naturally as above. In English we often use an Adjectival Phrase containing a Preposition to describe a Noun or Pronoun (e.g. *those on the right wing*), which we may call the *man-in-the-moon* construction; this must be avoided in Latin.

If a Preposition is used in Latin, it must be introduced by a **Verb,** and this means that a **Relative** (i.e. Adjectival) **Clause** must often be used where we would use an Adjectival Phrase. Thus, the *man in the moon* becomes **is qui in luna habitat;** *the road to the city,* **via quae fert ad urbem.**

(2) Demonstrative Pronouns and Pronominal Adjectives are often answered by corresponding Relative words, and the pairs that correspond with each other are known as **Correlatives:**

is quī, *he who.*	**tantus, quantus,** *as big as.*
īdem, quī, *the same as.*	**tantum, quantum** (with Gen.), *as much as, such a large amount as.*
tālis, quālis, *such as.*	**tot, quot,** *as many as.*

Note.—**Tantus exercitus** is the equivalent of *such a big army.*

Non est talis, qualem eum esse dixisti.
He is not the kind of man you said he was.

Eadem dixi, quae tu.
I said the same as you.

Tantas copias (tot naves) coegit, quantas potuit.
He collected as large forces (as many ships) as he could.

15

Mihi non est tantum pecuniae quantum Crasso.
I have not as much money as Crassus.

Note.—**Talis** means *such* in the sense of *of such a kind*; **tantus** can mean *such* in our sense of *so big*, e.g. **tantum periculum. Tantus,** and not **tot,** is used with **copiae** for *so many*.

Is, ea, id as Antecedents

Is, ea, id are often omitted as Antecedents in the Nom. and Acc. Cases, when they would be in the same Case as the Relative Pronoun:

Bis dat qui cito dat.
He gives twice who gives quickly.

Note.—**Is qui** or simply **qui** is the Latin for *the man who.*

Quos secum habebat, praemisit.
He sent forward the men he had with him.

Quae audiverunt, ad legatos deferunt.
They reported what they heard to the commanders.

It will be noticed that the form **quae** (neut. pl.) will often be the Latin for *what* not only in Indirect Questions, but also in Relative Clauses; in the sing., however, we must be careful to differentiate between **id quod** (Relative) and **quid** (Interrogative): **id quod dixisti est verum,** *what you said is true;* **nescio quid dixeris,** *I don't know what you said.*

Apart from the above usages, the normal practice is to express **is, ea, id** as the Antecedent:

Romani eos qui fugerant persequebantur.
The Romans were pursuing those who had fled.
   (**eos** and **qui** being in different Cases)

Laudatis eis qui negotio praefuerant, quid fieri velit ostendit.
After praising those who had been in charge of the business, he showed them what he wanted to be done.

EXERCISE 1.
1. Ei qui in muro erant, saxa deiciebant.
2. In hoc proelio non tantus exercitus erat Romanis, quantus Hannibali.
3. Ille tot bella gessit quot ceteri legerunt.
4. Scipio eandem visebat urbem, quam Hannibal.
5. Talis est liber quem misisti qualem speravi.
6. Quae ipse audiveris, statim ad me scribe.
7. Tantae erant nives, quantas Poeni non exspectaverant.
8. Qui hoc fecit dignus est praemio.
9. Caesari erat tantum audaciae, quantum scientiae.
10. Britanni impetum fecerunt in eos qui pro castris collocati erant.

EXERCISE 2.
1. The scout on the hill could see the enemy.
2. I am reading the same book as you.
3. Have we as many cavalry as the enemy?
4. The man who has many friends is happy.
5. What you have done is very useful to the state.
6. The road to Rome is long.
7. Few men have as much wisdom as Socrates.
8. Those whom Caesar sent forward crossed the river.
9. Those whom he captured, he soon set free.
10. This victory was such as the Romans had never hoped for.

Relative Clause preceding Main Clause

It will by now have been noticed that the Relative Clause is often placed first, so that the emphasis falls on the Main Clause containing the Demonstrative Pronoun:

Quos laborantes conspexerat, his subsidia submittebat.
Whatever men he saw in trouble, to these he sent up reserves.

Sometimes, when the Antecedent and the Relative Pronoun are both in the Nom. or in the Acc., we find the Antecedent placed inside the Relative Clause:

Quos tribunos militum circum se habebat se sequi iubet.
He ordered the military tribunes he had with him to follow him.

Note.—Very often a Present Participle in the Oblique Cases will be translated by a Relative Clause in English, and vice versa:

Caesar timentes confirmat.
Caesar encouraged those who were afraid.

Superlatives and Numerals in Relative Clause

Superlatives and Adjectives denoting Number or Amount are placed inside the Relative Clause, and not with the Antecedent as in English:

Urbem spectabat, quam pulcherrimam invenerat.
He was looking at the most beautiful city he had come across.

Cum equitibus, qui pauci supererant, profectus est.
He set out with the few cavalry who were left.

Id quod in Apposition

Id quod (or **quae res**), *a thing that, a happening that,* is often found introducing a clause which is in Apposition to the previous sentence:

Multae naves tempestate erant fractae, id quod Caesar non providerat.
Many ships had been broken by the storm, an event that Caesar had not foreseen.

Adverbial Correlatives

Demonstrative Adverbs of Place are answered by corresponding Relative Adverbs (according to the sense):

ibi, ubi, *in the place where.*	**eā, quā,** *by the same way as.*
inde, unde, *from where.*	**tam . . . , quam** (with Adj. or
eo or **illūc, quo,** *to the*	Advb.), *as . . . as.*
place to which.	**totiēs, quotiēs,** *as often as.*

Note.—**Tam altus murus** is the equivalent of the English *such a high wall.*

Eo se receperunt, unde egressi erant.
They retreated to the place from which they had started.

Tam stultus est quam dives.
He is as foolish as he is rich.

EXERCISE 3.
  1. Nihil de Britannia mercatoribus praeter eas regiones quae sunt contra Galliam notum est.
  2. Caesar easdem copias, quas ante, ut naves defenderent, reliquit.
  3. Falsa dicit, qui hoc affirmat.
  4. Haec lex non erat talis, qualem Romani probabant.
  5. Qui flumen petiverunt, ab hostibus oppressi sunt.
  6. Tot naves convenerunt, quot Caesar iusserat.
  7. Caesar eodem unde redierat proficiscitur.
  8. Caesar in Gallia reliquit legatum, quem fidissimum habebat.
  9. Hannibal non tantas copias, quantas speraverat, accepit.
  10. Qui Scipionem bello superaverit, ante omnes alios imperatores ponetur.
  11. Caesar quae audiverat, vera esse perspicit.
  12. Quos amicos iam habes, fidissimos esse invenies.
  13. Toties Romani imperatori gratias egerunt, quoties vicit.
  14. Non tam praeclarum est scire linguam Latinam, quam turpe nescire.
  15. Poeni Hannibalem revocaverunt, id quod ipse timuerat.
  16. Helvetiis non erat tantum agri, quantum cupiebant.

EXERCISE 4.
  1. Caesar himself saw the same things as he had found out by despatches.
  2. The ships in the harbour were now ready.
  3. Sixty ships, unable to hold their course, had returned to the place from which they had started.
  4. Caesar disembarked his troops in the place where he knew that the landing was easy.

5. The commander sent forward the few cavalry that he had.
6. Caesar left behind as many forces as he thought to be enough.
7. What Horatius did for his country will always be praised.
8. The daring of Hannibal was such as the Romans had never expected.
9. The Romans were terrified by the elephants, a thing that the enemy had hoped for.
10. Never had any commander conquered so many armies as Alexander.
11. The soldiers collected as much corn as they had been ordered.
12. Many of the men in Hannibal's army had not seen the snow before.
13. The enemy fought as bravely as our men.
14. Send the bravest soldiers you have.
15. The crowd of people waiting was such as I had never seen.
16. The man who prepares himself today will be safe tomorrow.

EXERCISE 5.

THE TRICKING OF THE TREVERI

The Trēveri, a tribe bordering on the Rhine, had caused considerable difficulty to Caesar, more particularly because they were frequently in league with German tribes on both sides of the river. On one occasion, in 53 B.C., the Treveri were daily expecting German reinforcements, and Labiēnus, Caesar's second-in-command, who was guarding the baggage of the whole army, spread a rumour that he was striking camp and retiring through fear of defeat.

Vix agmen novissimum extra munitiones processerat, cum Galli cohortati inter se, ne speratam praedam ex manibus dimitterent, flumen transire et iniquo loco committere proelium non dubitant; affirmant enim longum esse perterritis Romanis Germanorum auxilium exspectare, neque suam pati dignitatem ut tantis copiis tam exiguam manum praesertim

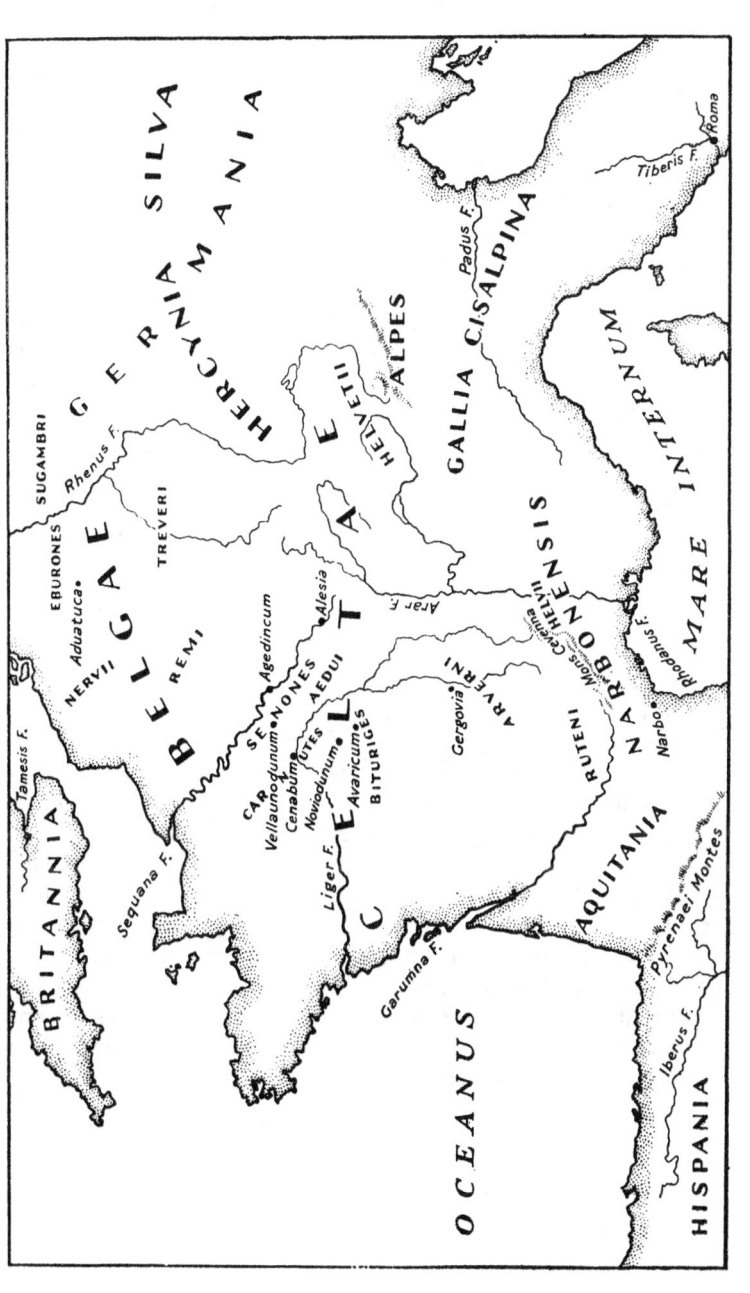

fugientem atque impeditam adoriri non audeant. Quae fore suspicatus Labienus, ut omnes citra flumen eliceret, eadem usus simulatione itineris placide progrediebatur. Tum praemissis paulum impedimentis atque in tumulo quodam collocatis 'Habetis', inquit, 'milites, quam petivistis facultatem: hostem impedito atque iniquo loco tenetis: praestate eandem nobis ducibus virtutem, quam saepe imperatori praestitistis, atque illum adesse et haec coram cernere existimate'. Simul signa ad hostem converti[1] aciemque dirigi iubet, et paucis turmis, quae impedimenta defenderent, dimissis, reliquos equites ad latera disponit. Celeriter nostri clamore sublato pila in hostes immittunt. Illi, ubi praeter spem quos fugere credebant infestis signis[2] ad se ire viderunt, impetum ferre non potuerunt ac primo concursu in fugam coniecti proximas silvas petiverunt. Germani percepta Treverorum fuga sese domum receperunt.

From Caesar, *Gallic War*, VI, 8.

[1] **signa convertere,** *to wheel.*
[2] lit. *with hostile standards,* and so *with the purpose of attacking.*

EXERCISE 6.

Not far away was a large amount[1] of booty, such as[1] the Gauls had never hoped to find. Since they did not wish to lose it, they decided to cross the river and advance to the place from where the Romans were already setting out, a thing which Labienus had already foreseen. After advancing with the same speed as before, he sent forward the baggage a little distance and then exhorted his men. 'The enemy you have been seeking', said he, 'you can now attack on favourable ground; fight today as courageously as you have fought under the eyes of Caesar himself.' He then ordered as many men as he thought to be sufficient to guard the baggage, and the rest to wheel and charge the enemy. The Gauls, panic-stricken by this sudden attack, made for the nearest woods they could see.

[1] Correlatives to be used.

Chapter 2
Further Uses of the Accusative

An Accusative is used:

(1) To express *motion towards*, where the exact sense requires it:

Elephanti in flumen inciderunt.
The elephants fell in the river.

Compare **impetum facere in** with Acc., *to make an attack upon.*

Carthaginem ad hiberna exercitus redit.
The army returns to winter-quarters at Carthage.

(Similarly, the Abl. must be used when required by the sense: **Carthagine ex hibernis exercitus discedit,** *the army leaves its winter-quarters at Carthage.*)

(2) With the Perfect Participle (or Tense) of **nascor,** to express **Age:**

Annos septuaginta natus hoc scripsit.
He wrote this when seventy years old.

Decem annos nata est.
She is ten years old.

(3) With **abhinc,** to express time *ago*:

Abhinc menses paucos Hispaniam superaverant.
A few months ago they had conquered Spain.
(**abhinc** is also, but less often, found with the Ablative)

(4) To express Dimension, Length, Breadth, Depth, or Height:

Caesar duas fossas quindecim pedes latas perduxit.
Caesar dug two trenches, fifteen feet broad.

The Genitive, however, is commonly used, without any Adjective to express, *high, deep, broad*, etc. :

Aggerem ac vallum duodecim pedum exstruxit.
He constructed a rampart and palisade twelve feet high.

EXERCISE 7.
1. Hannibal tandem ad suos Carthaginem rediit.
2. Abhinc biennium Romanos facile vicistis.
3. Murus in hoc loco erat duodecim pedes altus.
4. Sophocles nonaginta annos natus excessit e vita.
5. Nervii fossa pedum quindecim hiberna cingunt.
6. Cum ad uxorem Romam redisset, captivus gaudebat.
7. Abhinc unum et viginti dies Roma discessi.
8. Scisne quot pedes alta sit arbor illa?
9. Caesar sex et quadraginta annos natus Britanniam iterum invasit.
10. Romani non pransi in aquam se immiserunt.
11. Undique uno tempore in hostes impetus factus est.
12. Telum habebat ferrum tres longum pedes.

EXERCISE 8.
1. Scipio had led out his troops from the camp at Placentia.
2. My dog died at the age of seven.
3. We received the news three days ago.
4. Rich men have gone away to their houses in the country.
5. The Romans had fortified the camp with a ditch twenty feet deep.
6. Although he was already eighty, Sophocles was still writing plays.
7. Those who were in front fell on those who were behind.
8. How many feet wide is the Thames in that place?
9. Caesar persuaded a Gaul to convey a message to Cicero in the camp.
10. This road is five miles long.
11. That temple was built many years ago.
12. Dig a trench twelve feet wide.

Chapter 3
Further Uses of the Genitive (1)

(1) The Genitive of a Noun or Adjective to express **characteristic, mark, or duty**:

Est boni viri amicitiam magni aestimare.

It is a characteristic of a good man to value friendship highly.

Sapientis est corpus exercere.

It is the mark of a wise man to take exercise.

(2) The **Partitive** Genitive to express *a part less than a whole*:

Pars militum, *some of the soldiers.*

Tantum auxili, *so much help.*

Multi nostrum aderant, *many of us were present.*

But we find **vos omnes aderatis,** *all of you were present,* because *you* and *all* refer to the **same persons;** so too, **quot estis,** *how many of you are there?*

(3) The **Objective** Genitive, found not only after Nouns, e.g. **spes praedae,** *hope of (for) booty,* but also after many Adjectives expressing *desire, knowledge, memory, skill,* etc., and their opposites:

cupidus, *eager (for).*	**memor,** *remembering.*
avidus, *greedy (for).*	**immemor,** *unmindful (of).*
conscius, *having knowledge (of).*	**peritus,** *skilled (in).*
	imperitus, *unskilled (in).*
ignarus, inscius, *not knowing, ignorant (of).*	**insuetus,** *unaccustomed (to).*

Non sine causa Verres se cupidum pecuniae fuisse dicit.

Not without reason does Verres say that he was eager for money.

Further Uses of the Genitive (1)

Nostri huius generis pugnae imperiti erant.
Our troops were inexperienced in this kind of fighting.

EXERCISE 9.
1. Omnes nos in templum Iovis eamus.
2. Prudentis est canes ignotos cavere.
3. Ignari loci, Romani in insidias inciderunt.
4. Caesar sine dubio erat rei militaris peritissimus.
5. Est amicorum amicis succurrere.
6. In pugnam procedite, memores victoriarum priorum.
7. Quindecim milia Romanorum in acie caesa sunt.
8. Galli, quanquam laboris insueti erant, castra munire coeperunt.
9. Graeci putabant esse liberorum senes curare.
10. Romani praeter ceteras gentes sunt avidi laudis.

EXERCISE 10.
1. Is it not the duty of good soldiers to obey their officer?
2. Verres was so greedy for booty that he plundered Sicily.
3. It was characteristic of the Romans to spare the conquered.
4. The young men were being trained in order to become skilled in war.
5. All of us fought in that battle, but few of us escaped.
6. So great was his love for his country that he refused to surrender.
7. Having knowledge of Hannibal's trick, the citizens were able to overcome the Carthaginians.
8. The Britons often attacked from ambush our men, who did not know the country.
9. I do not think that it is always the mark of a wise man to be silent.
10. The enemy wanted to know how many of us there were.

EXERCISE 11.

THE GERMANS TURN THE TABLES
ON CAESAR

Led by their chief, Ambiorix, the Eburōnes, a tribe who lived to the north of the Treveri, had through treachery inflicted great loss upon Caesar and had later fled to forests and marshes. The following passage describes an episode that arose from Caesar's plan for exacting vengeance. He was for the moment hoist with his own petard, but the attack made by the Germans on Aduātuca was unsuccessful; the territory of the Eburones was completely devastated, though Ambiorix himself escaped.

Caesar impedimenta omnium legionum Aduatucam contulit. Id castelli nomen est. Hoc fere est in mediis Eburonum finibus. Erat in Eburonibus manus certa nulla, non oppidum, non praesidium, quod se armis defenderet, sed in omnes partes dispersa multitudo. Dimittit igitur ad finitimas civitates nuntios Caesar: omnes ad se vocat spe praedae ut Eburones diripiant, ut potius in silvis Gallorum vita quam legionarius miles periclitetur. Magnus undique numerus celeriter convenit.

Trans Rhenum ad Germanos pervenit fama, diripi Eburones atque ultro[1] omnes ad praedam evocari. Cogunt equitum duo milia Sugambri, qui sunt proximi Rheno. Transeunt Rhenum navibus ratibusque et Eburonum fines adeunt; multos ex fuga dispersos excipiunt, magno pecoris numero, cuius sunt cupidissimi barbari, potiuntur. Invitati praeda longius procedunt. Non hos palus in bello latrociniisque natos, non silvae morantur. Quibus in locis sit Caesar ex captivis quaerunt; profectum longius reperiunt omnemque exercitum discessisse cognoscunt. Atque unus ex captivis 'Quid vos,' inquit, 'hanc miseram ac tenuem sectamini praedam, quibus datur[2] iam esse fortunatissimos? Tribus horis Aduatucam venire potestis: huc omnes suas fortunas exercitus Romanorum contulit: praesidi tantum[3] est, ut ne murus quidem cingi possit, neque quisquam

[1] *actually.*

[2] Used impersonally: *the chance is now given.*

[3] **tantus** may be used meaning *so small* as well as *so large.*

egredi extra munitiones audeat.' Oblata spe Germani quam nacti erant praedam in occulto loco relinquunt; ipsi Aduatucam contendunt usi eodem duce, cuius haec indicio cognoverant.

From Caesar, *Gallic War*, VI, 32 and 34-35.

EXERCISE 12.

Messengers were sent out from the camp at Aduatuca to call out the Gauls to plunder the territories of the Eburones; for Caesar thought that the Gauls, having knowledge of the country and being greedy for booty, would accomplish this more quickly than his own men. The Sugambri, a German[1] tribe, who live across the Rhine, at once heard what the Gauls were going to do; crossing the river below the place where Caesar had left a garrison, they captured a large quantity of cattle. Led on by their desire for booty, they were hindered neither by forests nor by marshes. Then they found out from one of their prisoners that even more plunder could be easily obtained from the camp at Aduatuca. The prisoner said that they could reach the place in a short time and that it was guarded by so few troops that they all stayed inside the fortifications. The Germans hid their booty in the woods and left it there. Using the prisoner as a guide, they quickly reached the camp.

[1] *of Germans.*

Chapter 4
Further Uses of the Genitive (2)

The Genitive is used:

(4) To express abstract **Quality,** but always with an Adjective in agreement:

Erat vir magni animi et magnae inter Gallos auctoritatis.
He was a man of great courage and of great influence among the Gauls.

The Ablative with an Adjective in agreement is often used in the same way:

Vir acri ingenio, *a man of acute intellect.*

But two points must be carefully noticed:

(i) If the description is one of Number, Size, Weight, Age Time, etc., the Genitive is always used:

Puer annorum novem.	**Dierum iter quadraginta.**
A boy of nine years.	*A forty days' journey.*

(ii) If the description is of External Qualities or Appearance, the Ablative is always used:

Vultu erat tranquillo, *he was a man of serene countenance.*

(5) For the **Definition** of another Noun, instead of using Apposition:

Nomen regis.	**Virtus iustitiae.**
The name of king.	*The virtue of justice.*

N.B.—There are two important instances where a Genitive is **not** used:

(i) After **urbs, oppidum, insula,** etc., the proper name is always placed in Apposition, e.g. **urbs Roma,** *the city of Rome.*

(ii) Adjectives are used instead of place-names to describe origin, e.g. **civis Romanus,** *a citizen of Rome.*

(6) For expressing a **charge** after Verbs of *accusing* (**accuso**), *acquitting* (**absolvo**), *condemning for* (**damno, condemno**):

> **Ista veneficii accusata est (absoluta est).**
> *That woman was accused (acquitted) of poisoning.*

The **punishment** is sometimes expressed in the Genitive Case, but more often in the Ablative: **capitis** or **capite damno,** *I condemn to death,* but with **mors,** *death,* **vincula,** *imprisonment* (lit. *chains*), **pecunia,** *fine,* **exsilium,** *exile,* the Ablative is always used. **Multo** (1st Conjug.), *I punish,* is often used for judicial punishment:

> **Proditor capitis damnatus est.**
> *The traitor was condemned to death.*
> **Lacedaemonii ducem pecunia multaverunt.**
> *The Spartans fined the general.*

EXERCISE 13.
1. Horatius erat vir praestantis virtutis.
2. Multae statuae eximia pulchritudine Olympiae inventae sunt.
3. Labienus classem sescentarum navium aedificavit.
4. Marcus Manlius, qui Capitolium quondam servaverat, postea morte damnatus est.
5. Britanni se vitro inficiunt et capillo sunt promisso.
6. Themistocles, proditionis accusatus, ad urbem Magnesiam confugit.
7. In insula Britannia hominum est infinita multitudo.
8. Hi fratres erant singulari virtute homines.
9. Nomen regis populo Romano semper ingratum erat.
10. Caesar legatum castra munire fossa duodeviginti pedum iubet.
11. Ambiorix, princeps summae audaciae, Romanos fefellit.
12. Hannibal a Poenis exsilio damnatus est.

EXERCISE 14.
1. The armies of Carthage remained in Italy for many years.
2. Archimedes was a man of extraordinary ingenuity.

3. Many innocent citizens were accused of treason under Tiberius.
4. Augustus was a man of short stature and bright eyes.
5. Many statues were transported to Rome from the island of Sicily.
6. The Syracusans shot forth stones of great weight.
7. The name of freedom was sweet to the citizens of Syracuse.
8. Cassivellaunus was a chief of great influence among the Britons.
9. Most of those who had been accused were condemned to death.
10. Surely Verres, a man of the utmost shamelessness, will not be acquitted of theft?
11. Miltiades was punished by an exile of ten years.
12. Socrates was a man of remarkable wisdom.

EXERCISE 15.

RISING OF THE GAULS UNDER VERCINGETORIX

Caesar spent the winter of 53-52 in north Italy. Lack of settled government at Rome and the hope that Caesar would be detained beyond the Alps encouraged the Gauls to make a bid for freedom. The Carnūtes promised to begin the revolt if the other tribes swore to follow them.

Carnutes Cenabum¹ signo dato concurrunt civesque Romanos, qui negotii causa ibi constiterant, interficiunt bonaque eorum diripiunt. Celeriter ad omnes Galliae civitates fama perfertur. Nam ubicumque maior et illustrior incidit res, clamore per agros regionesque significant; hunc alii deinceps excipiunt et proximis tradunt, ut tum accidit. Nam quae Cenabi oriente sole gesta erant, ante secundam vigiliam in finibus Arvernorum audita sunt, quod spatium est milium passuum circiter centum LX.

Ibi Vercingetorix, Arvernus, summae potentiae adulescens, cuius pater principatum Galliae totius obtinuerat et, quod

¹ The capital of the Carnutes (Orleans).

regnum appetebat, ab civitate erat interfectus, convocatos suos clientes facile incendit. Prohibetur[1] ab Gobannitione, patruo suo, reliquisque principibus, qui nolebant eum hanc temptare fortunam; expellitur ex oppido Gergovia;[2] non destitit tamen atque in agris habet dilectum egentium ac perditorum. Hac coacta manu quoscumque adit ex civitate ad suam sententiam perducit; hortatur ut communis libertatis causa arma capiant, magnisque coactis copiis adversarios suos a quibus paulo ante erat eiectus expellit ex civitate. Rex ab suis appellatur. Celeriter sibi populos finitimos reliquosque omnes qui Oceanum[3] attingunt adiungit: omnium consensu ad eum defertur imperium. Omnibus his civitatibus obsides imperat, certum numerum militum ad se celeriter adduci iubet; in primis equitatui studet.

From Caesar, *Gallic War*, VII, 3-4.

[1] *restrained.*
[2] The capital of the Arverni.
[3] i.e. bordering on the Bay of Biscay.

EXERCISE 16.

The Carnutes swore to the tribes of Gaul that they would be the first to make war against Caesar, and put in charge of their troops two men of the utmost boldness. At dawn they captured the town of Cenabum without difficulty and killed the Roman citizens who were living there, among them a Roman knight,[1] a man of great distinction. Within a very short time the Arverni, who are a hundred and sixty miles away, heard what had been done at Cenabum; for such events are signalled across the fields by shouting and passed on from one state to another.

Hearing the message, an Arvernian chieftain, by name Vercingetorix, called his dependents to arms, although his father had himself been put to death, because he seemed too eager for kingly power. When, however, they had discovered his plan, his uncle Gobannitio and the rest of the chiefs drove him out of the town. Then Vercingetorix collected a band of

[1] The Equites or knights formed the second most important class at Rome after the Senators; this knight was in charge of the corn-supply.

rogues in the fields and urged both them and others to take up arms to drive out the Romans. With their help he drove out his uncle and the other chiefs. After receiving the title of king, he sent out ambassadors and persuaded the neighbouring tribes to remain loyal.[1] He then ordered troops and arms to be got ready and, since he was a man of the utmost strictness, he punished[2] those who wavered[3] with extreme penalties.

[1] Use **in fide maneo.**
[2] Use **afficio.**
[3] Use Present Participle of **dubito.**

Chapter 5
Further notes on Consecutive and Final Clauses

Relative Pronouns in Consecutive Clauses

We have already met such sentences as **Non erat is qui hoc faceret,** *he was not the kind of man to do this.*

The following examples should be carefully studied; in each of them the Relative Pronoun has the meaning *of such a kind as*, and is followed by a Consecutive use of the Subjunctive:

(1) **Sunt qui credant Romulum in caelum raptum esse.**
Erant qui crederent, etc.
There are some who believe that Romulus was snatched into the sky. There were some who believed, etc.

(2) **Dignus erat qui consul fieret.**
He was worthy to be made consul.

Indignus qui, *unworthy to* and **mereor qui,** *I deserve to* are similarly followed by the Subjunctive.

(3) **Hic dolor erat gravior quam quem Cicero ferre posset.**
This grief was too heavy for Cicero to bear.
(lit. *heavier than of such a kind as Cicero could bear*)

Ut is sometimes used after a Comparative with **quam** instead of a Relative, and this sentence would then run:

Hic dolor erat gravior quam ut Cicero ferre posset.

Two notes on Final Clauses

The use of the Relative Pronoun to introduce a Final Clause is already familiar, e.g. **legati Romam missi sunt, qui auxilium orarent,** *ambassadors were sent to Rome to ask for help.*

(1) When a Final Clause contains a **Comparative** Adjective or Adverb, Latin uses **quō**, lit. *by which means*, instead of **ut**:

> **Athenienses deos muris saepserant, quo facilius ab hoste possent defendere.**
>
> *The Athenians had protected their gods with walls, so that they might more easily defend them from the enemy.*

(2) A **Supine** in -um is frequently found after a Verb of **Motion,** to express Purpose; it is really a Verbal Noun of the fourth Declension in the Acc. Case; being partly Verbal, it can still govern a Direct Object:

> **Legati Romam missi sunt auxilium oratum.**
>
> *Ambassadors were sent to Rome to ask for help.*
>
> (lit. *were sent towards asking for help*, no Preposition being used with the Supine)

EXERCISE 17.
1. Sunt qui dicant Alexandrum fuisse imperatorem maximum.
2. Fortior est quam qui amicos in hoc discrimine relinquat.
3. Caesar, quo celerius in Galliam rediret, omnes milites in paucis navibus collocavit.
4. Cloelia erat digna quae laudaretur.
5. Caesar tres legiones pabulatum miserat.
6. Gallus quidam missus est qui ad Ciceronem epistolam deferret.
7. Fuerunt qui Placentiam tuti confugerent.
8. Cives prudentiores erant quam quos Hannibal litteris falleret.
9. Caesar milites ordines laxare iussit, quo facilius gladiis uti possent.
10. Equites exploratum erant praemissi.

EXERCISE 18.
1. Alexander deserved to be called Great.
2. There were some who thought that Hannibal would capture the city of Rome.

3. Numidians were sent to prepare an ambush (*to be done in three ways*).
4. The Romans were too tired to resist the Carthaginians.
5. In order to defend the ships more easily, Caesar ordered a fortification to be built round them.
6. Surely a woman of such bravery does not deserve to be punished?
7. There are some who believe that Hannibal will soon be recalled to Carthage.
8. This table is too heavy for me to carry.
9. Caesar sent Volusenus to reconnoitre the island (*to be done in three ways*).
10. To become wiser, read books more carefully.

EXERCISE 19.

CAESAR'S QUICK COUNTER-STROKE

The intention of Vercingetorix was to cut off Caesar from his legions, six of which were wintering at Agedincum in the territory of the Senones. The map will help to explain the actions both of Vercingetorix and of Lucterius.

Tum Vercingetorix Lucterium, summae hominem audaciae, cum parte copiarum in Rutenos mittit, ipse in Bituriges proficiscitur. Bituriges igitur ad Aeduos,[1] quorum erant in fide,[2] legatos mittunt subsidium rogatum, quo facilius hostium copias sustinere possint.

His rebus in Italiam Caesari nuntiatis, cum iam ille urbanas[3] res virtute Cn. Pompei commodiorem in statum pervenisse intellegeret, in Transalpinam Galliam profectus est.   Interim Lucterius in Rutenos missus eam civitatem Arvernis conciliat et in provinciam Narbonem[4] versus eruptionem facere con-

---

[1] A powerful tribe in the centre of Gaul, allied to Caesar.

[2] *under whose protection they were.* The Aedui did not send the help that was expected and the Bituriges joined the Arverni; later on the Aedui also joined in the revolt.

[3] Pompey restored order at Rome when he was made sole consul.

[4] The city of Narbonne, which gave its name to Gallia Narbonensis; this Roman province, founded in 121 B.C., is often referred to by Caesar, as here, simply as **provincia**; the latter word survives in the modern 'Provence' which its territory included.

tendit. Qua re nuntiata Caesar Narbonem pervenit, timentes confirmat, praesidia in Rutenis constituit, supplementum, quod ex Italia adduxerat, in Helvios, qui fines Arvernorum contingunt, convenire iubet.

Lucterio ita represso, quod[1] intrare intra praesidia periculosum putabat, in Helvios proficiscitur. Etsi mons Cevenna, qui Arvernos ab Helviis discludit, durissimo tempore anni altissima nive iter impediebat, tamen discussa nive sex in altitudinem pedum atque ita viis patefactis summo militum sudore ad fines Arvernorum pervenit. Quibus oppressis inopinantibus, quod se Cevenna ut muro munitos existimabant, ac ne singulari quidem unquam homini eo tempore anni semitae patuerant, equitibus imperat, ut quam latissime possint vagentur et quam maximum hostibus terrorem inferant. Celeriter haec fama ac nuntiis ad Vercingetorigem perferuntur; quem perterriti omnes Arverni circumsistunt atque obsecrant, ut suis fortunis consulat, neve ab hostibus diripiantur, praesertim cum videat omne ad se bellum translatum. Quorum ille precibus permotus castra ex Biturigibus movet in Arvernos versus.

From Caesar, *Gallic War* VII, 5-8.

[1] The subject of this clause is Lucterius.

EXERCISE 20.

Vercingetorix sent Lucterius to win over the Ruteni to the Arverni; he himself set off to attack the Bituriges. He adopted this plan in order that he might more easily cut off Caesar from his army. The Bituriges asked the Aedui for help; the latter, however, were too prudent to send troops across the Loire. There are some who think that they feared treachery. Vercingetorix thus won over the Bituriges. Meanwhile Lucterius, after winning over the Ruteni, collected a large force and hastened towards Narbo.

By now Caesar had set out from Italy for Transalpine Gaul and had reached Narbo. Here he posted garrisons in three places which were nearest the enemy, and thence advanced towards the Helvii. The Arverni thought that the Cevennes (this mountain divides the Arverni from the Helvii) were too difficult to be crossed in winter because of the deep snow. Caesar, however, not being the kind of man to be hindered by such a difficulty, cleared away snow six feet deep and reached the territories of the Arverni. He ordered his cavalry to wander far and wide so as to strike greater terror into the enemy. Panic-stricken at Caesar's arrival, the Arverni sent messengers to Vercingetorix to ask for help; they persuaded him to move his camp from the territory of the Bituriges back to his own.

Sentences for Revision

EXERCISE 21.

1. Abhinc horas duas una legio frumentatum emissa est.
2. Pars militum in saxa ceciderunt.
3. Non satis navium erat, quae milites portarent.
4. Multi Galli proditionis accusati erant.
5. Quo facilius hostibus timoris daret suspicionem, castra maiore strepitu moveri iussit.
6. Paucas equitum turmas, quae impedimenta defenderent, retinuit.
7. Hic murus duodecim pedum altior est quam quem sine scalis ascendere possimus.
8. Sunt qui divitias non magni aestiment.
9. Qui patriam prodiderunt merentur qui puniantur.
10. Multi, rerum novarum cupidi, ad urbem Romam confugerunt.

EXERCISE 22.

1. Cato was a man of great influence among the Romans.
2. The river was too deep for the soldiers to cross on foot.
3. There were some who thought that Hannibal was the greatest general.
4. Citizens of Athens condemned Socrates to death.
5. Cassivellaunus sent envoys to seek for peace (*to be done in three ways*).
6. It is the mark of a wise commander to send out scouts.

7. Helen is said to have been a woman of outstanding beauty.
8. Surely Socrates did not deserve to be condemned?
9. The island of Sicily was captured a few years ago.
10. At the age of seventy, he was not too old to give advice.

Chapter 6
Verbs of Fearing

(1) **Caesar tanto periculo exercitum obicere timebat.**
Caesar was afraid to expose his army to so great a danger.

Timeo and **vereor** are followed by a Prolative **Infinitive,** when someone *fears to do something*; the Infinitive must always be used in composition when an Infinitive in English follows a Verb of *fearing.*

(2) **Timemus ne circumveniamur.**
We fear (lest, that) we shall (may) be surrounded.

Here we have a fear expressed *lest something may happen* in the **Future;** the Verb in such dependent clauses is introduced by **nē** and is in the **Subjunctive Mood;** its Tense follows the rule for the Sequence of Tenses, the Present Subjunctive being used in Primary Sequence, and the Imperfect in Historic Sequence.

Here is an example in Historic Sequence:

Romani non timebant ne circumvenirentur.
The Romans were not afraid that they would be surrounded.

(For the sake of interest, it may be pointed out that a dependent clause after a Verb of *fearing* is in origin probably a negative wish: **ne circumveniamur,** *may we not be surrounded!* Then a fear clause is put in front of the wish: **timemus ne circumveniamur,** *we have a fear* about our wish (which is) *may we not be surrounded.*)

(3) **Nē ... nōn** is similarly used (but **ut** is often found instead of **nē nōn**) for a fear *that something may* or *might* **not** *happen*:

Labienus veritus est ne hostium impetum non sustinere posset (or **veritus est ut**).
Labienus feared that he would not be able to withstand the enemy's attack.

40

Nē **nōn** (rather than **ut**) is always used when both the main clause and the dependent clause are negatived:

Labienus non veritus est ne non vinceret.
Labienus did not fear that he would not win.

(4) **Timeo ne surda sit (facta sit).**
I fear she is (has become) deaf.

Hannibal timebat ne frater non pervenisset.
Hannibal was afraid that his brother had not arrived.

The Subjunctive with **nē** or **nē nōn** is also used to express fears for the **Present** or **Past**, with the ordinary Sequence of Tenses.

Note.—When a Participle is used, **veritus** is far more commonly found than **verens** or **timens,** which should be avoided; *fear* precedes the *action* which results from the *fear*; hence the use of the Perfect Participle:

Veriti ne circumvenirentur se fugae mandaverunt.
Fearing that they might be surrounded, they fled.

EXERCISE 23.
1. Treveri flumen transire non timebant.
2. Timemus ne ab hostibus diripiamur.
3. Galli timebant ne praedam dimitterent.
4. Hannibal veritus erat ne revocaretur.
5. Principes timebant ne Galli libertatem non reciperarent.
6. Timeo ne hostes iam adsint.
7. Veriti ut vincerent, Galli silvas petiverunt.
8. Caesar veretur ne multos milites amiserit.
9. Imperator timebat ne exploratores capti essent.
10. Germani silvas inire non timebant.

EXERCISE 24.
1. The Aedui were afraid that they would be betrayed.
2. Caesar was not afraid to endure dangers.
3. Our men feared that Caesar would not arrive.
4. I fear that many of our men have been wounded.
5. We are not afraid that the Romans will not win.

6. Fearing that the enemy had prepared an ambush, the general sent out scouts.
7. The chiefs were afraid that Vercingetorix would be made king.
8. Surely you are not afraid to sail today?
9. I am afraid the dog may attack you.
10. The citizens fear that the town is not now safe.

EXERCISE 25.
1. Caesar milites in silvas dimittere timebat.
2. Caesar timebat ne Galli ex insidiis exorerentur.
3. Timeo ne nobis non satis sit copiarum.
4. Milites qui sunt Aduatucae extra munitiones egredi timent.
5. Principes verebantur ne Vercingetorix regnum appeteret.
6. Arverni nunquam timuerant ne hostes hieme Cevennam transirent.
7. Num timetis ne Caesar auxilium nondum miserit?
8. Romani verebantur ut Samnites sibi parcerent.
9. Veritus ne capitis damnaretur, Hannibal in Asiam confugit.
10. Caesar timet ne multae naves inutiles sint.
11. Poeni timebant ne non domum rursus redirent.
12. Sapientis est aliquando vereri loqui.

EXERCISE 26.
1. The Carthaginians feared that they would be overcome by the cold and the snows.
2. Surely you are not afraid to cross the Alps, which many have crossed before?
3. Hannibal did not fear that he would not reach Italy with his army.
4. We fear that Vercingetorix is eager for kingly power.
5. Caesar no longer fears that his ships will be damaged by storms.
6. Our men were afraid to advance too quickly because they were ignorant of the locality.

7. The Syracusans feared that a new fleet would not arrive from Carthage.
8. Cassivellaunus, fearing that he could not now resist the Romans, disbanded most of his forces.
9. Verres is afraid he will be condemned to death.
10. Cicero feared that Caesar had not yet heard that he was in great danger.
11. Marcellus is afraid that someone will harm Archimedes.
12. The enemy fear that the bridge has already been broken.

EXERCISE 27.

THE FALL OF AVARICUM

Caesar left a small force to face Vercingetorix and safely reached his legions; then making Agedincum his base, he captured Vellaunodūnum, Cenabum, and Noviodūnum. Vercingetorix then decided upon a 'scorched earth' policy and the Gauls set fire to their towns. Against his will Vercingetorix made an exception of Avāricum (Bourges), the chief town of the Bituriges; Caesar did not capture it without difficulty; at one moment the inhabitants had decided to abandon it, and it is at this point that the following extract begins.

Iamque hoc facere noctu apparabant, cum matres familiae repente in publicum procurrerunt flentesque proiectae ad pedes suorum omnibus precibus petiverunt, ne se et communes liberos hostibus ad supplicium dederent; affirmabant infirmitatem virium fugam impedituram esse. Ubi eos in sententia perstare viderunt, conclamare et significare de fuga Romanis coeperunt. Quo timore perterriti Galli, ne ab equitatu Romanorum viae praeoccuparentur, consilio destiterunt. Postero die Caesar promota turri perfectisque operibus quae facere instituerat, magno coorto imbre non inutilem hanc tempestatem arbitratus est, quod paulo incautius custodias in muro dispositas videbat, suosque languidius in opere versari iussit et quid fieri vellet ostendit. Legionibusque intra vineas[1]

[1] *mantlets*, movable sheds for the protection of soldiers besieging a city.

clam expeditis, cohortatus ut aliquando[1] pro tantis laboribus fructum victoriae perciperent, militibus signum dedit. Illi subito ex omnibus partibus evolaverunt murumque celeriter compleverunt. Hostes re nova perterriti muro turribusque deiecti in foro ac locis patentioribus cuneatim constiterunt. Ubi neminem in aequum locum sese demittere, sed toto undique muro hostes circumfundi viderunt, veriti ne omnino spes fugae tolleretur, abiectis armis ultimas oppidi partes petiverunt, parsque ibi, cum angusto exitu portarum se ipsi premerent, a militibus, pars iam egressa portis ab equitibus est interfecta; nec fuit quisquam, qui[2] praedae studeret. Sic et Cenabi[3] caede et labore operis incitati non aetate confectis, non mulieribus, non infantibus pepercerunt. Denique ex omni numero, qui fuit circiter milium XL, vix DCCC, qui primo clamore audito se ex oppido eiecerunt, incolumes ad Vercingetorigem pervenerunt. Quos ille multa iam nocte silentio ex fuga excepit, veritus ne qua in castris ex misericordia vulgi seditio oreretur.

From Caesar, *Gallic War* VII, 26-28.

[1] When used in Commands **aliquando** means *now at last.*
[2] Probably a Consecutive use: *of such a kind as to,* i.e. *disposed to*; the context suggests that the booty would be money gained by the capture of prisoners.
[3] See Ex. 15.

EXERCISE 28.

The Gauls had resolved to escape from Avaricum, but the mothers persuaded them not to try; for they feared that they and their children would be hindered in flight and captured by the enemy; they had even made signals to the Romans about their husbands' plan. Next day it happened that a big storm arose and that the guards were posted on the wall with less caution. Caesar, taking advantage[1] of this weather, secretly got the legions ready inside the mantlets. 'At last,' said he, 'reap the fruit of victory in return for all your great toil; I will give rewards to those who first climb the wall.' At a given signal

[1] Use **utor.**

they quickly flew out and after scaling the wall, dislodged the enemy.

The Gauls waited for the Romans in the market-place, with the idea that[1] they should resist them there; but no one came. Then, fearing that they might not be able to escape, they rushed to the furthest gates of the city, but found that the enemy had by now manned all the walls. So great was the slaughter on that day that scarcely eight hundred reached the camp of Vercingetorix in safety. Since he was afraid that they would excite too much pity, he ordered them to be secretly conducted, each to his own friends.

[1] **eo consilio ut.**

Chapter 7
Further Uses of the Dative

(1) The Dative is used with most **compounds of sum;** the following examples are given to illustrate this:

Dux suis aderat, *the leader was present to help his men.*

Barbaris non deerat consilium, *the natives did not lack a plan.*
(lit. *a plan was not absent for the natives*)

Cicero amicis non deerat, *Cicero did not fail his friends.*

Druidae rebus divinis intersunt, *the Druids take part in divine worship.*

Eques Romanus rei frumentariae praeerat, *a Roman knight was in charge of the corn-supply.*

Nec sibi nec alteri prosunt, *they benefit neither themselves nor anybody else.*

Hasdrubal exercitui suo non superfuit, *Hasdrubal did not survive his own army.*

Note.—In the Conjugation of **prōsum,** *I am of advantage*, **d** is inserted for euphony before an **e,** e.g. **prodest.**

(2) The following uses of the Dative deserve attention:

(a) With **consulo: Medicus mihi consulit,** *the doctor consults my interests.* But **medicum consulo,** *I consult the doctor.*

(b) With **impero:** (i) **Caesar Britannis imperat ut obsides tradant,** *Caesar orders the Britons to hand over hostages,* (ii) **Caesar obsides Britannis imperat,** *Caesar requisitions hostages from the Britons.*

(c) With **minor: Mortem nobis minatus est,** *he threatened us with death.*

(d) With **nubo,** always used of a woman marrying a man:

46

Lavinia Aeneae nupsit, *Lavinia was married to Aeneas.*
In matrimonium duco is used of a man marrying a woman.

(3) (*a*) The Dative is used to express a **Purpose** or Result:
Receptui cano, *I sound (on the trumpet for) the retreat.*
Very often a Dative of Purpose is accompanied by a second Dative, the Dative of **Advantage** (or Disadvantage); this Dative is sometimes known as a Dative of **Reference**:

Caesar milites praesidio navibus reliquit.
Caesar left soldiers as (lit. *for*) *a garrison for the ships.*

Omnem equitatum suis auxilio misit.
He sent all his cavalry to help his men.

(*b*) When a Dative of Purpose is used with the Verb **sum,** the Verb together with the Dative forms a Predicate, and the Dative is called a **Predicative** Dative; it is found only with certain Nouns and only in the singular, and no Adjective is ever attached to the Noun except an Adjective expressing quantity, e.g. **magnus, tantus, summus.**

Common are:

auxilio esse ⎱ *to be a help.* **subsidio esse** ⎰	**impedimento esse,** *to be a hindrance.*
bono esse, *to profit, be of advantage.*	**odio esse,** *to be hated.*
damno esse ⎱ *to be hurtful* ⎰	**oneri esse,** *to be burdensome.*
detrimento esse ⎰ *or a cause of loss.*	**praesidio esse,** *to protect, guard.*
dedecori esse, *to be a disgrace.*	**saluti esse,** *to be a means of safety.*
documento esse, *to be a proof.*	**usui esse,** *to be useful.*

A Dative of Reference is often added:

Locus ipse erat praesidio barbaris.
The district itself gave protection to the natives.

Haec res saluti fuit nostris.

This event was a means of salvation to our men.

Odio est civitati.

He is hated by the state.

The last example should be particularly noticed; **ōdi,** *I hate,* a Defective Verb of the 3rd Conjug. has no Passive form, and Latin uses **odio sum,** lit. *I am for a hatred,* with a Dative of Reference, for *I am hated by.*

EXERCISE 29.

1. Lucterius parti copiarum praeerat.
2. Hannibal multis proeliis in Italia interfuit.
3. Vercingetorix omnibus his civitatibus obsides imperavit.
4. Caesar praesidio impedimentis legionem quartam decimam reliquit.
5. Nemo vult oneri esse amicis suis.
6. Hoc consilium vobis non proderit.
7. Caesar magno sibi usui fore arbitrabatur Britanniam perspexisse.
8. Hoc nuntio allato Arvernis spes omnino deerat.
9. Hoc erat documento barbarorum cupiditatis praedae.
10. Patruus eius exsilium Vercingetorigi minatus est.
11. Cum suos premi videret, dux receptui cecinit.
12. Cui bono est hoc dicere?

EXERCISE 30.

1. Caesar praised those soldiers who had been in charge of the business.
2. Caesar levies corn from the Trinobantes.
3. Hannibal hoped that the elephants would be a help to him.
4. Few of the Roman army survived that battle.
5. The Gauls considered their own interests, not Caesar's.
6. Caesar had left Labienus with three legions as a guard for the harbours.
7. Caesar's daughter was married to Pompey.

8. To defend Avaricum was not advantageous to the Gauls.
9. Hannibal said that he hated the Romans and was hated by them.
10. When about to cross to Britain, Caesar ordered all those things that are useful for ships to be got ready.
11. Geese are said to have been the salvation of the Romans on that day.
12. This method of combat proved a cause of great loss to the Romans.

EXERCISE 31.
1. Caesari e navi egresso deerant equites.
2. Caesar arbitrabatur Eburones persequi suis detrimento fore.
3. Hannibal, Carthaginem revocatus, nihilominus exercitui postea praefuit.
4. Verres propter avaritiam magno erat odio Siculis.
5. Milites verebantur ne Hannibal non satis sibi consuleret.
6. Roxane, virgo eximia pulchritudine, Alexandro nupsit.
7. Scientia militum saepe erat subsidio Caesari.
8. Consilium Fabii Romanis maxime profuit.
9. Romani non ignorabant maximo fore dedecori se dedere.
10. Multi cives Romani reipublicae superesse nolebant.

EXERCISE 32.
1. It is the mark of a wise man sometimes to consult a doctor.
2. A cohort had been left to guard the bridge.
3. The soldiers complained that Alexander was marrying a foreign woman.
4. Caesar thought that his own men's ignorance of the country would be both a hindrance and a source of loss to them.
5. There were some who thought that this chief would be hated by the Gauls.
6. The Bituriges hoped that forces would be sent to help them.

7. The chief's father had been in charge of the whole of Gaul.
8. This victory was a proof of the skill of the Romans.
9. Many men hope that they will not outlive their strength, so that they may not be a burden to others.
10. Roman citizens were taking part in business at Cenabum.

Chapter 8
The Gerund: (1) as a Verbal Noun

---

(1) The use of the Gerund in its Oblique Cases:

The Infinitive is only used as a Verbal Noun when it is in the Nom., or when it is in the Acc. in Indirect Statement, e.g. **videre est credere,** *seeing is believing* ; **dixit cedere esse turpe,** *he said that surrendering was disgraceful.*

When other Cases of a Verbal Noun are required, or when a Preposition is used which governs an Acc., then Latin uses the **Gerund,** e.g. **amandum,** *loving,* **monendum,** *advising,* declined in the sing. as a neuter Noun of the 2nd Declension; so, **regendi,** *of ruling.*

Examples :

Acc. **Caesar tempestatem idoneam ad navigandum nactus est.**
Caesar obtained suitable weather for sailing.

Gen. **Cupidus erat bellandi.**
He was desirous of making war.

Caesar pabulandi causa tres legiones misit.
Caesar sent three legions to forage (lit. *for the sake of foraging*).

Dat. **Operam damus legendo.**
We pay attention to reading.
(The Dat. of the Gerund is not common; it is found after **studeo,** *I am eager for, devoted to*)

Abl. **Fabius sedendo et cunctando bellum gerebat.**
Fabius carried on the war by sitting still and delaying.

Note.—The Gerund as a Verbal Noun may be qualified by an Adverb, but never by an Adjective; **celeriter currendo effugit,** *he escaped by running quickly.*

(2) **The Gerund of Intransitive Verbs, governing a Case:**
The Oblique Cases of the Gerund of an Intransitive Verb
may govern the same Case as the Verb from which it comes:

Ad subveniendum sociis, *for helping the allies.*
Amicis persuadendi causa, *to persuade one's friends.*
Captivis parcendo, *by sparing the prisoners.*

(3) **Common uses of the Genitive of the Gerund:**
The Genitive of the Gerund is often found:
  (*a*) with **causā** (which always follows the Gerund; see
      examples above) to express Purpose;
  (*b*) after Adjectives which take a Genitive, e.g. **cupidus,
      peritus, insuetus;**
  (*c*) after the following Nouns:

ars, *art, skill.*	**signum,** *signal.*
facultās ⎫	**spatium,** *time, space.*
occāsio ⎬ *opportunity, chance*	**spēs,** *hope.*
potestās ⎭	**studium,** *desire, enthusiasm.*
fīnis, *end.*	**tempus,** *time, right time.*
(**fīnem facio,** *I bring an end to*).	

In English, we use after these Nouns the Prepositions *in, for,
to,* or *of* according to the sense, e.g. **tempus scribendi,** *time for
writing*; **potestas oppugnandi,** *chance to attack*; it is important
to remember this use of the Gen. of the Gerund in composition.

EXERCISE 33.
  1. Nulla spes fugiendi nobis manet.
  2. Caesar locum ad egrediendum non idoneum arbitratus
     est.
  3. Regnum appetere exitio erat patri Vercingetorigis.
  4. Equites nostri praedandi vastandique causa in agros
     progressi erant.
  5. Dumnorix, Aeduorum princeps, dixit se navigandi
     insuetum esse.
  6. Volusenus non multa de Britannia explorando reperire
     potuit.

7. Parcendo hostibus Romani famam bonam consecuti sunt.
8. Caesar militibus oppugnandi signum dedit.
9. Britanni nostros in metendo occupatos subito oppugnaverunt.
10. Caesar naves paratas ad navigandum invenit.
11. Equites hostibus ex essedis desiliendi facultatem non dederunt.
12. Multi perditi ad subveniendum principi ex urbe fugerunt.
13. Carnutes Caesari resistendi causa praesidium comparabant.
14. Multi imperiti nandi in flumine perierunt.
15. Tempus est dormiendi, non agendi.
16. Sunt qui equitando studeant.

EXERCISE 34 (*Gerunds to be used where possible*).
1. The art of writing well is not easily learnt.
2. Many of the ships were useless for sailing.
3. Escaping from Avaricum was difficult.
4. Caesar gave the enemy a chance to fight.
5. Wise men pay attention to learning.
6. The hope of plundering and a desire for waging war had called out many Gauls from their daily toil.
7. Owing to the storm no opportunity to help was given to our troops.
8. The enemy were equal to us both in[1] valour and in enthusiasm for fighting.
9. The Carthaginians enticed our men across the river Trebia by retreating.
10. The soldiers were not overcome by the toil of rowing.
11. There was no space for flight.
12. Night brought an end to the fighting.
13. The citizens had no hope of resisting the enemy.
14. By obeying we learn to command.
15. The Britons were skilled in fighting from chariots.
16. I do not think that capturing this town will be easy.

[1] No Preposition.

Chapter 9

The Gerund: (2) expressing Obligation

Nobis properandum est (erit, erat).
We must (shall have to, had to) hurry.

The Nom. of the Gerund, together with the 3rd person sing. of the Verb **sum**, is used to express **Obligation**, i.e. the ideas of *should, must, ought.* This use is, however, confined to the Gerunds of **Intransitive Verbs** or of Transitive Verbs when used Intransitively, e.g. **vobis oppugnandum est,** *you must attack.*

The person on whom the Obligation falls, i.e. the person who *must do so-and-so*, is expressed in the Dative Case (e.g. **vobis** in the above example); this is called the **Dative** of the **Agent.**

In Indirect Statement the Acc. of the Gerund is used with an Infinitive of **sum**:

Dixit nobis properandum esse (fore, fuisse).
He said that we ought to hurry (would have to hurry, should have hurried).

If this construction is used with a Verb which governs the Dative, then, to avoid ambiguity, the person who *must do so-and-so* is expressed in the Abl. Case with **a** or **ab**:

Hostibus a nobis resistendum est.
We must resist the enemy.

Similarly this Gerund is used with the Subjunctive of **sum** in constructions involving the use of a Subjunctive:

Tot erant hostes ut nostris acerrime pugnandum esset.
The enemy were so numerous that our troops had to fight very fiercely.

Exercise 35.
1. Nobis Aduatucam statim contendendum est.
2. Militibus simul et de navibus desiliendum erat et in fluctibus consistendum.

3. Caesari in Helvios proficiscendum erit.
4. Cum multae naves essent fractae, Caesari ad mare redeundum erat.
5. Ciceroni ad Caesarem scribendum erat.
6. Romani timebant ne sibi cedendum esset.
7. Caesar arbitratus est sibi in Britannia non diutius morandum esse.
8. Nonne feminis et liberis a Caesare parcendum erat?
9. Romanis nondum pransis trans flumen natandum erat.
10. Nescio utrum nobis progrediendum an regrediendum sit.
11. Arverni putaverunt principi in patria manendum fuisse.
12. Scio illi puero a magistro saepe subveniendum fore.

EXERCISE 36.
1. The chief had to return to his own tribe.
2. The citizens have to give way to the prayers of the women.
3. Caesar said that he would have to set out at once.
4. The slave had to obey his master.
5. The legion must stay here to guard the baggage.
6. You should persuade your friends to go with you.
7. So many were the dangers that Caesar had to act quickly.
8. Soldiers know that they must obey their officers.
9. Ought you not to have written yesterday?
10. The Sicilians thought that the governor should be punished.
11. You will have to delay here for two days.
12. The storm is so great that we must go back home.

EXERCISE 37.

STRENGTH IN OLD AGE

Cicero wrote several philosophic books after his retirement from public life. Among them was a dialogue on Old Age, written in 44 B.C. The following extract comes from the mouth of Cato (234-149 B.C.), who fought under Fabius Maximus and later as censor upbraided the Romans for wastefulness and luxury.

56   *The Gerund: (2) expressing Obligation*

Audire te arbitror, Scipio,[1] quae faciat hodie Masinissa[2] nonaginta natus annos: si iter pedibus incipit, in equum omnino non ascendit; si equo, ex equo non descendit; nullo imbri, nullo frigore adducitur ut capite operto sit; summa est in eo corporis siccitas,[3] itaque omnia exsequitur regis officia. Potest igitur exercitatio et temperantia etiam in senectute conservare aliquid pristini roboris.

Resistendum est senectuti, pugnandum contra senectutem ut contra morbum, utendum exercitationibus modicis, tantum cibi et potionis adhibendum, ut reficiantur vires, non opprimantur. Nec vero corpori solum subveniendum est, sed menti atque animo multo[4] magis. Nam haec quoque, nisi tanquam lumini oleum instilles,[5] exstinguuntur senectute. Et corpora quidem exercitationum defatigatione ingravescunt, animi autem exercitando levantur. Quattuor robustos filios, quinque filias, tantam domum[6] Appius[7] regebat et caecus et senex; intentum enim animum tanquam arcum habebat nec languescens succumbebat senectuti. Tenebat non modo auctoritatem, sed etiam imperium in suos: metuebant servi, verebantur liberi, carum omnes habebant.

From Cicero, *De Senectute*, 34-37.

[1] Cato is addressing Scipio Africanus the Younger, who destroyed Carthage in 146.
[2] Masinissa, king of Numidia, gave help to the Romans in the Second Punic war.
[3] properly *dryness of body*, so almost *health*.
[4] To be taken with **magis**: *far more*.
[5] The Subjunctive is used here for a general Condition, *you* corresponding to the French *on*.
[6] *household*.
[7] Appius Claudius, censor in 312, built the Appian Way and was a noteworthy statesman.

EXERCISE 38.

If we wish to keep some of our former strength in old age, we must obey the laws of nature. Masinissa at the age of ninety still had the power of marching and of riding; such things are not demanded from[1] us all, but we should resist old age and live

[1] Use **postulo ab.**

wisely. We should help[1] our minds even more than our bodies. Now is the time for reading and learning, not only for exercising. Solon[2] said that he, while growing old, learned many things every day; surely there can be no pleasure greater than this pleasure of the mind! It is said that Appius, old and blind, directed a large household and kept command. I myself spend much time not only in writing, but also in reflecting, and whenever[3] I come into the senate, I help the state with the powers of my mind, not with those of my body.

[1] Use **subvenio** (Dat.).
[2] Athenian lawgiver (*c.* 600 B.C.)
[3] Use **quoties.**

Chapter 10
The Gerundive: (1) expressing Obligation

---

(1) **Delenda est (erit, erat) Carthago.**
   *Carthage must be (will have to be, ought to have been)
   destroyed.*

When a **Transitive Verb** is used, the commonest way in Latin
of expressing Obligation is by the use of the **Gerundive,** and by
a part of the Verb **sum.** The Gerundive is a Verbal Adjective
ending in **-ndus,** with a **Passive** meaning, e.g. **amandus, -a, -um,**
to be loved. All Transitive Verbs, including Deponents, have
Gerundives, e.g. **persequendus,** *to be pursued.*

In the above example **delenda** is the Gerundive of **deleo** and
agrees in Number, Gender, and Case with **Carthago.**

As with the Gerund, the person on whom the Obligation
falls is expressed by the **Dative** of the **Agent:**

   Carthago nobis delenda est.
   We must destroy Carthage.

For the sake of composition, it is worth noting what happens
when we translate *We must destroy Carthage* into Latin: as
deleo is a **Transitive Verb,** we use the **Gerundive** and put the
sentence in a **Passive** form; the **Object** in the English sentence
becomes the **Subject** in Latin, followed by the Gerundive in
agreement and the required part of **sum;** the **Subject** in the
English sentence takes its place as the Dative of the Agent;
Carthage is to-be-destroyed by us.

Whether, then, we use Gerund or Gerundive for expressing
Obligation depends upon whether the Verb is Intransitive or
Transitive; this can easily be remembered by

   Gerund—Intransitive
   Gerundive—Transitive
   (same number of syllables in each line!)
58

If, for example, we take the sentence *We must resist old age*, we must use the Gerund, because **resisto** takes the Dat. and is therefore Intransitive: **senectuti a nobis resistendum est** (see previous chapter).

The Gerundive (like the Gerund) is often used in Indirect Statement or with the Subjunctive:

Caesar cognovit naves sibi reficiendas esse.
Caesar realised that he had to repair the ships.

Arverni timebant ne extrema sibi patienda essent.
The Arverni feared that they would have to undergo extreme sufferings.

(2) A further use of the Gerundive of Obligation should be noted. It is often used in the Accusative after certain verbs, to express the Purpose of an action:

cūro, *I see to, cause.*	**relinquo,** *I leave.*
do, *I give.*	**suscipio,** *I undertake.*
mitto, *I send.*	**trādo,** *I hand over.*

Caesar exercitum transportandum curavit.
Caesar caused his army to be transported
or *saw to the transporting of his army.*

Centum obsides Aeduis custodiendos tradit.
He hands over a hundred hostages to the Aedui for custody.

EXERCISE 39.
1. Exercitus Caesari transportandus erat.
2. Haec urbs vobis expugnanda erit.
3. Nonne hoc heri tibi faciendum erat?
4. Tantum praedae nobis non dimittendum est.
5. Novae copiae imperatori exspectandae erant.
6. Galli dixerunt principem ex oppido expellendum esse.
7. Vercingetorix arma paranda curavit.
8. Cives timebant ne oppidum suum sibi incendendum esset.
9. Principes multas naves aedificandas susceperunt.
10. Arverni putaverunt se Caesari non deserendos fuisse.

EXERCISE 40.
1. We must reconnoitre the wood.
2. Caesar will have to send out scouts.
3. You ought to wait for a favourable wind.
4. The Gauls ought not to have killed Roman citizens.
5. These soldiers must guard the baggage.
6. We shall have to undergo great dangers.
7. So great was the storm that the ships had to be kept in the harbour.
8. Caesar caused garrisons to be posted in three places.
9. The general said that such an opportunity should not be neglected.
10. I know that I ought to have written a letter at once.

EXERCISE 41.
1. Patria nobis conservanda est.
2. Pabulum equitibus inveniendum est.
3. Multae naves Caesari parandae erant.
4. Fabri e Gallia arcessendi erant.
5. Milites in silvas ignotas non dimittendi sunt.
6. Subsidium quam celerrime Aeduis mittendum erit.
7. Magister dixit corpora pueris exercenda esse.
8. Caesar nivem discutiendam et vias patefaciendas curavit.
9. Vercingetorix ita egit, ut Caesari consilium celeriter capiendum esset.
10. Galli dixerunt Caesarem intercludendum fuisse.
11. Haec res per agros statim clamore significanda erit.
12. Hostes non diutius hodie vobis sunt persequendi.

EXERCISE 42.
1. We must send cavalry at once.
2. Caesar had to build a bridge over the Rhine.
3. Hannibal perceived that he ought to encourage his men.
4. We must free Gaul from the power of Rome.
5. The Gauls said that the villages and buildings should be burnt.
6. More ships ought to have been sent back.

7. Caesar was afraid that he would have to wage war against the Britons.
8. We must often neglect private advantages.
9. Caesar undertook the siege of Avaricum.
10. Hannibal had to make a new road in that place.
11. You must defend the camp.
12. This should not have been done so quickly.

Chapter 11
The Gerundive: (2) in Oblique Cases

---

(1) As explained in Chapter 10, the Acc. of the Gerundive is used in Indirect Statement, to express Obligation, and also after certain Verbs, such as **curo**.

(2) **Further uses of the Oblique Cases of the Gerundive:**
The Gen. and Abl. of the Gerund of a Transitive Verb **may** govern an Acc., e.g. **urbem capiendi causa,** *to capture the city*; **urbem capiendo,** *by capturing the city.*

The best Latin authors, however, preferred the use of the **Gerundive** in place of this construction; with **ad** and the Acc. and with the Dat. they always used it:

> **Marcellus ad urbem capiendam milites duxit.**
> *Marcellus led his soldiers to capture the city.*

> **Marcellus bello conficiendo studebat.**
> *Marcellus was keen on finishing the war.*

In these examples the Gerundive does not convey any sense of Obligation, but merely the **action** of the Verb; the Object and the Gerundive in agreement are placed in the Case that would have been occupied by a Gerund.

(This is sometimes called Gerundive Attraction, the Object being attracted to the Case of the Gerundive, which in turn agrees in Gender and Number with the Object.)

So with the Gen.: **urbis capiendae causa,** *to capture the city*, is preferred to **urbem capiendi causa;**

and with the Abl.: **urbe capienda,** *by capturing the city*, is preferred to **urbem capiendo.**

The only occasions when Latin prefers the Gerund to the Gerundive of a Transitive Verb in these constructions are (1) when the Object is a neuter Pronoun, e.g. **haec discendo,** *by learning these things*, because **his discendis** might stand for masc.

or fem., (2) when otherwise an ugly jingle of two Genitives Plural would arise; e.g. **socios iuvandi causa** is preferred to **sociorum iuvandorum causa.**

Note.—The Genitive of the Gerundive takes the ending of the following Genitives of Pronouns, **mei, tui, nostri, vestri, sui** (whether **sui** is sing. or plur.), irrespective of their logical gender or number:

> **Hortatur Gallos ne sui liberandi occasionem dimittant.**
> *He urges the Gauls not to let slip the chance of freeing themselves.*

As will be seen from examples in Chapters 8 and 11, the use of the Gerund or Gerundive with **ad** or **causā** provides variety in Latin in the expression of a Final Clause.

EXERCISE 43.
1. Caesar fabros ad naves reficiendas arcessivit.
2. Germani praedae petendae causa Aduatucam properaverant.
3. Helvetii finibus augendis studebant.
4. Caesar praesidiis constituendis timentes confirmat.
5. Haec faciendo matronae Gallis persuaserunt ne Avarico effugere conarentur.
6. Britanni oppida incursionum vitandarum causa munire solebant.
7. Caesar milites praemisit vias patefaciendi causa.
8. Tempus anni non idoneum erat ad bellum gerendum.
9. In agris vastandis nostri hostibus magnum terrorem intulerunt.
10. Caesar speravit Britannia superanda se facilius bellum Gallicum confecturum esse.
11. Facultatem sui colligendi Romani hostibus non relinquunt.
12. Hannibal ipse ad locum visendum digressus est.

EXERCISE 44.
1. Caesar summoned all the states to ravage the Eburones.
2. By clearing away the snow our men opened up the road.

3. That place did not seem suitable for landing troops.
4. We saw that the Gauls were occupied in burning their towns.
5. Ambassadors were sent to Caesar to seek peace.
6. The chiefs were eager for freeing Gaul.
7. By learning that you will become wiser.
8. Vercingetorix sent out messengers to win over the other states.
9. The Gauls tried to defend themselves by burning their buildings.
10. They saw that there was no chance of saving themselves.
11. The Romans, summoned to battle, had nothing to keep off the cold.
12. Archimedes was skilled in inventing engines of war.

EXERCISE 45.

VERCINGETORIX RESTORES MORALE

Himself undaunted, Vercingetorix rallied the Gauls after the disaster at Avaricum. He then successfully held Gergovia, the capital of the Arverni, and the whole of Gaul was now on his side, except the Rēmi and the Province. Caesar, however, with the help of German cavalry defeated him in battle and forced him back into his headquarters at Alesia. Here he besieged him and by routing a relief force of 250,000 men, brought about the collapse of the revolt.

Vercingetorix postero die concilio convocato Gallos consolatus cohortatusque est ne perturbarentur incommodo. Affirmavit non virtute neque in acie vicisse Romanos, sed artificio quodam et scientia oppugnationis. 'Nunquam' inquit, 'mihi placuit Avaricum defendi. Hoc tamen incommodum maioribus commodis sanabo; civitates quae ab reliquis Gallis dissentiunt, has mea diligentia vobis adiungam atque unum consilium¹ totius Galliae efficiam. Interea moneo ut castra muniatis, quo facilius repentinos hostium impetus sustineatis.'

Fuit haec oratio non ingrata Gallis, et maxime quod ipse

¹ *a single policy.*

animo[1] non defecerat tanto accepto incommodo neque se in occultum[2] abdiderat et conspectum multitudinis fugerat; plusque animo providere existimabatur, quod primo incendendum Avaricum, post deserendum esse censuerat. Simul in spem veniebant de reliquis adiungendis civitatibus; primumque eo tempore Galli castra munire instituerunt et adeo sunt animo confirmati, homines insueti laboris, ut omnia sibi patienda existimarent.

Nec minus quam est pollicitus Vercingetorix animo laborabat ut reliquas civitates adiungeret, atque eas donis pollicitationibusque alliciebat. Qui Avarico expugnato refugerant, armandos vestiendosque curat; simul, ut deminutae copiae redintegrarentur, imperat certum numerum militum civitatibus, sagittariosque omnes, quorum erat permagnus numerus in Gallia, conquiri et ad se mitti iubet. His rebus celeriter id quod Avarici deperierat expletur.

From Caesar, *Gallic War*, VII, 29-31 (adapted).

[1] *in spirit.*
[2] A Prepositional phrase, *into a secret place*, and so *away.*

EXERCISE 46.

On the next day Vercingetorix summoned a council to encourage the Gauls. He said that he had never voted that Avaricum should be defended. 'Do not be upset by this disaster; the Romans won because of their skill in besieging cities, not because of their courage.' He promised that he would remedy this disaster by winning over the rest of the states of Gaul, and urged them to defend themselves by fortifying the camp. The Gauls were encouraged by his words; for they now realized that they ought not to have tried to defend the city. Their hope of receiving the remaining states into an alliance was increased daily; although the work of fortifying the camp was not easy for them, they perceived that this must be done without delay. After arming and clothing those who had survived the siege, Vercingetorix caused a definite number of soldiers and all archers to be sought out and sent to him. By doing these things he soon renewed his diminished forces.

Additional sentences on Gerunds and Gerundives

EXERCISE 47.

1. Corpora nostra non nimia exercitatione fatiganda sunt.
2. Arverni dixerunt suis fortunis a Vercingetorige consulendum esse.
3. Appius servis metuendus erat.
4. Princeps in militibus puniendis severissimus erat.
5. Ars conservandi roboris senibus discenda est.
6. Cives senserunt nullam esse spem Avarico effugiendi.
7. Caesar arbitratus est opportunitate tempestatis sibi utendum esse.
8. Non nunc est tempus praedandi.
9. Galli dixerunt mulieribus a Romanis parcendum fuisse.
10. Caesar signum ineundae urbis militibus dedit.
11. Princeps sensit Gallorum animos confirmandos esse.
12. Vercingetorix erat in tanto periculo ut novae copiae ei arcessendae essent.

EXERCISE 48.

1. The time is not suitable for attacking.
2. We must finish this work without delay.
3. The Gauls sent ten thousand men to defend Avaricum.
4. So deep was the snow that the soldiers had to clear it away.
5. You ought to beware of the dog.
6. The Gauls roused the anger of the enemy by killing Roman citizens at Cenabum.
7. Vercingetorix said that the Romans must be resisted.
8. By defending Avaricum the Gauls lost many men.
9. We spend much time in learning Latin.
10. The chiefs shouted that Gaul must be freed.
11. You have no chance of saving the city.
12. The soldiers ought to have been given time for resting.

Chapter 12
Further Uses of the Ablative

Apart from those which have already been explained, the following uses of the **Ablative** call for notice:

(1) Abl. of **Origin** (the idea of *from* in *birth, descent*, etc.):

Princeps summo loco natus.
A chieftain born of highest station.

So **natus** with Abl. means *son of*, e.g. **Paulo natus,** *son of Paulus.*

(2) Abl. of **Cause** (*from*):

Multi pestilentia moriebantur.
Many were dying of the plague.

Hostes eadem re erant tardiores.
The enemy were slower for the same reason.

(3) Abl. of **Manner** (*how, in what way*); this is used *with* or *without* **cum**, if an Adjective is used, but *with* **cum**, if there is no Adjective:

Equites magno cum periculo dimicabant.
The cavalry were fighting with great risk.

Huc Caesar magnis itineribus contendit.
Caesar hurried to this place with forced marches.

Multi cum clamore in forum currunt.
Many run into the forum with a shout.

The following Ablatives of Manner (and some others) are, however, used *without* **cum**:

arte, *skilfully.*	**iūre,** *rightly.*
cāsu ⎫ *by chance.*	**iniūriā,** *unjustly.*
forte ⎭	**iussu,** *by order.*

iniussu, *without the order.*
mōre, *according to custom.*
nullo negōtio, *with no*
   trouble.
silentio, *in silence.*

sponte (with **meā, tuā, suā**),
   of one's own accord.
vi, *by force.*
vi et armis, *by force of arms.*

Iniussu imperatoris non de praesidio decedendum est.
We must not leave the garrison without the general's orders.

Ariovistus respondit se Rhenum transisse non sua sponte, sed rogatum a Gallis.
Ariovistus replied that he had not crossed the Rhine of his own accord, but at the request of the Gauls.

N.B. The Preposition **in** is never used with the Abl. of Manner, e.g. **omni modo,** *in every way.*

(4) Local Abl. of (*a*) Place (*where*), (*b*) Time (*when*):

(*a*) **Terrā marīque,** *by land and sea.* This Local Abl. is also used of parts of the body, e.g. **capite, pede, bracchio, aure, oculo vulnerari,** *to be wounded in the head, foot, arm, ear, eye.*

(*b*) **vēre,** *in spring.*
aestāte, *in summer.*
auctumno, *in autumn.*
hieme, *in winter.*

prīmā lūce, *at dawn.*
nocte, *by night.*
bello et pāce, *in war and peace.*

EXERCISE 49.
1. Erant qui dicerent Romulum deo natum esse.
2. Vercingetorix animos Gallorum confirmare magna cum diligentia conatus est.
3. Multi cives fame et siti moriebantur.
4. Caesar hoc oppidum nullo negotio cepit.
5. C. Mucius, adulescens nobili loco natus, propter magnam fortitudinem a Porsenna liberatus est.
6. Galli ex oppido Avarico silentio effugere constituerant.
7. Summa difficultate reliqui ad castra Vercingetorigis nocte pervenerunt.
8. Quo facilius Romanos impedirent, Galli multas urbes sponte sua incenderunt.

9. Hostes iniussu imperatoris armis abiectis portas petiverunt.
10. Omnis multitudo principis orationem Gallico more[1] approbant.
11. Prima luce imperator aciem instruxit.
12. Caesar magna cum celeritate ad legiones regressus est.

[1] This was by clashing their arms together.

EXERCISE 50.
1. Vercingetorix, son of a chieftain, was driven out of the state.
2. Caesar captured the town of Cenabum by force of arms.
3. According to the custom of their ancestors, the Gauls especially worship Mercury.
4. We must reach the town by forced marches.
5. Many had died of the plague in the autumn.
6. There are some who say that Hercules is a son of Jupiter.
7. With the utmost care Caesar kept the soldiers in the camp.
8. Themistocles was the salvation of his country both in peace and in war.
9. Some had been wounded in the arm, others in the leg.
10. I did this not by order of my master, but of my own accord.
11. We must conquer the Carthaginians by land and sea.
12. Seek your freedom in every way.

(5) Abl. of **Respect** (*in what point*):

aspectu ⎫	**nātu,**[1] *by birth.*
formā ⎬ *in appearance.*	**numero,** *in number.*
speciē ⎭	**rē vērā,**[2] *in truth, really.*

and the Abl. of many abstract Nouns:

Athenienses virtute valebant.

The Athenians were strong in courage.

Caesar hostes equitatu superiores esse intellegebat.

Caesar realized that the enemy were superior in cavalry.

[1] **natu maior,** *older*; **n. maximus,** *oldest*; **natu minor,** *younger*; **n. minimus,** *youngest.*

[2] Often written as one word **rēvērā.**

The Supine in **-ū** (cf. **natu,** above) comes under the heading of Abl. of Respect. It is not common, but should be noted for the purpose of recognition; it is found in certain authors after, e.g. **facilis, difficilis, mirabilis,** *wonderful,* **iucundus,** *pleasant*:

Difficile factu est, *it is difficult to do.*

(6) Abl. of **Measure of Difference** (*by how much*).

This is used (*a*) with Comparatives:

Multo, paulo, aliquanto, nihilo sapientior est quam tu.
He is much, a little, considerably, no wiser than you.
(lit. *by much, by a little,* etc.)

Hibernia est dimidio minor quam Britannia.
Ireland is half the size of Britain.
(lit. *smaller by half*)

Multis partibus maior, minor.	**Eo magis.**
Many times bigger, smaller.	*All the more.*

Latin uses this Abl. in Proportional sentences:

Quo longius procedebant, eo difficilior via esse videbatur.
The further they went, the more difficult did the journey seem to be.
(lit. *by what amount . . . , by that amount*)

Sometimes this Abl. is found with a Superlative, e.g. **simulacrum multo antiquissimum,** *by far the oldest statue.*

(*b*) with Verbs which imply Comparison, e.g. **supero,** *I surpass,* **antepono,** *I prefer* (*one thing to another*):

Virtutem omnibus rebus multo anteponunt.
They far prefer virtue to everything else.

Alter alterum paulo superat.
The one man slightly surpasses the other.

(*c*) before expressions of Time:

Multo ante noctem.	**Non multo post.**
A long time before night.	*Not long afterwards.*

Note.—**Multis ante annis,** *many years before*; **paucis post diebus,** *a few days later.*

EXERCISE 51.
1. Galli oppida sua omnia, numero ad duodecim, incendunt.
2. Quo plus habemus, eo plus cupimus.
3. Paulo post Arverni audiverunt quae Cenabi oriente sole gesta essent.
4. Britanni, vitro infecti, sunt in pugna horridi aspectu.
5. Gallia est multis partibus maior quam Britannia.
6. Hoc videtur difficile esse factu, revera est facile.
7. Galli erant et virtute et studio pugnandi nostris pares.
8. Caesar, cum paulo longius a castris processisset, suos ab hostibus premi vidit.
9. Quo acrius pugnabant, eo plures vulnerabantur.
10. Ciceronum natu maior erat orator, natu minor Caesaris legatus.
11. Nostri facile superabant, atque eo magis, quod in conspectu Caesaris res gerebatur.
12. Tribus post diebus domum rediimus.

EXERCISE 52.
1. The chief drove out of the state those by whom he had himself been driven out a short time before.
2. The enemy are superior in number, the Romans in courage.
3. Many things are pleasant in appearance, but really should be avoided.
4. The more often I hear him, the more I admire him.
5. Few cities surpass Athens in beauty.
6. Hasdrubal was younger than Hannibal.
7. Rome is by far the biggest city of Italy.
8. The horses of the Germans are distinguished neither in appearance nor in speed.
9. We far prefer friendship to wealth.
10. The more wine the sentries drank, the easier it was for the Romans to climb the walls.
11. This is easy to say, difficult to do.
12. Pompey excels not only in courage, but also in knowledge.

(7) **Abl. Absolute,** with a **Noun** or **Adjective,** instead of with a Participle; this use arises because **sum** has no Present Participle (except in the Compounds, **absens,** *absent,* and **praesens,** *present*):

> **me duce,** *with me as leader, under my leadership.*
>
> **me consule,** *in my consulship.*
>
> **rege Romulo,** *in the reign of Romulus.*
>
> **te auctore,** *at your suggestion* or *instigation.*
>
> **imperatore vivo, salvo, incolumi, superstite,** *as long as the general is alive, safe, survives.*
>
> **me invito,** *against my will.*
>
> **aequo Marte,** *on equal terms* (in battle).

(8) An Abl. is used with:

(a) **fruor,** *I enjoy.*   **ūtor,** *I use.*

   fungor, *I perform* (*an office*).   **vescor,** *I feed on.*

   potior, *I gain possession of.*

(b) Verbs denoting *fulness, need, deprivation, freedom* (these Verbs, when Transitive, may also have a Direct Object in the Acc.):

abundo, *I abound* (*in*), or *have plenty* (*of*).	**fraudo,** *I cheat* (*of*).
	nūdo, *I strip* (*of*).
compleo ⎫ *I fill* (*with*). **impleo** ⎭	**prohibeo,** *I debar, keep off* (*from*).
onero, *I load* (*with*).	**spolio,** *I rob* (*of*).
careo, *I lack* or *am free from something,* (e.g. *illness*).	**lībero,** *I free* (*someone from*). **vaco,** *I am free* (*from*).
egeo, *I need.*	

> **Oppidani frumento abundant.**
> *The townsfolk have plenty of corn.*
>
> **Collem vidit nudatum hominibus.**
> *He saw a hill stripped of defenders.*
>
> **Caesar equites hostium pabulatione prohibere conatus est.**
> *Caesar tried to cut off the enemy's cavalry from forage-supply.*

N.B. **Opus est mihi auxilio,** *I have need of help* (lit. *I have work with help*).

(c) the following Adjectives:

contentus, *satisfied* (*with*). **frētus,** *relying* (*on*).

dignus, *worthy* (*of*). **praeditus,** *endowed* (*with*).

indignus, *unworthy* (*of*).

EXERCISE 53.
1. Duce Vercingetorige multi Galli libertatis causa arma capere coeperunt.
2. Publio Valerio et Tito Lucretio consulibus Horatius Cocles Romam conservavit.
3. Princeps dixit frumentatione Romanos prohibere perfacile esse factu.
4. Ubi murus defensoribus nudatus est, homines testudinem faciunt.
5. Assentatio non amico digna est.
6. Caesare in Italia absente, Galli de bello consilia inibant.
7. Fretus eorum cupiditate, Caesar Gallos ad diripiendos Eburones vocat.
8. Germani lacte, caseo, carne vescuntur.
9. Opus erit nobis multis copiis, ut hac urbe potiamur.
10. Interdum medicina egemus, ut morbo careamus.
11. Me invito hos captivos armis spoliavistis.
12. Oppidum Avaricum magno tumultu impletum est.

EXERCISE 54.
1. Vercingetorix said that the Gauls had defended Avaricum against his will.
2. As long as both consuls were alive, the Romans fought bravely.
3. Caesar was a man endowed with great cleverness and foresight.
4. It is the mark of a good citizen always to perform his duties.

5. On that day the Romans were not able to fight against the Gauls on equal terms.
6. In order to be free from care, let us be content with little.
7. It was easy for the Gauls to keep the Romans from foraging, because they had plenty of cavalry.
8. The Arverni had need of reinforcements.
9. At the instigation of Vercingetorix many tribes began to resist Caesar.
10. The chief said that he was free from blame in this matter.
11. The Gauls thought that their leader was worthy of thanks.
12. The Britons used imported bronze.

EXERCISE 55.

ELKS AND BISON

In a digression about the Germans Caesar describes wild beasts to be found in the Hercynian forest, the wooded country of central Europe; the ūrus is bison europaeus and is still found in Lithuania.

Alces magnitudine capras paulo antecedunt mutilaeque sunt cornibus, et crura sine articulis habent, neque quietis causa procumbunt, neque si conciderunt, erigere sese aut sublevare possunt. His sunt arbores pro cubilibus: ad eas se applicant atque ita paulum modo reclinatae quietem capiunt. Quarum ex vestigiis cum est animadversum a venatoribus, quo se recipere consueverint, omnes eo loco aut ab radicibus subruunt aut accidunt arbores, tantum[1] ut summa species earum stantium relinquatur. Huc cum se consuetudine reclinaverunt, infirmas arbores pondere affligunt atque una ipsae concidunt.

Uri sunt magnitudine paulo infra elephantos, specie et colore et figura tauri.[2] Magna vis eorum est et magna velocitas, neque homini neque ferae quam conspexerunt parcunt. Hos studiose foveis captos Germani interficiunt. Hoc se labore durant adulescentes atque hoc genere venationis exercent, et qui plurimos ex his interfecerunt, relatis in publicum cornibus,

[1] **tantum,** *so far*; **summa,** *outward.*
[2] Gen. sing.

quae sint testimonio,[1] magnam ferunt laudem. Sed assuescere ad homines ne parvuli quidem excepti possunt. Amplitudo cornuum et figura et species multum a nostrorum boum cornibus differt. Haec studiose conquisita ab[2] labris argento circumcludunt atque in amplissimis epulis pro poculis utuntur.

From Caesar, *Gallic War*, VI, 27–28.

---

[1] Predicative Dat.

[2] For this use of ab, cf. **a dextra.**

Chapter 13
Impersonal Verbs

The **Impersonal** use in the 3rd person sing. in the Passive of Verbs which take the Dat. Case (and are therefore Intransitive) has already been noticed; e.g. **Caesari persuasum est,** *Caesar was persuaded.*

This same Impersonal construction is also found with the Passive of Verbs which are Intransitive in meaning:

Tres ferme horas pugnatum est.
The fighting went on for nearly three hours.

Curritur ad arma.   **In iugum Alpium perventum est.**
They run to arms.   *They reached the top of the Alps.*

It should be noticed that **videtur** and **dicitur** are not used in Latin for our *it seems, it is said (that)*; **videor** and **dicor** are used **personally:**

Socrates videtur (dicitur) fuisse hominum sapientissimus.
It seems (is said) that Socrates was the wisest of men.

We now pass to classes of Verbs which are only used **Impersonally:**

(*a*) **miseret,** *it moves to pity.*   **pudet,** *it shames.*
       paenitet, *it repents.*   **taedet,** *it wearies.*
       piget, *it displeases, vexes, irks.*

These Verbs belong to the 2nd Conjug. and have the 3rd person sing. of each tense, the Infinitives, and the Gerund; they govern the Acc. of the person who experiences the feeling of *pity, shame,* etc., and the Gen. of that which causes the feeling (or for which the feeling is felt):

Caesarem captivi miseret.
Caesar pities the prisoner.

Poeni dicunt se pugnandi (or **pugnare**) **taedere.**
The Carthaginians say that they are tired of fighting.

The above Impersonal Verbs (except **miseret**) may be followed by the Gen. of the Gerund or by the Infinitive (as in the last example); they are sometimes followed by **quod** with the Indicative:

> **Nos pudet quod iniussu ducis regressi sumus.**
> *We are ashamed that we returned without the general's order.*

Special care must be taken with the English word *sorry*; cf. *I am sorry for you* (**miseret**) with *I am sorry for my mistake* (**paenitet**).

N.B. Don't pity me must be turned by **ne te mei misereat; noli,** being Personal, cannot be used with Impersonal Verbs.

(b)	**oportet,** *it behoves.*	**dēdecet,** *it is unbecoming to.*
	decet, *it is becoming to.*	**iuvat,** *it delights.*

These are followed by the Acc. and an Infinitive Clause:

> **Nos nostra defendere oportet.**
> *It behoves us (We ought) to defend our own.*

> **Oratorem irasci minime decet.**
> *It is hardly becoming for an orator to get angry.*

Note.—(1) **Nos heri pugnare oportuit,** *we ought to have fought yesterday,* shows the use of the past tense (cf. the use of **potui**);

(2) The Gerund or Gerundive is far more commonly used than **oportet** to express Obligation.

(c) **libet,** *it pleases, is agreeable;* **licet,** *it is lawful, allowed.* These are followed by a Dative and an Infinitive:

> **Non libet mihi deplorare vitam neque me vixisse paenitet.**
> *It does not please me to complain about life nor am I sorry to have lived.*

> **Licet nemini contra patriam ducere exercitum.**
> *It is not lawful for anyone to (or No one may) lead an army against his country.*

Licet is also found with the Subjunctive, generally with **ut** omitted, e.g. **ludas licet,** *you may play.*

We may here conveniently mention the indefinite Pronoun, **quilibet**, which like **quivīs**, means *any one* or *any, you like.*

Hoc est tam clarum, ut quilibet intellegere possit.
This is so clear that any one can understand it.

(*d*) **Interest,** *it matters, is of importance*, is used with a Gen. of the person concerned, followed by an Infinitive or an Acc. and Infin. or **ut** with the Subjunctive or an Indirect Question. If, however, the person concerned is a Personal Pronoun, then **interest** is used with the Abl. of the Possessive Pronoun, **meā, tuā, nostrā, vestrā, suā** (the latter only if Reflexive, otherwise the Gen. of **is** or **ille**).

Interest may be qualified by an Adverb (e.g. **magnopere, multum**) or by a Gen. of Value (e.g. **magni, maximi**).

Quid illius interest ubi sis?
What does it matter to him where you are?

Mea magni interest ut te videam.
It matters a great deal to me that I should see you.

Dixit sua maxime interesse me valere.
He said that it was very important to him that I was well.

Rēfert, *it concerns, matters*, is also found with the Abl. of the Possessive Pronoun, but only rarely with the Gen. **Interest** is far more common.

(The origin of **meā rēfert** may be **ex meā rē fert,** *it follows from a view of my business* ; so **meā interest,** *it makes a difference in my business.*)

(*e*) The following Verbs of the 3rd Conjug. concerning time and weather need no explanation:

lūcescit, *it grows light.*	**ningit,** *it snows.*
vesperascit, *it becomes evening.*	**pluit,** *it rains.*

Verbs used Impersonally as well as Personally

There are some Verbs which, besides being used Personally, are also used Impersonally. The following examples show their use:

Me iuvat (or **delectat**) **venire.**
I am delighted to come.

Mihi placet hoc fieri.
It seems right to me that this should be done.

Senatui placuit ut ille mittatur.
The senate is resolved that he should be sent.
(lit. *it has pleased the senate that*)

Appāret (**constat**) **hoc esse verum.**
It is evident (*agreed*) *that this is true.*

Note.—**Constat inter omnes,** *all are agreed.*

Accidit ut ad eundem locum venirent.
It happened (*by chance*) *that they came to the same place.*

Evenit ut serius perveniret.
It turned out that he arrived too late.

EXERCISE 56.
1. Stultitiae nos paenitet.
2. Pugnatum est ab utroque exercitu acriter.
3. Videtur amicitia esse res maximi aestimanda.
4. Plurimos e Britannis belli taedebat.
5. Quod vesperascebat, Caesar suos longius progredi vetuit.
6. Sunt quos infamiae suae neque pudeat neque taedeat.
7. Verrem pro frumento civitatibus pecuniam dare oportuit.
8. Iniussu imperatoris militibus se recipere non licet.
9. Maximi nostra interest naves quam celerrime redire.
10. Aliquando nos desipere iuvat.

EXERCISE 57.
1. It is said that Archimedes helped the Syracusans with his skill.
2. This concerns you, not your father.
3. The senate was resolved that the command should be entrusted to Caesar.
4. A consul may not lead an army into Rome.

5. The Britons said that they were ashamed of such treachery.
6. I am tired of reading the same thing so often.
7. Fighting went on until sunset.
8. Since it was growing light, Caesar prepared to strike camp.
9. The farmer was sorry that he had not sown more corn.
10. The Carthaginians were resolved that Hannibal should be recalled.

EXERCISE 58.
1. Cum ningeret, Poenos itineris longi pigebat.
2. Principi nunquam placuit Avaricum defendi.
3. Defensores Avarici feminarum non miserebat.
4. Quid hanc miseram sectamini praedam, quibus licet iam esse fortunatissimos?
5. Legibus naturae nos oportet parere.
6. Arvernis apparebat nives Caesarem nequaquam impedivisse.
7. Magni nostra refert utrum Vercingetorix perventurus sit necne.
8. Evenit ut cives Avaricum defendere non possent.
9. Iam ad flumen Ligerem perventum erat.
10. Ne te huius rei paeniteat.

EXERCISE 59.
1. We should all fight against disease.
2. It is not unbecoming to an orator to feign anger.
3. It was important to the general to collect as many men as possible.
4. You may obtain as much plunder as you like.
5. It delighted Masinissa at the age of ninety to ride on horseback.
6. Caesar was sorry that he had invited the Germans to plunder the Gauls.
7. Do not be sorry for such a man.
8. It happened that the young men found the tracks of six elks.

9. The general thought that this was his business, not the senate's.

10. All are agreed that both Hannibal and Caesar were skilled in war.

EXERCISE 60.

WARFARE IN WINTER

In 403 B.C. the Romans were besieging Vēii; it was decided to continue the siege throughout the winter, instead of allowing the soldiers to return home as usual. This decision caused considerable grievances and agitation, although pay had been introduced in 406. In this passage Appius Claudius appeals for the more patriotic point of view.

Aut non suscipi bellum oportuit, aut geri pro dignitate populi Romani et perfici quam primum oportet. Perficietur autem, si urgemus obsessos, si non abscedimus antequam spei nostrae finem captis Veiis imposuerimus. Si hercules nulla alia causa,[1] ipsa indignitas perseverantiam imponere debuit. Decem quondam annos urbs oppugnata est ob unam mulierem ab universa Graecia. Quam procul ab domo? Quot terras, quot maria distans? Nos intra vicesimum lapidem, in conspectu prope urbis nostrae, annuam oppugnationem perferre piget? Scilicet quia levis causa belli est. Septies rebellaverunt; agros nostros milies depopulati sunt; Fidenates[2] deficere a nobis coegerunt; colonos nostros ibi[3] interfecerunt; auctores fuere contra ius caedis impiae legatorum nostrorum. Cum his molliter et per dilationes bellum geri oportet? Si nos tam iustum odium nihil movet, ne illa quidem, oro vos, movent? Operibus ingentibus saepta urbs est, quibus intra muros coercetur hostis; agrum non coluit, et culta evastata sunt bello; si reducimus exercitum, non differimus bellum, sed intra fines nostros accipimus.

From Livy, V, 4-5.

[1] Nom. Case, parallel with **indignitas.**
[2] Fīdēnae, which lay on the Tiber a few miles n. of Rome, revolted in 438; **Fīdēnātēs, -ium** (m.), *the inhabitants of Fidenae.*
[3] At Fidenae.

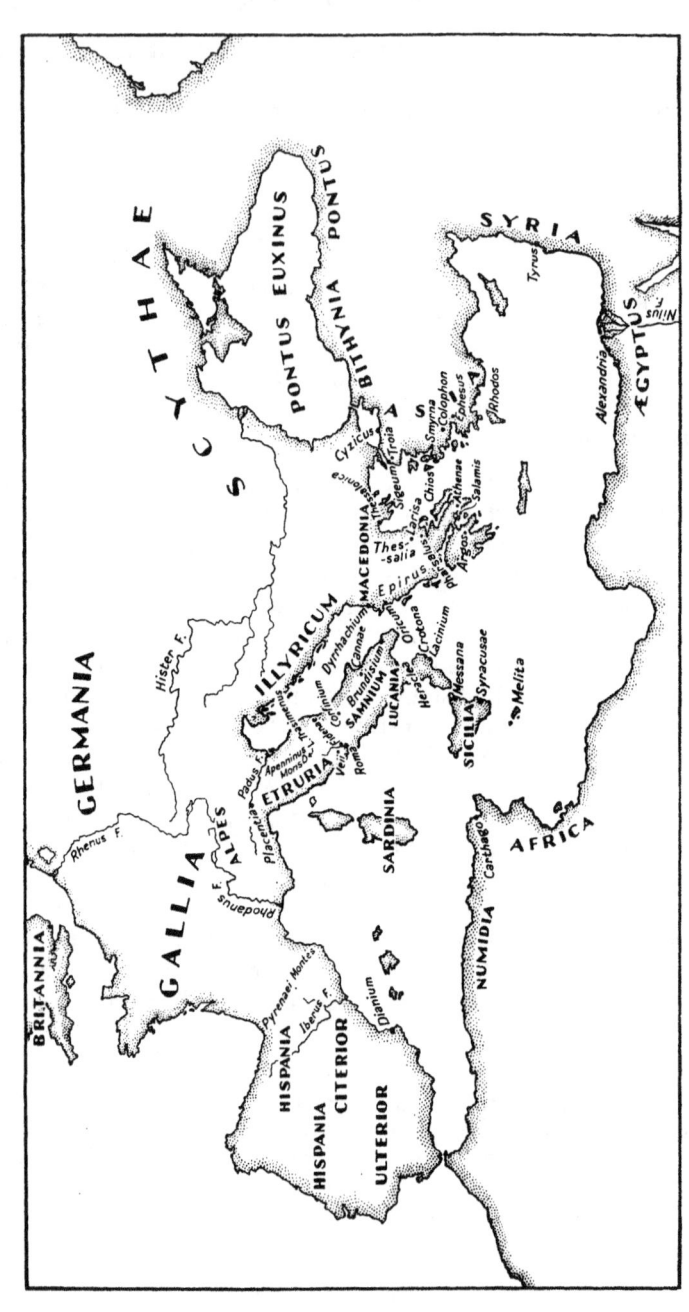

EXERCISE 61.

The senate thought that it was of great importance to the republic that the war should be continued during the whole winter; they therefore resolved that winter-tents[1] should be built for the soldiers. Since the latter saw that the Veientines were spending the winter under their own roofs, they were annoyed that they themselves should be overwhelmed by snows and frosts.[2] Appius Claudius, one of the tribunes, made the following speech to the citizens:

'The soldier formerly was delighted to till his own field for part of the year and seek food with which he might look after himself and his own; now he is delighted to receive pay; ought he not to perform a year's work[3] in return for a year's pay? Once upon a time the Greeks besieged Troy for ten years, a city which was many miles away. Surely we shall not be irked, fighting so near our own city? There are many reasons why we ought to persevere. The people of Veii have many times injured both us and our colonists. Besides, since the enemy is now being besieged, he is not allowed to till his fields; if we lead back the army, he will invade and plunder our own territory. Do not be weary of toiling and fighting; use your opportunity.'

[1] **hibernācula** (n. pl.).
[2] **pruīna** (f.).
[3] *to perform a year's work*, **annuam operam ēdere**.

Chapter 14
Subordinate Clauses in Indirect Speech

A. **Nuntii dixerunt naves, quas Caesar aedificavisset, fractas esse.**
The messengers said that the ships which Caesar had built had been broken.

The actual words of the messengers were **naves, quas Caesar aedificavit, fractae sunt;** the Dependent Clause introduced by **quas** forms part of the original Direct Speech. When the messengers' words are reported by the author, the Main Clause becomes an Indirect Statement in the Acc. and Infinitive, and the **Verb in the Dependent Clause** is now put in the **Subjunctive.**

Similarly **Naves fractae sunt, quod ancorae non subsistebant,** *the ships were broken because the anchors did not hold,* becomes in Reported Speech

> **Nuntii dixerunt naves fractas esse, quod ancorae non subsisterent.**

The guiding principle throughout Reported Speech or Thought is that when the Dependent (generally called the Subordinate) Clause formed part of the original Speech or Thought, and is not merely inserted as a remark of the author, then the Subjunctive is used in the Dependent Clause, whether it is introduced by a Relative or by a Conjunction.

Contrast

> **Nuntiatum est aedem Spei, quae est in foro, fulmine ictam esse.**
> *It was reported that the temple of Hope—which is in the Forum—was struck by a thunderbolt.*

Here the Relative Clause is in the Indicative, because it is a remark made by the author (Livy).

B. **Caesar imperavit ut naves quae fractae essent reficerentur.**
   Caesar ordered that the ships which had been broken should be repaired.

C. **Caesar rogavit num obsides quos imperavisset adessent.**
   Caesar asked whether the hostages whom he had demanded were there.

In B and C we see that the same principle applies to the choice of mood in a Clause Dependent upon an Indirect Command (or Petition) or an Indirect Question; if the words in the Dependent Clause form part of the original words of the speaker, then the Subjunctive mood is used.

To sum up, **Clauses Dependent upon Indirect Statements, Indirect Commands, and Indirect Questions have their Verb in the Subjunctive.**

Sequence of Tenses in Indirect Speech

(1) **Hannibal Poenis declaravit montes, quos viderent, non invios esse.**
   Hannibal declared to the Carthaginians that the mountains which they saw were not impassable.

The Sequence in the Dependent Clause will be Historic, if the Tense of the Verb of *saying* or *thinking* is Historic. As **declaravit** is Historic, **videret** is in Historic Sequence; the fact that **esse** is a Present Infinitive has no bearing upon the matter.

(2) Normally a Primary Tense of the Subjunctive follows a Primary Tense of the Main Verb:

Dicit librum quem invenerit esse tuum.
He says that the book which he has found is yours.

Sometimes, however, when a Perfect Infinitive is used, even if the Tense of the Verb of *saying* is Primary, the sense demands that the Sequence should be taken from the Infinitive and be Historic:

Dicit sese in terram esse egressum ut milites colligeret.
He says that he landed to collect soldiers.

(3) **Dixit eos, qui Alpes transissent, mox caput Italiae in potestate habituros esse.**
He said that those who crossed the Alps would soon have the capital of Italy in their power.

In the Direct Speech, *those who cross* would be in the Future Perfect Tense, **ei qui transierint;** in Reported Speech this becomes the Pluperfect Subjunctive after a Historic Verb of *saying.*

Substitute for Future Infinitive

At this point it is convenient to point out that in Reported Speech, where no Future Infinitive exists, a Future Infinitive is devised by using **fore** (the Fut. Infin. of **sum**) followed by **ut** and the Present or Imperfect Subjunctive (according to Sequence); this device is also used for the sake of variety even when a Fut. Infin. does exist; what would have been the Subject of the Infinitive Clause now becomes the Subject of the Subjunctive Clause:

Dixit fore ut urbs quam diutissime resisteret.
He said that the city would resist for as long as possible.
(lit. *that it would be that the city*, etc.)

Putasne fore ut bellum redintegretur?
Do you think that the war will be renewed?

EXERCISE 62.
1. Caesar dixit copias, quas misisset, mox adventuras esse.
2. Magister puerum rogavit num liber, quem legeret, esset iucundus.
3. Princeps imperavit ut ei qui ab oppido effugissent armarentur.
4. Vercingetorix affirmavit ea oppida incendi oportere, quae non ab omni periculo essent tuta.
5. Bituriges Gallos orant ne pulcherrimam prope totius Galliae urbem, quae praesidio sit civitati, suis manibus incendere cogantur.
6. Principes putabant consilium, quod Vercingetorix cepisset, stulti esse.

7. Cives dixerunt se facile sese defensuros esse, quod prope ex omnibus partibus urbs flumine circumdaretur.
8. Captivus Sugambros rogavit cur praedam, quae Aduatucae esset, non peterent.
9. Hannibal dixit Gallos quondam eas Alpes transisse, quas Poeni adire timerent.
10. Dumnorix petivit ut in Gallia relinqueretur, quod mare timeret.
11. Caesar promisit se praemia daturum esse eis qui primi murum ascendissent.
12. Caesar rogavit cur ei qui pacem petivissent bellum sine causa intulissent.
13. Princeps cives hortabatur ne incommodo quod accepissent perturbarentur.
14. Galli sciverunt fore ut Caesar obsides posceret, quod ei non paruissent.
15. Britanni quae Caesar imperavisset sese facturos polliciti sunt.

EXERCISE 63.
1. The Gauls said that they would do everything which Caesar wished.
2. Cicero begged that reinforcements should be sent as soon as possible, because he was in danger.
3. Ariovistus asked Caesar why he had entered territory which was not ours.
4. Hannibal said that he would give his men land in Italy, Africa, Spain, where each man preferred.
5. Caesar asked why the ships which he had ordered had delayed.
6. Caesar ordered the lieutenant-generals to build as many ships as they could.
7. Vercingetorix said it was easy to hinder the Romans, because the Gauls had plenty of horsemen.
8. Caesar asked how the Gauls were wont to capture the elks which they found in the forest.
9. I asked the boy why he had not done what I had ordered.

10. The chieftain said that he would win over those states which disagreed with the rest of the Gauls.
11. Hannibal asked when the reinforcements he had sent for would arrive.
12. Caesar realized that our men could not win, because their arms were too heavy.
13. Messengers said that many of the ships in which the Romans had been transported could be repaired.
14. Appius Claudius said that the Romans ought not to leave the city which they were now besieging.
15. The Gauls hoped that Hannibal would fall into the ambush which they had prepared.

Note on Continuous Narration

In the narration of a story in Latin, as in English, it is unnecessary to repeat a Verb of Saying after the first sentence; in Latin the constructions (Acc. and Infin., with Dependent Clauses in the Subjunctive) will show that the narration is being continued; this point must be kept in mind in turning an English story into Latin.

EXERCISE 64.

(a) A DREAM SAVES A STATUE

Hannibalem Coelius[1] scribit, cum columnam auream, quae esset in fano Iunonis Laciniae,[2] auferre vellet dubitaretque, utrum ea solida esset an extrinsecus inaurata, perterebravisse; cumque solidam invenisset, statuisse tollere; ei secundum[3] quietem visam esse Iunonem praedicere, ne id faceret, minarique, si fecisset, se curaturam, ut eum quoque oculum,[4] quo bene videret, amitteret. Idque ab homine acuto non esse

---

[1] L. Coelius Antipater wrote a history of Rome c. 120 B.C.
[2] *of Lacinium*, a cape in S. Italy, on which was a temple to Juno.
[3] **secundum** is here a Preposition: *after going to sleep.*
[4] Hannibal had lost an eye from ophthalmia while crossing the Apennines before the battle of Lake Trasimene in 217.

neglectum; itaque ex auro quod exterebratum esset buculam curasse[1] faciendam et eam in summa columna collocavisse.

From Cicero, *De Divinatione*, I, 48.

[1] The Subject of the Infinitive must be supplied.

(b) ONE GOOD TURN DESERVES ANOTHER

Hoc somnium de Simonide[1] commemoratur: qui cum ignotum quendam proiectum mortuum vidisset eumque humavisset haberetque in animo navem conscendere, moneri visus est, ne id faceret, ab eo, quem sepultura affecerat; si navigasset, eum naufragio esse periturum; itaque Simonidem redisse, perisse ceteros, qui tum navigassent.

From Cicero, *De Divinatione*, I, 56.

[1] Simonides was a Greek lyric poet, b. 556 B.C.

EXERCISE 65. (*See note preceding Exercise* 64.)

(a) Coelius, the famous historian, relates that Hannibal, who at that time was fighting near Crotona, entered the temple of Juno and coveted a column which appeared to be made of gold; he found by boring that the column was solid. When he had already decided to take it away, Juno seemed to say to him in his sleep that if he took it away, he would lose his second eye (he had lost one already). Warned by the dream, Hannibal consecrated to the goddess the gold which he had bored out, by making a heifer out of it.

(b) They say that Simonides buried a dead man, whom he had found by chance, and that the same man advised him in a dream not to undertake a voyage which he at that time had in mind. Simonides obeyed the advice that had been given him and returned safe home, but the ship in which he was about to sail was sunk.

Chapter 15
Temporal Clauses (1)

---

(1) The general principle underlying Adverbial Clauses of Time or **Temporal** Clauses is that **if Time alone** is concerned, then the **Indicative** is used, unless, of course, the Temporal Clause is also a Clause Subordinate to an Indirect Statement, Command, or Question (see Chapter 14) and for that reason has its Verb in the Subjunctive. A Future Perfect is used where the exact sense requires it.

This principle holds good for Clauses introduced by :

antequam *before.* **priusquam**	**ubi,** *when, as soon as.*
postquam,[1] *after.*	**dum** **dōnec** *until.* **quoad**
simul ac[1] *as soon as.* **simul atque**[2]	

[1] These Conjunctions are used with the Perfect Tense in Latin where English would often use the Pluperfect, e.g. **simul ac vēnit,** *as soon as he had come.*

[2] **simul atque** must be used before vowels.

Pure Time

Reges erant Romae antequam consules creati sunt.
There were kings at Rome before consuls were elected.

Ego scribam ad Antonium, sed non antequam te videro.
I will write to Antony, but not before I have seen you.

Caesar, postquam (simul ac, ubi) copias exposuit, castra munivit.
After (as soon as, when) Caesar had landed his troops, he fortified a camp.

Impetum facite, simul atque (ubi) hostes conspexeritis.
Attack as soon as (when) you see the enemy.

Pavebamus, dum tempestas quievit.
We were in a panic until the storm died down.

But **Dixit reges fuisse Romae antequam consules creati essent.**

Ut (and sometimes **ut primum**) meaning *when, as soon as,* will also be met, followed by a Perfect Indicative:

Consules, ut ad Cannas ventum est, et in conspectu Poenum habebant.
When the consuls reached Cannae, they beheld the Carthaginians as well.

(2) When, however, some further idea than that of simple time is implied, e.g. of **Purpose** or **Result**, then **antequam, priusquam,** and **dum** (*until*) are followed by the Subjunctive. In fact, when Clauses introduced by these three Conjunctions refer to the Future, the Verb is more often than not in the Subjunctive (*someone is waiting or refuses to wait for something to happen,* i.e. *for a* **purpose**):

Some idea besides that of Time

Scipio cum uno dimicare duce malebat, priusquam iungerentur hostium exercitus.
Scipio preferred to fight against one general, before the enemy's armies joined up.

Manete, dum signum videatis.
Wait till you see the signal.

Caesar exspectavit dum reliquae naves convenirent.
Caesar waited till the rest of the ships should assemble.

Note on antequam and priusquam

These two Conjunctions are often written as two words, the **ante** and the **prius** being placed in the Main Clause in anticipation of the Temporal Clause:

Romani prius Placentiam pervenere, quam satis sciret Hannibal ab Ticino profectos.
The Romans reached Placentia, before Hannibal could be aware that they had started from the Ticinus.

In translating into English, therefore, **ante** or **prius** should be observed as signposts and not translated until the **quam** has been reached.

EXERCISE 66.

1. Caesar, postquam per exploratores comperit Germanos sese in silvas recepisse, constituit non progredi longius.
2. Nostri non finem sequendi fecerunt, quoad praecipites hostes egerunt.
3. Adventus eius ab omnibus visus est, priusquam nuntius adferretur.
4. Princeps Treverorum, simul atque de Caesaris adventu cognitum est, ad eum venit.
5. Ubi descenderitis, uno aut altero proelio Romanos superabitis.
6. Postquam vulneratos ambo consules viderunt, socii effugerunt.
7. Caesar ad Galliam pervenire volebat, antequam ab exercitu intercluderetur.
8. Simul ac litteras scripsero, rus ibo.
9. Hannibal in Italia mansit, donec a legatis revocatus est.
10. Hic vobis manendum est, dum reliqui viam hostibus a tergo intercludant.
11. Non prius fuga destiterunt quam in conspectum agminis nostri venerunt.
12. Dux summae dementiae esse iudicabat exspectare dum hostium copiae augerentur.

EXERCISE 67.

1. The Germans did not stop fleeing until they reached the river Rhine.
2. After Caesar had reached the territory of the Treveri, he decided to cross the Rhine.
3. Hannibal waited for a long time, till reinforcements should arrive.
4. Write to me as soon as you reach home.

5. When the enemy realized that they could not cross the river, they decided to return home.
6. The elks fall down as soon as they have leant against the trees.
7. The German cavalry were not seen until they approached the camp.
8. When I have finished this, I shall do that.
9. The Romans tried to reach the enemy's camp before they could be seen by them.
10. Caesar told the commanders to hold their ground until he came nearer with his army.
11. As soon as the enemy had recovered from their rout, they at once sent ambassadors to Caesar.
12. Caesar made many preparations before he set sail.

Chapter 16
Temporal Clauses (2): **cum**

The uses of **cum** (or **quum**) are various and deserve separate treatment.

We are already familiar with two uses:

(*a*) **Cum** meaning *since*[1] (Causal), always used with the Subunctive;

(*b*) **Cum** meaning *when*, used with the Imperfect or Pluperfect Subjunctive, in Past Time.

> [1] *Note.*—*Since* in a purely Temporal sense, meaning *from the time when*, is **ex quo tempore** or simply **ex quo**, e.g. **Non me iuvare destitit, ex quo pervenit**, *he has not ceased to help me since he arrived.*

Further uses

(*c*) **Cum,** *when*, is regularly used with the Future Tenses of the **Indicative,** especially with the Future Perfect, when that Tense precisely represents the time of the action; *when you go to Rome* or *when you have reached Rome, you will be happy* becomes *When you will have gone* or *will have reached*, etc., in Latin:

Inspiciam hortos, cum venero.
I will have a look at the gardens when I come.

If the time is really Present, the Present Indicative is used:

Coram cum sumus, sermo nobis deesse non solet.
When we are face to face, we do not usually lack conversation.

(*d*) **Cum,** *when*, is also used with the **Past Tenses** of the **Indicative** in certain circumstances:

(1) In a **Frequentative** sense, to express Repeated Actions, to be translated by *whenever* or *as often as*; the Latin Perfect cor-

94

responds to the English Present in this use, and the Latin Pluperfect to the English Perfect:

> **Gubernatores, cum delphinos se in portum conicientes viderunt, tempestatem significari putant.**
> *Whenever helmsmen see dolphins hurling themselves towards the harbour, they think that a storm is portended.*

> **Cum equitatus noster se in agros eiecerat, Cassivellaunus essedarios ex silvis emittebat.**
> *Whenever our cavalry made a dash into the fields, Cassivellaunus would launch his charioteers from the woods.*

(2) When the most important fact in a sentence is contained in the Temporal Clause and not in the Main Clause, i.e. when the Clauses are **inverted**:

> **Iam nona ferme diei hora erat, cum Romanus signum receptui dedit.**
> *It was already about the ninth hour of the day, when the Roman gave the signal for retreat.*

(3) When the **cum** Clause refers to a **definite** *time at which* (= **quo tempore**) something occurred (this use should be recognized rather than imitated); it is not used for *while* with the Past Tenses of the Indicative:

> **Cum Caesar in Galliam venit, alterius factionis principes erant Aedui, alterius Sequani.**
> *At the time when Caesar arrived in Gaul, the leaders of one party were the Aedui, of the other the Sequani.*

Cum primum (like **ut primum**) is used with the Perfect Indicative meaning *as soon as*:

> **Cum primum pati laborem viae potuit, venit.**
> *As soon as he could stand the fatigue of the journey, he came.*

(*e*) **Cum** often has a **Concessive** use; when it means *although*, it always takes the **Subjunctive** (it is mentioned here for the sake of convenience):

Cum maxima telorum multitudine premerentur, nemo de vallo discessit.

Although they were sore pressed by a huge number of javelins, nobody left the rampart.

EXERCISE 68.

1. Tuas cotidie litteras exspectabo. Ad has autem, cum poteris, rescribes.
2. Caesar, cum Vellaunodunum venisset, oppugnare instituit.
3. Cum te videbo, omnia narrabo.
4. Cum se inter equitum turmas insinuaverunt, ex essedis desiliunt.
5. Cum Athenas veneris, ad me scribe.
6. Appius, cum esset et caecus et senex, domum regebat.
7. Cum iam hostes essent in prospectu, nuntii ad Caesarem venerunt.
8. Etrusci iam impetu conabantur detrudere virum, cum fragor rupti pontis impetum sustinuit.
9. Cum eo unde erant egressi reverti coeperant, nostri circumveniebantur.
10. Plura scribam ad te, cum constitero.
11. Vixdum satis patebat iter, cum perfugae certatim ruunt per portam.
12. Cum Placentiam consul venit, iam castra moverat Hannibal.

EXERCISE 69.

1. You will find more booty when you reach Aduatuca.
2. Our men had caught sight of the enemy, when messengers came to say that many ships had been damaged.
3. The Bituriges defended Avaricum, although the chief had warned them not to do this.
4. Since he had been warned in a dream, Hannibal did not remove the golden column.
5. Whenever the Britons fortify woods with rampart and ditch, they call it a stronghold.
6. Set out when you have obtained suitable weather.

7. Scarcely had the rearguard advanced outside the fortifications, when the Gauls began to cross the river.
8. When Simonides was about to go on a voyage, he was warned not to do so.
9. Although the snow is very deep, we must remove it at once.
10. Whenever the roads were blocked with snow, the Arverni thought they were safe.
11. When I have won over the other states, we Gauls will recover our power.
12. Caesar decided to return to his legions as soon as possible, since the Gauls were beginning to revolt.

Chapter 17

Further uses of **dum,** and Revision of Temporal Clauses

Besides being used in Temporal Clauses in its meaning of *until* (see Chapter 15), **dum** has three further uses:

(1) Meaning *while* in the sense of **during** *the time that*, always with the **Present Indicative:**

> **Dum haec in his locis geruntur, Cassivellaunus ad Cantium nuntios mittit.**
> *While this was happening here, Cassivellaunus sent messengers to Kent.*

(2) Meaning *while* in the sense of **all** *the time that, as long as*, with **any tense** of the **Indicative:**

> **Dum intolerabilia frigora erant, quies militi data est.**
> *While the cold was unbearable, rest was given to the soldiers.*

Quamdiu, *as long as*, might have been used here instead of **dum.**

A further illustration will help to make clear these two uses of **dum:**

> **Dum pluit, exiimus,** *while it was raining, we went out*; here the action of *going out* happens in the middle of the *raining*;
> **Dum pluebat, domi manebamus,** *while it was raining, we stayed indoors*; here the actions of *raining* and *staying* are of the same duration.

(3) Meaning *provided that*, with the **Subjunctive** (negative **nē**), often lengthened to **dummodo,** *provided that only, if only*:

Nonnulli omnia honesta neglegunt, dummodo potentiam consequantur.

Some men are regardless of everything honourable, provided that they obtain power.

EXERCISE 70.

1. Abite, dum est facultas, vosque ad legionem recipite.
2. Amicos nostros, dum poterimus, iuvemus.
3. Ne moremur, dum Germani auxilium mittant.
4. Dum Fabius cunctabatur, Hannibal vincere non poterat.
5. Senectus est iucunda, dummodo mens vigeat.
6. Gaudeamus igitur, dum iuvenes sumus.
7. Rure manebo, quamdiu mihi licebit.
8. Hostes oppugnemus, dum adhuc itinere sunt defessi.
9. Illa nocte scribebam, dum illuxit.
10. Dummodo ne nimium roges, pecuniam tibi dabo.

EXERCISE 71.

1. While this was going on in Italy, Scipio was sent with a fleet and an army to Spain.
2. While I breathe, I hope.
3. Caesar could not conquer Gaul as long as the Britons sent reinforcements for the enemy.
4. We can bear even the worst troubles, provided that we have friends.
5. Stay where you are as long as you can.
6. The Gauls said that they would not wait until the Germans arrived.
7. While Hannibal was staying at Ephesus, he met Publius Africanus.
8. If only you cross the Alps, you will conquer the Romans.
9. Horatius resisted the enemy as long as he could.
10. While the elephants were being taken across, Hannibal had sent cavalry to reconnoitre.

Miscellaneous Sentences on Temporal Clauses

EXERCISE 72.

1. Simul ac Romani impetum fecerunt, Treveri in fugam coniecti silvas petiverunt.
2. Germani sese domum receperunt, antequam ad castra Treverorum pervenerunt.
3. Dummodo properetis, omnes fortunas exercitus Romanorum vobis diripere licebit.
4. Cives Romani Cenabi interfecti sunt, priusquam effugere possent.
5. Lege hunc librum, simul atque domum perveneris.
6. Ubi nuntium ex captivis audiverunt, Germani Aduatucam contenderunt.
7. Cives montem Cevennam putaverant esse insuperabilem hieme, dum subito Romanos adesse viderunt.
8. Non prius regrediendum est, quam dux receptui cecinerit.
9. Dum Romani urbem intrant, hostes ultimas partes petebant.
10. Cum satis pecuniae ei esset, parum ei erat sapientiae.
11. Huc redi, cum portus et aditus insulae exploraveris.
12. Dum vires ei supererant, Masinissa etiam in extrema senectute se exercebat.

EXERCISE 73.

1. Free yourselves from the power of the Romans, while you have an opportunity.
2. Whenever Caesar distrusted the enemy, he always demanded hostages.
3. As soon as he could, the chieftain saw to the clothing and arming of the survivors.
4. We can resist the enemy, provided that reinforcements are sent soon.
5. Do not advance until I tell you to.
6. While the Romans were still disembarking, the Britons attacked them.
7. The Greeks besieged Troy till they captured it.

8. Rome flourished as long as luxury did not corrupt her citizens.
9. I read your letter before I had dinner.
10. Come when you have finished your work.
11. Although he wanted to take away the golden column, Hannibal obeyed the advice of the goddess.
12. Since you have received a year's pay, you ought to fight throughout the whole year.

EXERCISE 74.

VERRES: SOFT LIVING OF A GOVERNOR

Verres was governor of Sicily from 73 B.C. for three years, and made a large fortune by means of bribes and confiscations. He was tried on a charge of extortion in 70. Cicero was chosen to be prosecutor in the case and in the following passage makes fun of Verres' unsoldierly manner of life. Verres withdrew into exile in the middle of the proceedings and the parts of Cicero's speech to be found in this book were never actually delivered.

Itinerum laborem, qui vel maximus est in re militari, iudices, et in Sicilia maxime necessarius,[1] accipite quam facilem sibi iste[2] et iucundum ratione consilioque[3] reddiderit. Primum temporibus hibernis ad magnitudinem frigorum et tempestatum vim ac fluminum praeclarum hoc sibi remedium compararat. Urbem Syracusas elegerat, cuius hic[4] situs atque haec[4] natura esse loci caelique dicitur ut nullo die solem homines non aliquo tempore viderint. Hic ita vivebat iste bonus imperator hibernis mensibus ut eum non facile non modo extra tectum sed ne extra lectum quidem quisquam videret.

Cum autem ver esse coeperat (cuius initium iste non a Favonio neque ab aliquo astro notabat, sed cum rosam

[1] The governor had to see that tithes of corn were collected and be on the look out for rebellions among the slaves.
[2] *that person near you*, i.e. *the defendant.*
[3] *method and policy*, so *methodical policy.*
[4] *such.*

viderat, tum incipere ver arbitrabatur), dabat se labori atque
itineribus; in quibus eo usque[1] se praebebat patientem atque
impigrum ut eum nemo unquam in equo sedentem viderit.
Nam ut mos fuit Bithyniae[2] regibus, lectica octaphoro fere-
batur, in qua pulvinus erat perlucidus Melitensis rosa[3] fartus;
ipse autem coronam habebat unam in capite, alteram in collo,
reticulumque ad naris sibi admovebat plenum rosae. Sic
confecto itinere cum ad aliquod oppidum venerat, eadem
lectica usque ad cubiculum deferebatur.

From Cicero, *In Verrem, Actio II,* V, 26-27.

[1] *right up to this point,* so *to such an extent.*
[2] This kingdom, south of the Black Sea, was bequeathed to Rome
in 75 B.C.
[3] *rose-petals.*

EXERCISE 75.

As soon as he saw that winter was at hand, Verres retired to
Syracuse, although he knew well that it was the part of a good
praetor to endure cold and even long journeys. So lazy was he
that, whenever the inhabitants wanted to consult him, they
found him in bed; here he remained until spring approached.
Then what toil, what journeys he devoted himself to! When he
had to make a journey, he did not, as was the custom for old-
time generals, ride on horseback. He used to order his litter to
be got ready nor was he willing to be carried in it, until his
slaves had stuffed his Maltese cushion with rose-petals! He was
so effeminate that he had two garlands, so idle that he would
not leave his litter until he had been carried to his very bedroom;
hither would come the magistrates of the Sicilians and Roman
knights!

EXERCISE 76.

VERRES: HOW HE SPENT THE SUMMER

Cum vero aestas summa esse coeperat, quod tempus omnes
Siciliae semper praetores[1] in itineribus consumere consuerunt,

[1] This was the title by which governors were styled in the pro-
vinces; strictly speaking, he was a pro-praetor.

propterea quod tum putant obeundam esse maxime provinciam, cum in areis frumenta sunt, quod et familiae[1] congregantur et magnitudo serviti perspicitur et labor[2] operis maxime offendit, frumenti copia commonet, tempus anni non impedit: tum, inquam, cum concursant ceteri praetores, iste novo quodam genere imperator pulcherrimo Syracusarum loco stativa sibi castra faciebat. Nam in ipso aditu atque ore portus tabernacula carbaseis intenta[3] velis collocabat. Huc ex illa domo praetoria, quae regis Hieronis[4] fuit, sic emigrabat ut eum per illos dies nemo extra illum locum videre posset. Huc homines digni istius amicitia, digni vita illa conviviisque veniebant. Ac per eos dies, cum iste cum pallio[5] purpureo talarique tunica[5] versaretur in conviviis muliebribus, non offendebantur[6] homines neque moleste ferebant abesse a foro magistratum, non iudicia[7] fieri; locum illum litoris percrepare totum mulierum vocibus cantuque[8] symphoniae, in foro silentium esse summum causarum atque iuris, non ferebant homines moleste; non enim ius abesse videbatur a foro neque iudicia, sed vis et crudelitas et bonorum acerba et indigna direptio.

From Cicero, *In Verrem, Actio II*, V, 29-31.

[1] *household establishments*, including slaves (not *family*, which is **domus**); **magnitudo** here means *number*.
[2] Probably **labor operis** means *the fruits of toil*, i.e. the harvest; **praetores** should be supplied as the object of **offendit**, *strikes the eye of*, **commonet**, *forcibly reminds* (that they should inspect), and **impedit**.
[3] *roofed.*
[4] Hiero was a famous tyrant of Syracuse in the fifth cent.
[5] Greek dress, regarded as effeminate.
[6] **offendo** here has the meaning of *displease*.
[7] *that no trials should be held.*
[8] Probably *playing*.

EXERCISE 77.

Verres was well aware that when summer had begun he ought to undertake journeys throughout the province. It is very important that governors should travel about while the corn is on the threshing-floor, while many slaves are still in one place, while there is danger that[1] a rebellion may arise. But though this was obvious to him, the defendant did not leave Syracuse. He set up tents at the mouth of the harbour and here spent those days not in duties, but in pleasure and in banquets. But the citizens were not annoyed that Verres thus wasted his time.

They were so afraid that their goods would be plundered, that whenever they heard the shore ringing with songs and music and saw the forum empty, they rejoiced.

[1] **nē,** as after a Verb of Fearing.

Chapter 18
Further Frequentative Usages

We have already met **cum** with the Pluperfect Indicative, expressing a Repeated Action (in past time), e.g. **cum rosam viderat,** *whenever he saw a rose.* Latin also uses the Pluperfect in the same way with **si quis,** *if anyone*; **si quando,** *if ever*; **quicumque** (and less commonly **quisquis**), *whoever*; **qui** (when used for *whoever*); **ut quisque,** *whenever anyone*; the corresponding Verb in the Main Clause is always in the Imperfect, corresponding to the English *would do so-and-so*:

Si quando desperare coeperant, se in proxima oppida recipiebant.

If ever they began to despair, they would withdraw to the nearest strongholds.

Quos laborantes conspexerat, his subsidia submittebat.

He sent help to any whom he saw in difficulty.

EXERCISE 78.

VERRES: HIS BOUNDLESS GREED

Cicero deals at great length with the statues and with the gold and silver works of art which Verres stole from the Sicilians; Verres' greed extended to the valuable cargoes of Roman shipmasters who put in at Sicilian ports.

Carcer ille qui est a crudelissimo tyranno Dionysio[1] factus Syracusis, quae[2] lautumiae vocantur, in istius imperio domicilium civium Romanorum fuit. Ut quisque istius animum

---

[1] Tyrant of Syracuse, 405-367 B.C.

[2] When the Relative Pronoun is the Subject of a Copulative Verb, e.g. **sum** or the Passives of Verbs of *calling*, it may agree in Gender and Number with the Complement.

The survivors of the disastrous Athenian expedition were imprisoned in the stone-quarries in 413 B.C.

aut oculos offenderat, in lautumias statim coniciebatur.
Quaecumque navis ex Asia, quae ex Syria, quae Tyro, quae
Alexandria venerat, statim tenebatur; vectores omnes in
lautumias coniciebantur, onera atque merces in praetoriam
domum deferebantur. At quae causa tum subiciebatur ab ipso, iudices, huius tam
nefariae crudelitatis? Eadem quae nunc in defensione com-
memorabitur. Quicumque accesserant ad Siciliam paulo
pleniores,[1] eos Sertorianos[2] milites esse atque a Dianio fugere
dicebat. Illi ad deprecandum periculum proferebant alii
purpuram Tyriam, tus alii atque odores vestemque linteam,
gemmas alii et margaritas, vina nonnulli Graeca venalisque
Asiaticos, ut intellegeretur ex mercibus quibus ex locis
navigarent. Non providerant eas ipsas sibi causas esse periculi,
quibus argumentis[3] se ad salutem uti arbitrabantur. Iste enim
haec eos ex piratarum[4] societate adeptos esse dicebat; ipsos
in lautumias abduci iubebat, navis eorum atque onera diligenter adservanda curabat. His institutis cum completus iam
mercatorum carcer esset, tum cervices in carcere frangebantur
indignissime civium Romanorum, ut iam illa vox et imploratio,
'Civis Romanus sum', quae saepe multis in ultimis terris opem
inter barbaros et salutem tulit, ea mortem illis acerbiorem et
supplicium maturius ferret.

From Cicero, *In Verrem, Actio II*, V, 143-147.

[1] Referring to the **vectores** in charge of the cargo; *rather well laden.*
[2] Sertorius supported the cause of the democrats in Spain and
was murdered there in 72 B.C. Verres pretended that even though
Pompey had settled the 'rebellion' in Spain, the soldiers of Sertorius
were still public enemies. Dianium was on the east coast of Spain.
[3] To be taken Predicatively, *as evidence.*
[4] The pirates who infested the Mediterranean were suppressed by
Pompey in 66.

EXERCISE 79.
Whomsoever Verres found standing in the way of his own
greed, he at once hurled into the stone-quarries, the famous
prison constructed by Dionysius. From whatever land a ship
arrived, Verres saw that it was at once detained; his spies[1]

[1] Use **custōdes.**

would imprison the passengers and carry off the goods to the governor. How slight a pretext did he suggest for cruelty so great! If ever a merchant brought to Sicily purple from Tyre, slaves from Asia, pearls from Alexandria, the defendant would pretend that he was an associate of pirates and would seize not only the cargoes, but also the ships themselves. The famous cry, 'I am a Roman citizen', has been the means of salvation to many men throughout the whole world; if, however, any of these merchants ever dared to utter it, then his neck was broken and he was put to death.

Chapter 19
Some Uses of the Independent Subjunctive

The **Subjunctive** Mood is mostly used, as its name implies, in clauses *subjoined* to Main Clauses, many types of which have already been illustrated.

The Subjunctive is also used **Independently**, not, as the Indicative, to indicate facts, but to present **ideas**; we may summarize these uses as follows:

(1) **Exhortation: Resistamus,** *let us resist.*
Command: Ne redeat, *let him not return* (this is often called the **Jussive** Subjunctive).

(2) **Wish: Redeat victor!** *May he come back victorious!*
A wish expressed by the Subjunctive is often introduced by **utinam,** *would that, I wish that!* The Negative is **nē.**

   (*a*) Wishes for the Future are expressed by the Present Subjunct.:
   Utinam redeas! *Would that you would come back!*

   (*b*) Wishes for the Present are expressed by the Imperfect Subjunct.:
   Utinam adesses! *Would that you were here now!*

   (*c*) Wishes for the Past are expressed by the Pluperfect Subjunct.:
   Utinam ne hoc fecisses! *I wish you had not done this!*

(3) **Direct Deliberative Questions,** questions asked in perplexity, when no answer is expected: **Quid faciamus?** *What are we to do?*
(*Let us do—what?* It is easy to see that this is really the same use of the Subjunctive as the Jussive use.)
So, in Past Time, **Quid faceremus?** *What were we to do?*

In **nesciebat quid faceret,** *he did not know what to do,* we have an example of an Indirect Deliberative Question; the Latin could equally mean *he did not know what he was doing*, but the context would show whether the question was deliberative.

(4) The **Potential** Subjunctive, used to make statements in a halting or polite way; this use is mainly confined to (*a*) certain phrases and (*b*) Verbs of *wishing*:

(*a*) **Ausim dicere,** *I would venture to say* (**ausim** is an archaic form of **audeam**).

Facile crediderim, *I could easily believe.*

Vix crederes, *you would hardly believe.*

Putares, *you would have thought.*

Dixerit quispiam, *some one might say.*

(*b*) **Velim** is used (i) with a Prolative Infinitive, e.g. **velim scire,** *I should like to know*; (ii) with the 2nd and 3rd persons of the Present Subjunct. to express a polite wish for the Future (**ut** being omitted):

Velim mihi ignoscas, *I should like you to forgive me.*

Velim Mago respondeat, *I should like Mago to reply.*

Vellem is used with the 2nd and 3rd persons of the Imperfect and Pluperfect Subjunct. to express polite wishes for the Present and Past respectively:

Vellem tu adesses, *I wish you could be present.*

Vellem adesset Antonius, *I wish Antony could be present.*

Vellem me ad cenam invitasses, *I wish you had asked me to dinner.*

Prohibitions and Polite Commands

(*a*) It is convenient at this point to mention the use of **nē** with the 2nd persons of the Perfect Subjunctive, as an alternative to **noli, nolite** with the Pres. Infin., to express Prohibitions:

Ne transieris Hiberum, *do not cross the Ebro.*

(*b*) Mention should be made, too, of the way in which the Romans expressed a polite Command by **fac** with the 2nd person of the Present Subjunctive (**ut** being generally omitted, but **nē** being used if the Subjunct. Clause is negatived):

Fac mihi perscribas, *see that you write me a full account.*

Fac ne obliviscaris, *see that you don't forget.*

Cura ut or **nē** are similarly used:

Cura, si me amas, ut valeas.
Do see to it, if you have any love for me, that you keep well.

EXERCISE 80.

1. Quaeramus igitur quot itinera per provinciam Verres aestate fecerit.
2. Utinam Verres in tecto maneat, ne res male in foro administret!
3. Quid faciant Siculi? Omnia bona diripiuntur.
4. Vix crederes qualis imperator esset iste.
5. Ne rescripseris, dum litteras alias acceperis.
6. Fac mihi quam primum respondeas.
7. Velim scire quid Romae agatur.
8. Utinam Verres hanc provinciam nunquam praetor obtinuisset!
9. Non ausim credere qualis fuerit istius avaritia.
10. Vellem novae copiae antea pervenissent.
11. Siculi nesciebant isto praetore quomodo se conservarent.
12. Quid in hoc discrimine facerent defensores Avarici?
13. Velim ad me scribas, ut de his rebus me certiorem facias.
14. Hoc tibi heri faciendum erat; cura ut cras facias.

EXERCISE 81.

1. Would that we were now together in Rome!
2. When are we to have a just praetor?
3. You would have thought that such a man could not have been elected.
4. Would that I had received your letter yesterday!
5. I should like Verres to try to deny this.
6. Do not blame him; first see that you know everything.
7. When are we to see the praetor again?

8. Let us hide our corn while Verres is engaged in his banquets.
9. See that you send help as soon as possible.
10. The inhabitants did not know where to hide their goods.
11. We should like you to have been there to see.
12. I could easily believe that all you have said is true.
13. Would that I might see my friends again soon!
14. Someone might say that we have no witnesses.

EXERCISE 82.

THE LETTER OF AN EXILE

The last hundred years of the Republic, which ends in 31 B.C. with the rise of Augustus as the first emperor, sees the gradual decay of the authority of the Senate, revolutionary attempts at popular reform, and the attachment of citizens to parties and generals rather than to the state. Cicero's aim was to reconcile the Senate and the Equites, the big business men, but this attitude stood in the way of the ambitions of the individualistic Pompey, Caesar, and Crassus, and he was banished on a pretext in 58. This letter, written en route for Thessalonīca, is addressed to his wife and children.

Tullius Terentiae et Tulliolae[1] et Ciceroni suis S.D.P.[2]

Ego minus saepe do[3] ad vos litteras quam possum propterea quod cum[4] omnia mihi tempora sunt misera tum vero, cum aut scribo ad vos aut vestras lego, conficior lacrimis sic, ut ferre non possim. Utinam minus vitae cupidi fuissemus! Si haec mala fixa sunt, ego vero te quam primum, mea vita, cupio videre et in tuo complexu emori, quando neque di, quos tu castissime coluisti, neque homines, quibus ego semper servivi, nobis gratiam rettulerunt. Nos Brundisii apud M. Laenium Flaccum dies XIII fuimus, virum optimum, qui

---

[1] A diminutive form of Tullia.

[2] Abbrev. for **salutem dicit plurimam,** *sends warmest greetings,* the conventional beginning of a letter, which is often ended by **valē,** *farewell.*

[3] **litteras do,** *I write to,* hence **ad.**

[4] **cum . . . tum,** *both . . . and, not only . . . but also.*

periculum fortunarum et capitis sui prae mea salute neglexit. Huic utinam aliquando gratiam referre possimus! Brundisio profecti sumus,[1] per Macedoniam Cyzicum[2] petebamus. O me perditum! O afflictum! Quid enim? Rogem te ut venias? Mulierem aegram et corpore et animo confectam? Non rogem? Sine te igitur sim? Unum hoc scito: si te habebo, non mihi videbor plane perisse. Sed quid Tulliola mea fiet?[3] Iam id vos videte: mihi deest consilium. Quid, Cicero meus quid aget? Iste vero sit in sinu semper et complexu meo. Non queo plura iam scribere: impedit maeror. Nunc, miser quando tuas iam litteras accipiam? Quis ad me perferet? Cura, quod potes,[4] ut valeas, et sic existimes, me vehementius tua miseria quam mea commoveri. Mea Terentia, fidissima atque optima uxor, et mea carissima filiola, et spes reliqua nostra, Cicero, valete.

From Cicero, *Epistolae ad Familiares*, XIV, 4.

[1] This would be **proficiscor**, if Cicero were speaking; but he is writing a letter, and uses an Epistolary Aorist because the action would be past by the time Terentia received the letter; **petebamus** corresponds to **petiturus sum** in the same way.
[2] Island city on s. side of the Propontis (Sea of Marmora).
[3] *What will become of . . . ?* Tulliolā meā is Abl. (lit. *What will be done with?*).
[4] **quod** is here equivalent to **quantum**, *as far as*.

EXERCISE 83.

My dear Terentia, little Tullia, and Cicero,

I should like to write to you more often. But whenever I write to you, I am overcome by your troubles and my own, and the task is very difficult. Provided that there is no chance of returning, I should like to see you, my darling, and die, rather than be away from home. Would that gods and men had shown thanks to me! I am now off[1] to Cyzicus from Brundisium. Poor me! What am I to do? I don't know whether to ask for you to come or not! What will become of the two children? I should like to have had you with me, but you must look after them. See that you all keep well, and write as soon as possible.

Yours ever
Tullius

[1] For tense see note 1 above.

Chapter 20
Conditional Sentences: (1) Open

A **Conditional** Clause, generally introduced by **sī,** *if,* is an Adverbial Clause, depending upon a Main Clause.

The Main Clause in a Conditional sentence is often called the **Apodosis,** the Conditional Clause the **Protasis;** together, they form a Conditional sentence.

It is true that in Latin, as in English, the *if* Clause generally precedes the Main Clause, e.g. *If I don't hurry, I shall be late* (and the truth of the Main Clause depends upon the *if* Clause), but in studying the way in which Conditional Sentences are written, we must be concerned first of all with the **Mood** of the **Main Clause.**

Conditional sentences fall into two chief types, according to whether the Mood of the Main Clause is the **Indicative** (or **Imperative**), which we will call the **Open** type, or the **Subjunctive,** which we will call the **Remote** type.

Type A. Open Conditional Sentences

If the **Main Verb** makes a matter-of-fact statement and is in the **Indicative** (or is in the form of a command and is in the **Imperative**), then the Verb of the Conditional Clause is also in the Indicative. In other words, if the Apodosis is in the Indicative, the Protasis will be in the Indicative.

The Tense of the Indicative corresponds to the sense; **nisi** is generally used for *unless, if . . . not:*

Si vos valetis, nos valemus.
If you are well, we are well.

Nisi tu vales, ego non valeo.
Unless you are well, I am not well.

Si opus perfecisti, licet abire.
If you have finished the work, you may go.

113

Si me diligis, rescribe.
If you are fond of me, write back.

Rempublicam, si licebit, tuebimur.
We will look after the state, if we are allowed.

Si quem cum eo sermonem habueris, scribes ad me.
If you have any conversation with him, you will write to me.

Notes.—(1) Latin uses the Future or Future Perfect in the Conditional Clauses, if this tense is required by the sense.

(2) The Indefinite Pronoun (and Adjective), **quis, qua, quid (quod)**, is used for *anyone* or *any* after **si** and **nisi.**

(It is worth stressing at this point that **quis** is always used for *any* in Dependent Clauses introduced by **sī, nisi, num, nē,** and **cum,** *when.*)
A **double** Conditional Clause is expressed by **sive . . . sive (non),** *whether . . . or (not)* (sometimes, **seu . . . seu**):

Sive tu medicum adhibueris sive non, convalesces.
Whether you summon a doctor or not, you will get better.

N.B. Great care should be taken in translating *whether* into Latin. **Utrum . . . an,** *whether . . . or,* is only used in Indirect Questions.

Sin means *but if* in a contrasted Conditional Clause:

. . . , sin tu iam Roma profectus eris, curabis ut hoc ita fiat.
. . . , but if you have already left Rome, you will see that this is done so.

Sī nōn is used in place of **nisi,** if the *not* applies to a single word:

Si ad villam non veneris, Romae te fortasse videbo.
If you do not come (i.e. fail to come), perhaps I shall see you in Rome.

EXERCISE 84.
1. Si nescis, tibi ignosco.
2. Desilite, milites, nisi vultis aquilam hostibus prodere.

3. Si nunc cessavero, quando vobis gratiam pro beneficiis vestris referam?
4. Si iam senex Sophocles fabulam pulchram scripsit, non desipiebat.
5. Si quid cognovero, scies.
6. Nisi oppida vestra incenderitis, Caesar facile vos superabit.
7. Si Verres haec fecit, dignus est poena gravissima.
8. Sive pedibus ibat sive in equo vehebatur, Masinissa se durissimum praestitit.
9. Castra defendite diligenter, si quid durius acciderit.
10. Si navem conscenderis, peribis.
11. Sive ningit sive non, Veii obsidendi sunt.
12. Nisi hic auream columnam relinques, alterum oculum amittes.
13. Si quis hoc iam fecit, maxime gaudeo.
14. Si via patefacta erit, Arvernos inopinantes oppugnare poterimus.
15. Sive vobis opus est armis sive vestitu, ego omnia parabo.

EXERCISE 85.
1. If you are ill, you ought to remain at home.
2. If you desire more plunder, hurry to Aduatuca.
3. Unless you have read my letter, you cannot know what I want.
4. Whether the litter is ready or not, I will set off at once.
5. If you come to Cyzicus, I shall be happier.
6. If spring was at hand, why did you not make journeys through the province?
7. See that you come if you can.
8. We will banish Vercingetorix, if he does not obey.
9. If the bridge has been broken, we must build another.
10. If any of the enemy cross the river, attack them at once.
11. If this is so, we must send help.
12. If he was a help to you, you ought to thank him.
13. Unless we receive reinforcements soon, we shall not be able to escape.

14. Whether we defend the city or burn it, we shall be in great danger.
15. If anyone comes, tell him I am sleeping.

EXERCISE 86.

CICERO'S APPEAL FOR A KINDLY HEARING

Cicero in his twenty-seventh year successfully appeared as counsel for the defence in a murder trial; a young man had been falsely accused of killing his father. These words occur near the beginning of Cicero's speech.

Fide sapientiaque vestra fretus, iudices, plus oneris sustuli quam ferre me posse intellego : hoc onus si vos aliqua ex parte adlevabitis, feram ut potero studio et industria, iudices; sin a vobis, id quod non spero, deserar, tamen animo non deficiam et id, quod suscepi, quoad potero, perferam; quod si perferre non potero, opprimi me onere officii malo, quam id, quod mihi cum fide semel impositum est, aut propter perfidiam abicere aut propter infirmitatem animi deponere. Te quoque magno opere, M. Fanni,[1] quaeso, ut qualem te iam antea populo Romano praebuisti, cum huic eidem quaestioni iudex praeesses, talem te et nobis et rei publicae hoc tempore impertias.

From Cicero, *Pro Roscio Amerino*, 10-11.

[1] M. Fannius was the praetor, who presided over the court.

EXERCISE 87.

Gentlemen of the jury, the burden which I have undertaken is heavier than I can bear alone; it will at once become lighter, if you will help me; but if in this crisis you desert me, yet I will still try to do that which I ought to do; if I cannot do this, at least I shall not have failed my client through weakness of spirit; for if anyone has once laid upon me a burden together with his trust, I would rather be crushed by it than lay it down. I shall be most grateful to you also, M. Fannius, who preside over[1] this court, if you will listen to my words with attention and kind indulgence.

[1] praesum.

EXERCISE 88.

NO GOLD IN BRITAIN

Trebātius, a distinguished lawyer, was a great friend of Cicero's. Cicero recommends him to Caesar during his Gallic campaigns. There was evidently some idea of Trebatius accompanying Caesar to Britain in 54, and the following is an extract from a letter sent to him by Cicero.

Ego te commendare non desisto, sed quid proficiam, ex te scire cupio. Illud soleo mirari, non me toties accipere tuas litteras, quoties a Quinto mihi fratre afferantur. In Britannia nihil esse audio neque auri neque argenti. Id si ita est, essedum aliquod suadeo capias, et ad nos quam primum recurras. Sin autem sine Britannia[1] tamen assequi, quod volumus, possumus, perfice ut sis in familiaribus Caesaris.

From Cicero, Epistolae ad Familiares, VII, 7.

[1] i.e. without going to Britain.

Chapter 21
Conditional Sentences: (2) Remote

Type B. Remote Conditional Sentences

If the **Main Verb** only makes a suggestion, more **remote** in its wording than an open statement, and is in the **Subjunctive Mood,** then the Verb of the Conditional Clause is also in the Subjunctive.

An example in English will make this clear: *we would go home, if we could.* It is just an idea—not *we will go home, if we can,* but simply *we would.* This word *would* or *should* is always used in translating the Apodosis of any kind of Remote Conditional Sentence.

Latin uses three Tenses of the Subjunctive to express Remote Conditional Sentences, corresponding to the **time:**

Time	Tense of Subjunctive
(a) Future	Present
(b) Present	Imperfect
(c) Past	Pluperfect

Examples:

(a) **Si pueros bene doceas, discant.**
If you were to teach (or, more commonly, *if you taught*) *boys well, they would learn* (in the Future).

(b) **Si pueros bene doceres, discerent.**
If you were teaching boys well, they would be learning (in the Present).

(c) **Si pueros bene docuisses, didicissent.**
If you had taught boys well, they would have learnt (in the Past).

Sometimes, according to the sense, we have a mixture of Past Time and Present Time in a Conditional Sentence:

118

Si magister pueros bene docuisset, hoc scirent.
If the master had taught the boys well, they would know this.

Si insons esset, non effugisset.
If he were innocent, he would not have run away.

It will have been seen by now that Latin uses the same Tense of the Subjunctive in the Protasis of a Remote Conditional Sentence as it does in expressing Wishes (see Chapter 19). Such a Protasis, uttered in a certain tone of voice, becomes a Wish, e.g. *If you were to teach boys well!*

Exceptional use of Indicative in a Remote Apodosis

When the Verb of the Apodosis of a Remote Conditional Sentence is **debeo, possum, oportet,** or a Tense formed by the use of the **Gerund** or **Gerundive** of Obligation, then the Verb of the **Apodosis** is in the Indicative:

Deleri totus exercitus potuit, si victores persecuti essent fugientes.
The whole army could (or *might*) *have been destroyed, if the conquerors had pursued those in flight.*

Nisi hoc fecisset, non puniendus erat.
Unless he had done this, he ought not to have been punished.

EXERCISE 89.
1. Si hostes flumen transeant, eos statim oppugnemus.
2. Non desperaremus, si Marcellus hodie superesset.
3. Si consules emisissent exploratores, exercitus Romanus non circumventus esset.
4. Si respublica in periculum veniat, optimus quisque ei subveniat.
5. Nisi Verres provinciam obtinuisset, multi cives adhuc viverent.
6. Hostes intra fines nostros accipiamus, si exercitum Romam reducamus.
7. Nisi Veios capere constituissemus, hoc bellum non suscipi oportuit.
8. Nonne gauderetis, si iam domi essetis?

9. Si naviges, naufragio pereas.
10. Si Verres in forum veniat, hoc moleste feramus.
11. Cives, si Vercingetorigi paruissent, non oppidum defendissent.
12. Si te haberem, non mihi viderer plane perisse.
13. Si castra muniatis, hostium impetus facilius sustineatis.
14. Nisi propter hiemem pugnare destitissent, nostri urbem capere potuerunt.
15. Si Veios cepissemus, iam pace frueremur.

EXERCISE 90.
1. If you were to go there, you would find more booty.
2. If you had written, I should have known this before.
3. If I were now in Rome, I should be helping you and the children.
4. We should hinder Caesar, if we were to burn the town.
5. Had the citizens not lost all hope, they would have resisted longer.
6. The farmer would not be so rich today, if he had not tilled the fields so carefully.
7. If we had started before, we could have reached the city before night.
8. If Verres were a good general, he would not always be riding in a litter.
9. If you were to come to me in Thessalonica, I should rejoice.
10. The soldiers ought not to have been sent from the camp, if they had not had breakfast.
11. If Hannibal had removed the statue, he would have lost his other eye.
12. If you were to hide the corn, you would have enough for[1] the winter.
13. If the boy had not brought the book, he would have had to fetch it.
14. If the scout had seen us, we should now be in the hands of the enemy.
15. If I had the book, I should be reading it.

[1] **ad**

EXERCISE 91.

VERRES: HIS CONDUCT SHOULD SHOCK THE WORLD

Si qui rex, si qua civitas exterarum gentium, si qua natio fecisset aliquid in civis Romanos eius modi, nonne publice vindicaremus, nonne bello persequeremur? possemus hanc iniuriam ignominiamque nominis Romani inultam impunitamque dimittere? Quot bella maiores nostros et quanta suscepisse arbitramini, quod cives Romani iniuria affecti, quod navicularii retenti, quod mercatores spoliati dicerentur? At ego iam retentos[1] non queror, spoliatos[1] ferendum[2] puto; navibus, mancipiis, mercibus ademptis in vincla mercatores esse coniectos et in vinclis civis Romanos necatos esse arguo. Si haec apud Scythas[3] dicerem, non hic in tanta multitudine civium Romanorum, non apud senatores, lectissimos civitatis, non in foro populi Romani de tot et tam acerbis suppliciis civium Romanorum, tamen animos etiam barbarorum hominum permoverem; tanta enim huius imperi amplitudo, tanta nominis Romani dignitas est apud omnis nationes ut ista in nostros homines crudelitas nemini concessa esse videatur.

From Cicero, *In Verrem, Actio II,* V, 149-150.

[1] **esse** must be supplied; likewise the Subject of the Infinitive.
[2] Again **esse** must be supplied: *I think we must put up with the fact that.*
[3] Nomadic tribes who lived in the Danube basin and north of the Black Sea.

EXERCISE 92.

If any Roman citizen were to be thrown into prison and killed by a foreign king, would we not avenge such a wrong by waging war? Even if merchants had only been robbed, our ancestors would have undertaken a war and not left such a dishonour to the name[1] of Rome unpunished. If Roman citizens have not only been robbed, but thrown into chains and killed, all the more ought we to take vengeance. I am speaking today

[1] Gen.

among senators in the forum of the Roman people about the bitter tortures of Roman citizens; but the name of Rome has such weight that even if Scythians were listening to me, yet their anger would be aroused.

Chapter 22
Miscellaneous Conditional Sentences (Revision)

1. Responde, si potes.
2. Si viam patefaciatis, hostes facile opprimatis.
3. Si quis in conspectum venerit, da signum statim.
4. Si hoc heri didicisses, nonne hodie scires?
5. Nisi sapientium verba legeris, nunquam sapiens fies.
6. Si Graeci domo diu abesse noluissent, Troiam non cepissent.
7. Sive iuvenes sumus sive senes, mens nostra exercenda est.
8. Si Poeni novas copias ad Hannibalem misissent, bellum fuisset longius.
9. Si forum silet, Syracusani non queruntur.
10. Si me sententiam roges, eadem quae tu respondeam.
11. Nisi Caesar celeriter redisset, in Britannia per hiemem ei manendum erat.
12. Si quis civibus Romanis iniuria nocet, puniendus est.
13. Si opus prius confecissetis, nunc otio frueremini.
14. Oppida vestra Caesari auxilio erunt, nisi ea incenderitis.
15. Sive hostes appropinquant sive non, moneo ut omnes caveatis.

1. If you advance quickly, you will soon catch sight of the enemy.
2. If you wish to become happy, do not neglect your work.
3. If he committed such crimes, Verres is worthy of severe punishment.
4. I should be less wretched, if you were to write more often.
5. Whether Caesar is present or not, we shall try to win a victory.

6. If Verres had not been so lazy, he would have undertaken long journeys.
7. The Germans would now be arriving, if they had not heard the news.
8. If this news is true, we ought to advance without delay.
9. If he had lived longer, Alexander might have conquered the whole world.
10. We will surrender, if you promise to spare the citizens.
11. If you have not seen the show, I advise you to see it today.
12. If you were to see the show, you would laugh.
13. Whether it rains or snows, we will go home tomorrow.
14. If you had written, I should have replied at once.
15. If, soldiers, you use your opportunity, you will easily take the city by storm.

Chapter 23
Concessive Clauses

(1) **Romani, quanquam itinere fessi erant, tamen instructi procedunt.**
Although the Romans were tired from the march, yet they advanced in battle formation.

Etsi in his locis maturae sunt hiemes, tamen in Britanniam proficisci contendit.
Although the winters are early in this part of the world, he made haste to set out for Britain.

The **Indicative** is used in clauses introduced by **quanquam** (often **quamquam**), *although*, **etsī, etiamsī**, *although*, *even if*, when the statement in the *although* clauses is granted or *conceded* to be **true**.

Note.—When a Concessive Clause is opposed to a Main Clause, **tamen**, when used in the Main Clause, comes first word.

(2) The **Subjunctive** is used in an *although* or *even if* clause, when the clause merely contains an **idea** which may or may not be true; such a clause may be introduced by **etsī** or **etiamsī**; often by **quamvīs**, *although* (lit. *however much you like*); sometimes by **cum** or by **licet**, *although*. **Quanquam** is not used with the Subjunctive except in a Dependent Clause in Reported Speech:

Haec ego non rideo, quamvis tu rideas.
I do not laugh at this, although (however much) you may laugh.

Cum primi ordines hostium concidissent, tamen acerrime reliqui resistebant.
Although the first ranks of the enemy had fallen, nevertheless the remainder put up a very fierce resistance.

Licet mihi pericula impendeant omnia, succurram.
Though every danger may overhang me, I will come to the rescue.

125

Quamvīs is naturally used to qualify an Adjective in a Concessive Clause:

Assentatio, quamvis perniciosa sit, nocere tamen nemini potest nisi ei qui eam recipit.

Flattery, however ruinous it may be, can hurt no one except him who receives it.

(3) When both the Concessive Clause and the Main Clause present suggested ideas, then the Subjunctive is used in both clauses, as in the Remote type of Conditional Sentence:

Etiamsi tu imperes, hoc non faciamus.

Even if you were to order us, we would not do this.

EXERCISE 95.

1. Caesar, etsi multis rebus in Italiam revocabatur, tamen constituerat nullam partem belli relinquere.
2. Verres, quanquam itinera per Siciliam facere eum oportuit, Syracusis mansit.
3. Quamvis velim huc venias, Romae tibi manendum est.
4. Etiamsi a vobis deserar, hoc onus non deponam.
5. Cicero, cum tenuissima valetudine esset, ne nocturnum quidem sibi tempus ad quietem relinquebat.
6. Ferunt Masinissam, quanquam nonaginta annos natus esset, senectuti restitisse.
7. Vercingetorix, quanquam ei non placuerat Avaricum defendi, tamen incommodo accepto civium animos confirmavit.
8. Licet civitas in maximo sit periculo, ego non ei deero.
9. Etsi exspectabam epistolam a te longiorem, tamen ad brevem rescribendum esse putavi.
10. Quamvis pauci simus, Romanis a nobis fortiter resistendum est.
11. Quanquam Bituriges subsidium rogaverunt, Aedui erant prudentiores quam qui flumen transirent.
12. Etiamsi Galli noctu ex oppido effugissent, Romani vias praeoccupavissent.

EXERCISE 96.

1. Although the work was difficult, the boy did not despair.
2. Sophocles was still writing plays, although he was an old man.
3. However weary you may be now, victory will soon be yours.
4. Even if Verres comes, he will not find our corn.
5. Although you may wish to defend your town, I advise you to burn it.
6. Although I want to write a longer letter, I have not enough time today.
7. Even if you were skilled in swimming, you would not be able to cross this river.
8. Although only a small part of the summer was left, Caesar started for Britain.
9. Even though you may despise the small numbers of the enemy, you must be on your guard.
10. The general told his men that, although they had been defeated, he would remedy the disaster.
11. Although he was still a boy, Hannibal swore that he would always be an enemy to the Romans.
12. Even if foreigners were listening, I should persuade them that Verres ought to be punished.

EXERCISE 97.

THE CLEMENCY OF A CONQUEROR

Civil war broke out in 49 between Julius Caesar and Pompey. It was not until after campaigns in Italy, Spain, Gaul, and Africa, that Caesar finally defeated Pompey at the battle of Pharsālia in Thessaly, in July 48. The following passage describes the 'mopping up' operations after the capture of Pompey's camp and the surrender of fugitives. Pompey himself escaped to the sea and fled to Egypt, where he was assassinated.

Caesar castris potitus a militibus contendit, ne in praeda occupati reliqui negotii gerendi facultatem dimitterent. Qua re impetrata montem[1] opere circummunire instituit. Pompeiani, quod is mons erat sine aqua, diffisi ei loco relicto monte universi iugis[2] eius Larisam[3] versus se recipere coeperunt. Qua re animadversa Caesar copias suas divisit partemque legionum in castris Pompei remanere iussit, partem in sua castra remisit, quattuor secum legiones duxit commodioreque itinere Pompeianis occurrere coepit et progressus milia passuum VI aciem instruxit. Qua re animadversa Pompeiani in quodam monte constiterunt. Hunc montem flumen subluebat. Caesar milites cohortatus, etsi totius diei continenti labore erant confecti noxque iam suberat, tamen munitione flumen a monte seclusit, ne noctu aquari Pompeiani possent. Quo perfecto opere illi de deditione missis legatis agere coeperunt. Pauci ordinis senatorii, qui se cum iis coniunxerant, nocte fuga salutem petiverunt.

Caesar prima luce omnes eos, qui in monte consederant, ex superioribus locis in planitiem descendere atque arma proicere iussit. Quod ubi sine recusatione fecerunt passisque palmis proiecti ad terram flentes ab eo salutem petiverunt, consolatus consurgere iussit et pauca apud eos de lenitate sua locutus, quo minore essent timore, omnes conservavit militibusque suis commendavit, ne qui eorum violaretur, neu quid sui[4] desiderarent. Hac adhibita diligentia ex castris sibi legiones alias occurrere et eas, quas secum duxerat, in vicem requiescere atque in castra reverti iussit eodemque die Larisam pervenit.

From Caesar, *Civil War*, III, 97-98.

[1] Behind Pompey's camp.
[2] Abl. of Separation.
[3] Some twenty miles n. of the battlefield.
[4] Neuter: *of their property*.

EXERCISE 98.

Although Caesar had routed the troops of Pompey and captured their camp, he was unwilling to allow his men to rest until they had captured the fugitives. Because it turned out that the mountain to which these had fled was waterless, they had retired towards Larissa; then seeing that Caesar was pursuing them with four legions, they betook themselves to a second mountain, at the foot of which there ran[1] a river. In spite of a whole day's fighting, Caesar's troops were easily persuaded to keep the Pompeians away from the water-supply. As soon as the entrenchment had been completed, they sent ambassadors to sue for peace, although it was still night.

When dawn came, orders were given for all who had bivouacked on the mountain to come down and hand over their weapons. The Pompeians at once obeyed Caesar's order, showing by their tears that they were afraid that they would be punished, even if they did not refuse. Caesar, however, showed such clemency that he not only spared them all, but ordered his troops not to hurt any of them.

[1] See Ex. 97.

Translation piece for purposes of Revision

There are no fresh constructions in this piece, which is a fine piece of oratorical writing, but it contains several longish sentences which take a little patience in working out.

EXERCISE 99.

VERRES: CICERO UPHOLDS THE RIGHTS OF CIVIS ROMANUS

Gāvius, an innocent Roman citizen, had escaped from the stone-quarries at Syracuse and reached Messāna, a Sicilian town about five miles across the sea from Italy. Here he begàn to complain of his treatment, was at once arrested, and ordered by Verres to be flogged. His plea of Roman citizenship availed him nothing. Verres, without any evidence, denounced him as a spy, and, when Gavius renewed his plea, had him crucified.

Si tu apud Persas aut in extrema India deprensus, Verres, ad supplicium ducerere,[1] quid aliud clamitares nisi te civem esse Romanum? et si tibi ignoto apud ignotos, apud barbaros, apud homines in extremis atque ultimis gentibus positos,

[1] Alternative form of **ducereris**.

nobile et inlustre apud omnis nomen civitatis tuae profuisset, ille, quisquis erat, quem tu in crucem rapiebas, qui tibi esset[1] ignotus, cum civem se Romanum esse diceret, apud te praetorem, si non effugium, ne moram quidem mortis mentione atque usurpatione civitatis adsequi potuit? Homines tenues, obscuro loco nati, navigant, adeunt ad ea loca quae nunquam antea viderunt, ubi neque noti esse iis quo[2] venerunt, neque semper cum cognitoribus esse possunt. Hac una tamen fiducia civitatis non modo apud nostros magistratus, qui et legum et existimationis periculo continentur, neque apud civis solum Romanos, qui et sermonis et iuris et multarum rerum societate iuncti sunt, fore se tutos arbitrantur, sed quocumque venerint, hanc sibi rem praesidio sperant futuram. Tolle hanc spem, tolle hoc praesidium, civibus Romanis constitue nihil esse opis in hac voce, 'Civis Romanus sum', posse impune praetorem aut alium quempiam supplicium quod velit in eum constituere qui se civem Romanum esse dicat, quod qui sit ignoret: iam omnis provincias, iam omnia regna, iam omnis liberas civitates, iam omnem orbem terrarum, qui semper nostris hominibus maxime patuit, civibus Romanis ista defensione praeclūseris.

From Cicero, *In Verrem, Actio II*, V, 166-168.

[1] Subjunctive, because Verres only *alleged* that Gavius was unknown.

[2] *to whom*: the Adverb is sometimes used of Persons.

Chapter 24
Causal Clauses

(1) **Quod ad hostes appropinquabat, Caesar legiones expeditas ducebat.**
Because he was approaching the enemy, Caesar was leading the legions without baggage.

Hannibal, quia fessum militem proeliis habebat, iis quietem dedit.
Because Hannibal had soldiers who were tired with fighting, he gave them a rest.

When a **definite** Cause or reason is stated by the writer or speaker, then the Verb of the **Causal Clause** is in the **Indicative**, as in the above examples. **Quod** is rather more common than **quia**. **Propterea quod,** *on account of the fact that*, **quoniam,** *since*, are also used with the Indicative.

When, however, **cum** is used in the sense of *since* or *because*, the Verb is always in the Subjunctive:

Caesar, cum non multum aestatis superesset, obsides imperavit.
Since there was not much summer left, Caesar demanded hostages.　　　　　．

Particularly common at the beginning of a sentence is the phrase, **quae cum ita sint,** *in these circumstances (since these things are so)*; this becomes **quae cum ita essent,** when the Main Verb is Historic:

Quae cum ita sint, quid dubitatis?
In this case, why do you hesitate?

(2) The **Subjunctive** is used in a Causal Clause (apart from its use with **cum**)

(*a*) if the clause forms part of Reported Speech:

131

Nuntiaverunt prope omnes naves afflictas esse, quod ancorae non subsisterent.
They said that nearly all the ships had been damaged, because the anchors did not hold.

(*b*) if the Cause is **alleged** by someone other than the writer; in such a case the Subjunctive is introduced by **quod** (meaning here *on the ground that*). This construction is common after Verbs of *accusing, admiring, blaming, complaining, condemning, praising, wondering* :

Lacedaemonii Themistoclem accusaverunt, quod societatem cum Xerxe fecisset.
The Spartans accused Themistocles of having made an alliance with Xerxes.

Caesar querebatur quod Britanni bellum sine causa intulissent.
Caesar complained that the Britons had started a war without cause.

(*c*) if the Cause is **rejected** (i.e. negatived); the Subjunctive is then introduced by **nōn quod** or **nōn quō**, *not because* :

Hoc fecit, non quo vellet, sed quia coactus est.
He did this, not because he wanted to, but because he had to.

Further uses of quod

(1) Verbs of *rejoicing* (**gaudeo**), *grieving* (**doleo, maereo**), *congratulating* (**grātulor** with Dat.), *thanking* (**grātias ago**), are often followed by **quod** and the **Indicative** (i.e. the cause of the *rejoicing*, etc. is taken as a fact) :

Quod Brundisii moratus es, gaudeo.
I am glad that you have stayed on at Brundisium.

Even more common, however, after Verbs of *rejoicing* and *grieving* is an Accusative and Infinitive Clause :

Gaudeo tibi iucundas esse meas litteras.
I am glad that you like my letters.

(2) **Quod** is often equivalent to *the fact that*, and so a clause

in the Indicative introduced by **quod** may stand as the Subject or Object of a Verb:

Multum Gallos adiuvabat, quod Liger ex nivibus creverat.
The fact that the Loire had risen after the snows gave the Gauls much help.

Praetereo quod non scripsisti.
I pass over the fact that you have not written.

Qui in a Causal usage

Maluimus iter facere pedibus, qui incommodissime navigassemus.
We preferred to travel on foot, seeing that we had had a most uncomfortable passage.

Here **qui** is used in a Causal sense and not purely as a Relative Pronoun; when it is thus used, it is generally followed by the Subjunctive; sometimes we find **quippe qui** or **utpote qui** (*as one in fact who*) in the same sense and with rather more emphasis.

EXERCISE 100.
1. Quia inopia frumenti erat, Caesar tres legiones emisit.
2. Caesar nostros hostes longius prosequi vetuit, quod loci naturam ignorabat.
3. Cum longinqua a domo instet militia, si quis vestrum suos invisere vult, commeatum do.
4. Caesar non anxius erat, quoniam Ciceronem obsidione liberatum esse sciebat.
5. Vercingetorix a Gallis accusatus est, quod castra propius Romanos movisset.
6. Intellectum est nostros propter gravitatem armorum, quod insequi cedentes non possent, minus aptos esse ad huius generis hostem.
7. Nervii reliquos Belgas culpabant, qui se populo Romano dedidissent.
8. Gratulor tibi quod ex provincia salvum te ad tuos recepisti.

9. Quae cum ita essent, praefectus suis imperavit, ut se reciperent.
10. Quia civis Romanus erat, Gavius speravit se tutum fore.
11. Galli Avaricum defenderant, non quo princeps imperavisset, sed quia ipsis hoc placuerat.
12. Populus deis gratias egit, quod exercitus vicerat.
13. Miror quod ad me nihil scripsisti.
14. Verres accusatus est quod multa templa spoliavisset.
15. Adiuvabat Caesaris consilium, quod barbari erant cupidissimi praedae.
16. Hannibal, cum oculum alterum amittere nollet, templum Iunonis non spoliavit.

EXERCISE 101.
1. The Gauls did not fight on that day, because they were waiting for reinforcements.
2. Since night was at hand, they decided to stay this side of the river.
3. The Aedui said that they had returned home because they feared treachery.
4. Because he was lazy, Verres was carried in a litter.
5. Cicero complained that his friend had not written to him.
6. In these circumstances Caesar determined to set out for Gaul at once.
7. The general rejoiced that our men had captured the town so easily.
8. Hannibal accused himself for not having led his troops to Rome after his victory at Cannae.[1]
9. Because he had determined to spend the winter in Gaul, Caesar led his army back to the sea.
10. O wretched man, who has not seen that wisdom is better than wealth.
11. Cicero thanked his friend for having sent him a book.
12. In this case, we had better retreat at once to the nearest hills.
13. The chieftain was accused of aiming at the kingship.

[1] Adj., **Cannensis.**

14. I pass over the fact that you threw a Roman citizen into chains.
15. Hannibal returned to Carthage, not because he had been completely defeated, but because he had been recalled.
16. Simonides returned home because he had been warned in a dream.

EXERCISE 102.

IN PRAISE OF POETRY

Archias, a native of Syria and apparently a poet of repute, had been enrolled as a citizen at Hēraclēa in Lūcānia, and, subject to certain conditions, was entitled to the rights of Roman citizenship, which he had in fact exercised. Cicero defends him in 62 B.C. when he is prosecuted for illegally claiming these rights. In the absence of documentary proof, Cicero devotes most of his speech to a panegyric upon Greek and Roman literature and upon the talents of Archias.

Saxa et solitudines voci respondent, bestiae saepe immanes cantu flectuntur atque consistunt[1]: nos instituti rebus optimis non poetarum voce moveamur? Homerum Colophonii[2] civem esse dicunt suum, Chii suum vindicant, Salaminii repetunt, Smyrnaei vero suum esse confirmant, itaque etiam delubrum eius in oppido dedicaverunt; permulti alii praeterea pugnant inter se atque contendunt.

Ergo illi alienum, quia poeta fuit, post mortem etiam expetunt: nos hunc vivum, qui et voluntate et legibus noster est, repudiabimus? Praesertim cum omne olim studium atque omne ingenium contulerit Archias ad populi Romani gloriam laudemque celebrandam?

Nam si quis minorem gloriae fructum putat ex Graecis[3] versibus percipi quam ex Latinis, vehementer errat, propterea quod Graeca leguntur in omnibus fere gentibus, Latina suis

---

[1] cf. the story of Orpheus.

[2] Colophon, Chios, and Smyrna were all towns in Ionia, in Asia Minor; Salamis is an island opposite Athens.

[3] Archias wrote in Greek, his native language.

finibus,[1] exiguis sane, continentur. Qua re[2] si res eae, quas gessimus, orbis terrae regionibus definiuntur, cupere debemus, quo manuum nostrarum tela pervenerint, eodem gloriam famamque penetrare, quod cum ipsis populis, de quorum rebus scribitur, haec ampla sunt, tum eis certe, qui de vita gloriae causa dimicant, hoc maximum periculorum incitamentum est et laborum. Quam multos scriptores rerum suarum magnus ille Alexander[3] secum habuisse dicitur! Atque is tamen, cum in Sigeo ad Achillis[4] tumulum adstitisset: 'O fortunate' inquit 'adulescens, qui tuae virtutis Homerum praeconem inveneris'! Et vere. Nam nisi Ilias illa exstitisset, idem tumulus, qui corpus eius contexerat, nomen etiam obruisset.

From Cicero, *Pro Archia*, 19-24.

[1] i.e. Latium.
[2] Often written in one word, **quārē**.
[3] Alexander the Great, king of Macedon 336-323 B.C.
[4] Achilles avenged the death of his friend Patroclus at the siege of Troy by killing Hector. Sigeum was a town on the coast near Troy.

EXERCISE 103.

It is said that seven[1] cities claimed Homer as their own citizen after his death, because he was a poet: are we, who value Greek and Latin literature so highly, to reject Archias who is alive and is our own? Nor indeed does my client[2] deserve less renown, because he has celebrated the praise of the Roman people in Greek verse rather than in Latin. Nay, all the more, since men understand the Latin tongue almost in Latium alone, Greek almost everywhere. Because Archias has committed to poetry the praise of Marius[3] and Lucullus, very brave and famous men, he has celebrated also the renown of the Roman people; for ours are the trophies, ours the triumphs. Wherever

[1] Smyrna, Rhodos, Colophon, Salamis, Chios, Argos, Athenae, according to an epigram quoted by Aulus Gellius (d. A.D. 175).
[2] hic.
[3] Marius for his victory over the Cimbri, a German tribe, in 101; Lucullus for his victories from 74 to 69 over Mithridates, King of Pontus, which lies to the south of the Black Sea.

our generals are successful, thither also will our glory and fame penetrate, provided that our poets embellish our victories. Even Alexander the Great envied Achilles, because he had Homer to celebrate his glory. In this city in which generals still almost in arms have honoured the name of poets, judges in civilian dress should not cast out the poets themselves.

Chapter 25
Quominus and quin

Quōminus and quīn used after Verbs of *hindering* and *preventing.*

(1) **Caesar vento impeditus est quominus solveret.**
Caesar was prevented by the wind from setting sail.

Aetas non (vix) impedit quominus agri colendi studium teneamus.
Age does not hinder (scarcely hinders) us from keeping up the pursuit of agriculture.

Quominus (sometimes written **quo minus**), meaning literally *whereby the less,* is used with the Subjunctive after Verbs of *hindering* and *preventing* when these Verbs are (*a*) Positive, (*b*) Negative, (*c*) virtually Negative, i.e. used with a quasi-negative, e.g. **vix, aegrē,** *scarcely, with difficulty,* or used in a question of which the answer, if given, would be in the Negative.

Prohibeo is generally followed by an **Infinitive,** though the construction with **quominus** is also commonly found with it:

Galli Germanos Rhenum transire prohibebant.
The Gauls tried to stop the Germans from crossing the Rhine.

Further use of quominus

Non per populum Romanum stetit, quominus perpetua cum Samnitibus amicitia esset.

It was not due to the Roman people that they did not have everlasting friendship with the Samnites.

This use of **stat per** and the Acc., followed by **quominus** and the Subjunctive is quite common, to express *it is someone's* **fault** *that something does not happen.* **Caution.** It is **never** used to express *it is to someone's* **credit** *that something does not happen.*

(2) **Quīn** (= **quī-ne,** a Consecutive Conjunction), *whereby not,* is also used with the Subjunctive after Verbs of *hindering* and *preventing,* but it is **only** used when the Verb is **Negative** or **virtually Negative** (see above):

> **Germani retineri non poterant quin in nostros tela conicerent.**
> *The Germans could not be restrained from hurling javelins upon our men.*

EXERCISE 104.
1. Reliqui principes conabantur Vercingetorigem impedire quominus arma caperet.
2. Mons Cevenna Caesarem non impedivit, quin ad Arvernos perveniret.
3. Matronae de fuga significando Romanis Gallos effugere prohibuerunt.
4. Naves onerariae vento deterrebantur quominus in portum venirent.
5. Tantum incommodum principem non deterruit quominus Gallorum animos confirmaret.
6. Si exercitum reducemus, quid Veientes impediet quin agros nostros depopulentur?
7. Stetit per Verrem quominus mercatores Romam tuti pervenirent.
8. Hannibal somnio impeditus est, quominus columnam auream auferret.
9. Ne Archiam prohibeamus quominus civitate fruatur.
10. Caesar vix poterat suos deterrere, quin hostes statim persequerentur.

EXERCISE 105.
1. The enemy hindered our men from foraging.
2. Appius Claudius was not hindered by old age from ruling a large household.
3. Even winter does not prevent a good praetor from making a long journey.
4. Simonides was prevented by a dream from sailing.

5. It was due to the Cathaginian senate that Hannibal did not stay longer in Italy.
6. Surely the Roman people does not prevent conquered tribes from using their own customs?
7. With difficulty did Hannibal stop his men from throwing away all hope of winning.
8. What can prevent us, who have crossed the Alps, from capturing Rome itself?
9. Even if a merchant was a Roman citizen, this did not stop Verres from throwing him into prison.
10. Nothing will prevent me from accomplishing what I have undertaken.

Further uses of quin

Quin, meaning *but that*, is used with the Subjunctive after Verbs and phrases of *doubting*, and by later authors after Verbs of *denying*, when they are Negative or virtually Negative:

(*a*) **Homines non dubitant quin di vota exaudiant.**
Men do not doubt that the gods listen to their vows.

(*b*) **Agamemnon non dubitat quin Troia brevi peritura sit.**
Agamemnon does not doubt that Troy will soon perish.

So, too, after **non dubium est,** *there is no doubt* (lit. *it is not doubtful*), **non dubitari potest,** *it cannot be doubted.*

It should be noticed from example (*b*) above, that the compound Future Subjunctive is used after **quin,** as in Indirect Questions.

(*c*) **Non negari potest quin melius sit exercitum mitti.**
It cannot be denied that it is better that an army should be sent.

(but **melius esse** is probably better Latin)

For various idiomatic uses of **quin,** *but that*, after Negative Verbs and phrases, the following examples should be studied:

Haud multum (or minimum) afuit (abfuit, or aberat) quin periret.
He very nearly died.

Non possum facere quin cotidie ad te litteras mittam.
I can't help sending letters to you every day.

Num barbari sibi temperabunt, quin in Italiam contendant?
Surely the barbarians will not stop short of (lit. *control themselves from*) *marching into Italy?*

Vix potuit fieri quin Verres damnaretur.
It was scarcely possible that Verres should not be condemned.

Nunquam eum video, quin delecter.
I never see him without being delighted.

Quin is also used as a Relative Pronoun in the Nominative followed by a Negative (= **qui non**), with the Subjunctive Mood :

> **Nemo fuit omnino militum, quin vulneraretur.**
> *There was absolutely not one of the soldiers who was not wounded.*

So too :

> **Nemo est quin sciat, putet.**
> *All the world knows, thinks.*

Quin rarely stands for **quae non** or **quod non** (which we must, therefore, use instead) ; the Acc. of **quin** (standing for **qui non**, masc.) is **quem non**:

> **Nullus dolor est quem non longinquitas temporis minuat.**
> *There is no grief that lapse of time does not lessen.*

Quin is sometimes used for **quo non** in the Abl. (**qui** being an old form of the Abl. of the Relative) :

> **Nullum intermisi diem quin scriberem.**
> *I allowed no day to pass without writing.*

Without

At this point it is worth noticing several ways of expressing *without* in Latin, varying according to the sense :

> **Sine mora contendit** } *he hastened without delay.*
> **Non moratus**

> **Haud locutus** or **tacitus abiit,** *he went away without a word.*

Nullo certo ordine, *without definite order* (e.g. in battle).

Iniussu }
Nullo imperante } *without orders.*

Huius ingenium ita laudo ut non pertimescam, *I admire his ability without fearing it.* (Main Verb Positive)

Nunquam pugnat, quin vincat, *he never fights without winning.* (Main Verb Negative)

EXERCISE 106.
1. Non dubito quin hoc tibi molestum sit.
2. Nunquam mihi dubium fuit, quin a te diligerer.
3. Non multum abfuit quin opera desererentur.
4. Nemo fuit quin sciret ubi Verres lateret.
5. Num dubitas quin ille nos in hostium numero habeat?
6. Nunquam ad te scribo quin te videre cupiam.
7. Prope nullum fuit templum quod Verres non spoliaret.
8. Non poteramus facere quin ob hoc rideremus.
9. Non dubitabam quin te Romae visurus essem.
10. Non potuit fieri quin Caesar Gallos tandem superaret.
11. Magister ita severus est, ut non sit iniustus.
12. Paulum afuit quin hostem fugientem interficeret.

EXERCISE 107.
1. I do not doubt that you were very busy.
2. All the world knows that Caesar is dead.
3. There is no doubt that Archias is a good poet.
4. They were very nearly driven out of the camp.
5. There was no one whom Cicero's words did not move.
6. The Carthaginians could not help longing for their homes.
7. You cannot deny that you put to death a Roman citizen.
8. Our men could not leave the camp without being attacked by the enemy.
9. He blamed me without punishing me.
10. We did not doubt that you would read the letter with pleasure.

11. It is impossible for them not to be caught.
12. There was no day when I did not receive a letter.

EXERCISE 108.

A STATUE TO A BRAVE AMBASSADOR

After the murder of Julius Caesar in 44 B.C. Antony and Octavian, Caesar's great-nephew, both made bids for power. Antony himself obtained Cisalpine Gaul, and hurried there to crush Decimus Brūtus to whom it had been assigned by Caesar. Without declaring Antony a public enemy, the Senate sent three ambassadors to call upon him to give up the province and submit to the authority of the Senate and the Roman people. Cicero had called for far sterner measures, and when one of the ambassadors, Servius Sulpicius, died before reaching Antony's camp, he maintained that he had died in the service of his country and successfully pleaded that a statue should be erected in his honour. The following passages form part of the Ninth of Cicero's speeches against Antony, commonly known as the Philippics (the term coming from the speeches of Demosthenes against Philip of Macedon in the 4th cent. B.C.).

Vellem di immortales fecissent, patres conscripti,[1] ut vivo potius Ser. Sulpicio gratias ageremus quam honores mortuo quaereremus. Nec vero dubito quin, si ille vir legationem renuntiare potuisset, reditus eius et vobis gratus fuerit et rei publicae salutaris futurus, non quo L. Philippo et L. Pisoni[2] aut studium aut cura defuerit in tanto officio tantoque munere, sed cum Ser. Sulpicius aetate illos anteiret, sapientia omnes, subito ereptus e causa totam legationem orbam et debilitatam reliquit. Quod si cuiquam[3] iustus honos habitus est in morte legato, in nullo iustior quam in Ser. Sulpicio reperietur. Ceteri, qui in legatione mortem obierunt, ad in-

[1] A common way of addressing senators: lit. *chosen*; trans. *my lords*.
[2] His colleagues in the embassy.
[3] **cuiquam,** which is used after a negative for *anyone*, is used here instead of **cui,** because Cicero feels that no such honour has been deserved until now.

certum vitae periculum sine ullo mortis metu profecti sunt:
Ser. Sulpicius cum aliqua perveniendi ad M. Antonium spc
profectus est, nulla revertendi. Qui cum ita affectus esset, ut,
si ad gravem valetudinem labor accessisset, sibi ipse diffideret,
non recusavit quo minus vel extremo spiritu, si quam opem
rei publicae ferre posset, experiretur. Itaque non illum vis
hiemis, non nives, non longitudo itineris, non asperitas
viarum, non morbus ingravescens retardavit, cumque iam ad
congressum colloquiumque eius pervenisset, ad quem erat
missus, in ipsa cura ac meditatione obeundi sui muneris
excessit e vita.

Si Ser. Sulpicio casus mortem attulisset, dolerem equidem
tanto rei publicae vulnere, mortem vero eius non monimento,
sed luctu publico esse ornandam putarem. Nunc autem quis
dubitat quin ei vitam abstulerit ipsa legatio? Secum enim ille
mortem extulit: quam, si nobiscum remansisset, sua cura,
optimi filii fidelissimaeque coniugis diligentia vitare potuisset.
At ille cum videret, si vestrae auctoritati non paruisset, dis-
similem se futurum sui, sin paruisset, munus sibi illud pro re
publica susceptum vitae finem fore, maluit in maximo rei
publicae discrimine emori quam minus quam potuisset videri
rei publicae profuisse. Multis illi in urbibus, iter qua[1] faciebat,
reficiendi se et curandi potestas fuit. Aderat hospitum invitatio
liberalis pro dignitate summi viri et eorum hortatio, qui una
erant missi, ad requiescendum et vitae suae consulendum. At
ille properans, festinans, mandata vestra conficere cupiens, in
hac constantia morbo adversante perseveravit.

From Cicero, *Philippic*, IX, 1-2 and 5-6.

[1] Understand **viā**, *along the road by which.*

EXERCISE 109.

There is no doubt, my lords, that if Servius Sulpicius had
survived, we should have assembled here to render him thanks.
But since the embassy itself brought death to him, today we
owe him more than thanks. Other ambassadors have died on an
embassy, but they have set out with some hope of returning:
although Servius Sulpicius knew, before he set out, that owing

to ill-health he would not come back, this did not stop him from trying to help the state, so long as he could. We seek honours on his behalf, not because he surpassed his colleagues in enthusiasm and diligence, but because in spite of his increasing illness he did not shrink from his task and died in undertaking it.

I cannot help believing that his life could have been saved by the care of his wife and his son, if he had stayed here. But to him, to be of use to the state was a nobler thing than the saving of one life. There was no city through which he journeyed in which either hospitality or an opportunity of resting was not offered. But he was not the kind of man to consult his own interests in such a crisis of the state : without delaying, he hurried to complete your commission.

Chapter 26
Comparative Clauses

Comparative Clauses are Adverbial Clauses of Manner, which point out the *likeness* or *unlikeness* of what is expressed in them, *compared* with what is expressed in the Main Clause.

We have already met a very simple kind of Comparative Clause (Chap. 1), expressed by a Relative: **Tantas copias coegit, quantas potuit,** *he collected as large forces as he could.*

Comparative Clauses fall into two main groups, according to whether the comparison is stated as *real* or *imaginary*.

(1) Real Comparisons

The Verb of the Comparative Clause is in the **Indicative**; among the commoner words of comparison are:

> **ut,** *as*; **sīcut, perinde ac (atque** before a vowel), *just as*;
> **aequē** or **pariter ac,** *equally as, in the same manner as*;
> **īdem ac,** *the same as*; **alius ac,** *other than*;
> **aliter ac,** *otherwise than*; **contrā ac** (or **quam**), *contrary to.*

> **Faciam sicut (perinde ac) promisi.**
> *I will do just as I promised.*

> **Alia (aliter) ac promisit, fecit.**
> *He acted differently from what he promised.*

Sometimes the Verb in the Comparative Clause is omitted, because it can be understood from the sense:

> **Me colit aeque atque patronum suum.**
> *He looks up to me as much as to his own patron.*

(2) Imaginary Comparisons

The Verb of the Comparative Clause is in the **Subjunctive**, introduced by **quasi, tanquam** (often **tanquam si**), **velut si** (sometimes **velut**), **proinde ac si,** all meaning *as if, just as if, as though.*

Normally, the Tense of the Subjunctive follows the rule for Sequence of Tenses:

Hic est obstandum, milites, velut si ante Romana moenia pugnemus.
We must make a stand here, my men, just as if we were fighting before the walls of Rome.

Quam maximas pecunias mutuati sunt, proinde ac si restituere vellent.
They borrowed as much money as possible, as if they wanted to make a repayment.

Istum, tanquam si esset, consulem salutaverunt.
They greeted him as consul, as though he still were one.

When introduced by **si**, a Comparative Clause is by origin the Protasis of a Conditional Clause of the Remote type (see Chap. 21), and occasionally such examples will be met as: **Me utitur, velut si inimicus essem,** *he treats me as if I were an enemy.* Here the normal Tense for this particular type of Conditional Clause is used, an Apodosis, *he would treat me*, being suppressed after **velut** (*he treats me as he would treat me, if I were an enemy*).

Quasi, velut and **tanquam** are often used to qualify a Noun, Adjective, or Participle, without any Finite Verb:

Quasi luce libertatis recreatus revixit.
He came back to life, as if revived by the light of freedom.

Repente te tanquam serpens intulisti.
Suddenly you bore down like a snake.

EXERCISE 110.
1. Britanni obsides tradiderunt, sicut Caesar imperaverat.
2. Eo die Romani pugnaverunt proinde ac si Caesar ipse adesset.
3. Alia fecerunt cives atque Vercingetorix monuerat.
4. Eaedem statuae nos delectabant atque Verrem.
5. Velim vos pugnare, velut si servos videatis vestros arma contra vos ferentes.
6. Nonnulli homines loquuntur, quasi omnia sciant.

7. Germani proelium commiserunt contra atque Caesari promiserant.
8. Verres in Sicilia se gessit, quasi quoddam novum monstrum esset.
9. Romani, a Samnitibus circumventi, castra munire coeperunt, proinde ac si consules imperavissent.
10. Sulpicius rempublicam tanquam parentem colebat.

EXERCISE 111.

1. The elk fell, just as we expected.
2. Vercingetorix called the Gauls to arms contrary to his uncle's orders.
3. The Gauls feared the cruelty of the chief when absent, just as though he were present.
4. The same things do not delight youth as old age.
5. The women made signals as if they were about to betray the town.
6. I am reading a different book from you.
7. Appius kept his mind taut like a bow.
8. The enemy retreated just as Caesar had expected.
9. So great a panic seized the senators, just as though the enemy had already reached the gates.
10. The Roman citizen escaped from the stone-quarries, as though from the underworld.[1]

[1] Use **inferi** (m. pl.), lit. *the inhabitants of the underworld.*

EXERCISE 112.

A GRANDMOTHER'S COURAGE

This extract comes from one of the letters of Pliny the Younger, who was born in A.D. *62, became consul in* 100, *and was appointed governor of Bīthȳnia by the emperor Trajan. Caecīna Paetus committed suicide in* 42, *when accused of taking part in a revolt led by Scrībōniānus against the Emperor Claudius. He belonged to a family famous for their individualistic or Stoic philosophy and republican ideals.*

Adnotasse videor facta dictaque virorum feminarumque illustrium alia clariora esse, alia maiora. Confirmata est opinio mea hesterno Fanniae sermone. Neptis haec[1] Arriae illius, quae marito et solatium mortis et exemplum fuit. Multa referebat aviae suae non minora hoc, sed obscuriora: quae tibi existimo tam mirabilia legenti fore, quam mihi audienti fuerunt. Aegrotabat Caecina Paetus, maritus eius; aegrotabat et filius, uterque mortifere, ut videbatur: filius decessit, eximia pulchritudine, pari verecundia, et parentibus non minus ob alia carus, quam quod filius erat. Huic illa ita funus paravit, ita duxit exsequias, ut ignoraret maritus. Quin immo, quoties cubiculum eius intraret,[2] vivere filium atque etiam commodiorem esse simulabat, ac persaepe interroganti, quid ageret puer, respondebat: 'Bene quievit, libenter cibum sumpsit'. Deinde, cum diu cohibitae lacrimae vincerent prorumperentque, egrediebatur. Tunc se dolori dabat. Satiata, siccis oculis, composito vultu redibat, tanquam orbitatem foris reliquisset. Praeclarum quidem illud eiusdem, ferrum stringere, perfodere pectus, extrahere pugionem, porrigere marito, addere vocem immortalem ac paene divinam: 'Paete, non dolet'.[3] Sed tamen ista facienti, ista dicenti gloria et aeternitas ante oculos erant: quo maius est, sine praemio aeternitatis, sine praemio gloriae abdere lacrimas, operire luctum, amissoque filio matrem adhuc agere. Scribonianus arma in Illyrico contra Claudium moverat: fuerat Paetus in partibus[4]; occiso Scriboniano Romam trahebatur. Erat ascensurus navem: Arria milites orabat, ut simul imponeretur. 'Nempe enim', inquit 'daturi estis consulari viro servulos aliquos, quorum e manu cibum capiat, a quibus vestiatur, a quibus calcietur: omnia sola praestabo'. Non impetravit.

---

[1] **erat** must be supplied, as in another sentence later.

[2] In the golden age of Latin literature, 80 B.C. to A.D. 14, which included Cicero, Caesar, and Livy, the Indicative would have been used; in the silver age which followed and to which Tacitus and Pliny belong among prose writers, we find greater latitude and variety in syntax.

[3] **doleo** here has the meaning of *hurt*; the poet Martial (A.D. 40-102) also commemorates this heroism:

> 'Si qua fides, vulnus quod feci non dolet,' inquit,
> 'Sed quod tu facies hoc mihi, Paete, dolet.'

[4] *in the faction.*

Conduxit piscatoriam naviculam, ingensque navigium minimo secuta est. Quin etiam, cum Thrasea, gener eius, deprecaretur, ne mori pergeret, interque alia dixisset: 'Vis ergo filiam tuam,[1] si mihi pereundum fuerit, mori mecum?' respondit: 'Si tam diu tantaque concordia vixerit tecum, quam ego cum Paeto, volo'.

From Pliny's Letters, III, 16.

[1] Her name also was Arria; Thrasea was condemned in A.D. 66 for his opposition to Nero; he forbade his wife to follow her mother's example, when he committed suicide.

EXERCISE 113.

Sometimes deeds which are unknown seem to me to be equally great as those which are famous. Yesterday Fannia told me a wonderful story about her grandmother. It happened that her husband, Caecina Paetus, and her son were ill at the same time. When the son, who was extremely dear to them, died of his illness, Arria behaved herself and spoke to her husband as if the boy were still alive and even a little better. So well did she conceal what had happened that the funeral was carried out without her husband's knowledge. To act as though she were still a mother was, I think, a far greater thing than what she did, when she herself faced death. Everyone knows how she pierced her own breast with a dagger and what words she spoke while she handed it to her husband; she might, however, have said these words as if she knew that they would win praise among posterity. No one except her relations knew how bravely she had behaved over her son's death; she had then no object[1] except to comfort and save her husband.

[1] *to make it one's object to*, **id agere ut;** here we would use **nihil agere nisi ut.**

Chapter 27
Oratio Obliqua (1)

(1) Direct Speech

When the actual words of a speech are reproduced by a Latin author, the Verbs **inquit, inquiunt** (or **ait, aiunt**) are inserted after the first or second word of the speech; Direct Speech or **Oratio Recta** is, as its name implies, straightforward; many examples of this have already been met.

(2) Indirect Speech

In Latin, even more often than in English, it was usual in reporting speech to omit the Verbs of *saying, asking, commanding*, etc., and to report the substance of the speech in the third person; this use of Indirect Speech is known as **Oratio Obliqua.** We generally, of course, find one Verb of *saying* at the very beginning or else some indication that a speech is about to be delivered.

Here is a condensed extract from a speech of Winston Churchill's in Oratio Recta:

'It is an alert I am sounding, yet it is more than an alert—it is an alarm. We have never been beaten yet, and now we fight for our survival as an independent, self-supporting nation.'

This passage reported in Oratio Obliqua would run:

It was an alert he was sounding, yet it was more than an alert—it was an alarm. They had never been beaten yet, and at that time they were fighting for their survival, etc.

Change of Persons and Structure

Here is part of a message sent by a Gallic chief to Caesar, as it would be in Oratio Recta:

Civitas est in mea potestate, et si, Caesar, permittes, ad te in castra veniam, meas civitatisque fortunas tuae fidei committam.

The state is in my power, and if you allow it, Caesar, I will come to you in your camp and entrust my fortunes and those of the state to your protection.

This Sentence in Oratio Obliqua would run as follows, **dixit** being understood:

Civitatem esse in sua potestate, seseque, si Caesar permitteret, ad illum (or **eum**) **in castra venturum, suas civitatisque fortunas illius** (or **eius**) **fidei commissurum.**

The state was in his power, and if Caesar allowed it, he would come to him in the camp and entrust his fortunes and those of the state to his protection.

A comparison of these passages shows us:

(*a*) that the 1st person (the speaker) now becomes the Reflexive 3rd person (**sua, sese, suas**);

(*b*) that the 2nd person becomes a Demonstrative Pronoun of the 3rd person (**illum, illius; eum, eius** would be used, if less emphasis were required);

(*c*) that **Main Clauses** which are **Statements** (**civitas est, veniam, committam**) become **Accusative and Infinitive Clauses;**

(*d*) that the **Clause** which is **Dependent** on or **Subordinate** to the Accusative and Infinitive Clause, namely the Conditional Clause, is put in the **Subjunctive,** the Tense being **Historic,** because the Main Verb **dixit** is Historic;

(*e*) that the original Vocative Case, **Caesar,** is dropped, and **Caesar** appears in the Nominative as the Subject of the Conditional Clause.

If the above remarks have been understood, then the main elements of Oratio Obliqua have been grasped.

Summary of changes in Pronouns and Adverbs in Oratio Obliqua

Oratio Recta	*Oratio Obliqua*
Ego, nos; meus, noster	**se (ipse, ipsi** in Nom.); **suus**

Even though **ego** and **nos** may not have been required in *oratio recta*, **se** is necessary as the Subject of the Infin.; **se** and **suus** often include his audience with the speaker.

Tu, vos; tuus, vester	**ille, illi; illius, illorum** or, less emphatically **is, ei; eius, eorum**
Hic; iste	**ille; is**

Is is often used for what was already a 3rd person in *oratio recta*.

Hodie	**illo die, eo die**

So **heri** becomes **pridie, cras** becomes **postridie; hic,** *here,* becomes **ibi,** *there,* etc.

Nunc	**iam** or **tunc, tum**

Example: *If I stay here today, we shall all be safe.*
Si ipse eo die ibi maneret, se omnes futuros esse tutos.

Further note on the Reflexive Pronoun

Although **se** and **suus** generally refer to the speaker, they may, where there can be no ambiguity in the meaning, refer to someone else who is the Subject of an Infinitive Clause or of a Subordinate Clause:

Neminem secum sine sua pernicie contendisse.
(Ariovistus said that) *no one had fought with him without his* (i.e. the fighter's) *own destruction.*

Changes in Main Clauses

Oratio Recta	*Oratio Obliqua*
(1) **Statements** in the **Indicative** (so also **denials**)	**Accusative and Infinitive** (the Tense following the sense)

O.R.   **Nulla spes superest, omnis cibus est consumptus.**
There is no hope left, all the food has been eaten.

O.O. **Nullam spem superesse, omnem cibum esse consumptum.**
There was no hope left, all the food had been eaten.

(2) **Direct Commands** and **Prohibitions**   **Imperfect Subjunctive**

(**imperavit ut** being omitted, but **ne** retained for Prohibitions)

O.R. **Nolite hosti cedere; totis viribus resistite.**
Do not yield to the foe; resist with all your might.

O.O. **Ne hosti cederent; totis viribus resisterent.**
They were not to yield to the foe; they were to resist, etc.

(3) **Exhortations**   **Imperfect Subjunctive**
(Jussive Subjunctive)   (**ne**, if Negative)

O.R. **Milites domum redeant,** *let the soldiers return home.*

O.O. **Milites domum redirent** (understanding **oravit ut**).

O.R. **Eis succurramus,** *let us help them.*

O.O. **Ipsi eis succurrerent** (understanding **hortatus est ut**).

If there is emphasis on the sense of duty, then this could become an Indirect Statement with the Gerund, **eis a se succurrendum esse.**

(4) **Questions**

(*a*) If asked (i) for obtaining   **Subjunctive**
information, or (ii) **in the**   (usual Sequence of Tenses)
2nd person

O.R. **Cur in meas possessiones venis?**
Why are you coming into my territory?

O.O. **Cur in suas possessiones veniret?**
(**rogavit** being understood)

O.R. **Quid mihi faciendum est?** *What should I do?*

O.O. **Quid sibi faciendum esset?** *What should he do?*

It should be noticed that interrogation marks are retained in Oratio Obliqua.

(*b*) If **Rhetorical,** not expecting   **Accusative and Infinitive**
an answer   (the Tense following the sense)

Note.—Most quoted questions in the 1st and 3rd persons are rhetorical.

O.R.   **Num desperamus?** *Are we downhearted?*

O.O.   **Num se desperare?**

O.R.   **Quid teritur tempus? Qui alius exercitus ex-spectatur?**
       Why is time being wasted? What other army is awaited?

O.O.   **Quid teri tempus? Quem alium exercitum ex-spectari?**

(c) If **Deliberative**   **Imperfect Subjunctive**

O.R.   **Quid faciamus?** *What are we to do?*

O.O.   **Quid facerent?** (or **quid sibi faciendum esset?** or, if the Question is really Rhetorical, **quid sibi faciendum esse?**)

(5) **Wishes**   **Utinam** and **Imperf.** or
  (**utinam** and Subjunctive)   **Pluperf. Subjunctive**

Sometimes a Wish for the Present or Future may be turned into an Acc. and Infin. Clause, e.g. **se velle.**

O.R.   **Utinam redeas, redires!** *Would that you might return, were now returning!*

O.O.   **Utinam ille rediret** or **se velle illum redire.**

Utinam adfuisses! would become **utinam ille adfuisset.**

Subordinate Clauses in Oratio Obliqua will be dealt with in the next chapter.

EXERCISE 114. (*Translate both into English O.O. and into English O.R.*)

1. Transisse Rhenum sese non sua sponte, sed rogatum.
2. Feminis liberisque milites parcerent.
3. Quot naves tempestate essent fractae?
4. Num recentium iniuriarum se memoriam deponere posse?
5. Se diem ad deliberandum sumpturum esse.
6. Ille novas copias eo quam celerrime ad se mitteret.
7. Illo die aut hostes vincendos esse aut sibi moriendum.

8. Utinam pridie frater illius ad se scripsisset.
9. Cur illi tam miseram praedam sectarentur?
10. Se velle illos solitam virtutem eo die praestare.
11. Nunquam sibi placuisse Avaricum defendi.
12. Ne Galli sui liberandi occasionem dimitterent.
13. Illud incommodum se facile sanaturum esse.
14. Quid ipse, tanto impeditus maerore, scriberet?
15. Aut non suscipi bellum oportuisse aut perfici quam primum oportere.
16. Postridie in campos Italiae sibi fore descendendum.
17. Num sapientis esse senectuti cedere?
18. Eum neque vim hiemis neque longitudinem itineris retardavisse.
19. Milites desilirent neve aquilam hostibus proderent.
20. Cur Fabius cunctaretur? Ipsi Hannibalem statim oppugnarent.

EXERCISE 115. (*Translate into Oratio Obliqua*)
1. I am a Roman citizen.
2. Burn all the towns, but leave the forage in the fields.
3. I did not make war upon the Gauls, but they upon me.
4. Why are you frightened by the Alps, my men?
5. Let us make for the nearest woods.
6. This work must be done today.
7. Where are we to seek safety?
8. The enemy have ravaged our fields and killed our settlers.
9. Shall we allow the enemy to invade our country?
10. Our son is alive and even a little better.
11. Do not let slip an opportunity of finishing this business.
12. Why do you refuse citizenship to this poet, O senators?
13. Would that you and the children might come here to me!
14. You will soon conquer the enemy and reach Rome itself.
15. Show your bravery under our leadership.
16. We shall set sail for Britain tomorrow.
17. When shall we see our homes again?
18. Are you going to desert your country in this danger?
19. Not without great hope have I left my home.
20. We must resist the enemy now in this very place.

Exercise 116.

CAESAR COUNTS THE COST

During his campaign against the forces of Pompey in Spain in 49 B.C. Caesar manoeuvred his army between that of Afrānius, Pompey's commander, and the river Ebro, with the result that the Pompeians were cut off from supplies of forage and water. It was tempting for Caesar to finish the campaign at once; this temptation, however, he resisted in order to avoid unnecessary casualties; his decision was justified by the surrender of the Pompeians two days later.

Erat occasio bene gerendae rei. Neque vero id[1] Caesarem fugiebat, tanto sub oculis accepto detrimento perterritum exercitum sustinere[2] non posse, praesertim circumdatum undique exercitu, cum in loco aequo atque aperto confligeretur: idque ex omnibus partibus ab eo flagitabatur. Concurrebant legati, centuriones tribunique militum[3]: Ne dubitaret proelium committere. Omnium esse militum paratissimos animos. Afranianos contra multis rebus sui timoris signa dedisse: quod suis non subvenissent, quod de colle non decederent, quod vix equitum incursus sustinerent collatisque in unum locum signis[4] conferti neque ordines neque signa servarent. Quod si iniquitatem loci timeret, datum iri tamen aliquo loco pugnandi facultatem, quod certe inde decedendum esset Afranio nec sine aqua permanere posset.

Caesar in eam spem venerat, se sine pugna et sine vulnere suorum rem conficere posse, quod re frumentaria adversarios interclusisset. Cur etiam secundo proelio aliquos ex suis amitteret? cur vulnerari pateretur optime de se meritos milites? cur denique fortunam periclitaretur? praesertim cum non minus esset imperatoris consilio superare quam gladio. Movebatur etiam misericordia civium, quos interficiendos videbat: quibus salvis atque incolumibus rem obtinere malebat.

From Caesar, *Civil War*, I, 71-72.

[1] **id** is anticipatory.   [2] Intransitive.

[3] There were six military tribunes to a legion; in Caesar's time they assisted the **legatus**, who was in command.

[4] *with their standards crowded* and so ineffective; **signa servare** seems to mean *to keep military formation*.

EXERCISE 117. (*Translate direct speech into Oratio Obliqua*)

The lieutenants said that there was now an opportunity of fighting on level ground and that the enemy could not resist their cavalry. 'We are all ready to fight; lead us into battle at once; let us not delay longer. The soldiers of Afranius are afraid to bring help to their own men, they are unwilling to come down from the hill, they do not even keep their ranks. Surely you do not fear the disadvantage of ground? Anyhow Afranius needs water and will have to come down soon.'

Caesar, however, did not approve of this plan. 'I have shut off the army of Afranius from water and from corn-supply; I can finish this business without a battle. My men have deserved well of me; since this is so, is it the mark of a good general to allow them to be wounded and killed? Furthermore, am I also to allow citizens to be killed? By a wise plan both my own men and the citizens can be saved.'

Chapter 28
Oratio Obliqua (2)

Subordinate Clauses

The **Verbs** of Dependent or **Subordinate Clauses** go into a **Historic** Tense of the **Subjunctive** (the Imperfect or Pluperfect, according to the time); all such Subordinate Clauses depend upon an original Historic Verb of *saying*, even though it is not expressed:

Habere sese, quae de re communi dicere vellent, quibus rebus controversias minui posse sperarent.

They had (they said) something to say for the common good, by which they hoped that the differences could be lessened.

It should be particularly noticed that the Tense of **vellent** and **sperarent** depends not on the Present Infinitive **habere**, but on a Historic Verb **dixerunt**, which has to be supplied.

Qui eius consili principes fuissent, in Britanniam profugisse.

Those who had been the ringleaders of this plot had fled to Britain.

Vereri se, ne per insidias ab eo circumveniretur.

He was afraid that he (Ariovistus) might be surrounded by Caesar by a trick.

An Imperfect Subjunctive corresponds to a Future Simple in *O.R.*, but a Pluperfect Subjunctive takes the place of a Future Perfect in *O.R.*, so far as Subordinate Clauses are concerned:

I will give you land in Italy, Africa, Spain, where anybody wants it, tax-free to the man who receives it, and to his children

becomes

Agrum sese daturum esse in Italia, Africa, Hispania, ubi quisque vellet, immunem ipsi, qui accepisset, liberisque.

In Direct Speech we should have had **acceperit** (Fut. Perfect).

Exceptions to the above rule

(1) When **dum** means *while* in the sense of *during the time that*, the Verb with **dum** remains in the **Present Indicative**:

> **Hostes, dum in opere sunt occupati, oppugnarent.**
> *They were to attack the enemy while they were still busy with their earthworks.*

(2) If the Relative Pronoun merely stands for **et is** (i.e. **is** Co-ordinate), then the Verb of the Relative Clause is sometimes attracted into the Infinitive; this use should be noticed rather than imitated:

> **Conspectos esse equites, quos auxilium laturos esse.**
> *The cavalry had been sighted, who would bring help.*

Conditional Sentences in Oratio Obliqua

The **Main Clause** or Apodosis becomes an **Acc. and Infin. Clause,** and the Verb of the **Conditional Clause** or Protasis will be in either the Imperfect or the Pluperfect **Subjunctive,** according to the time; the following scheme sets out the conversion of Mood and Tense, after **dixit**:

O.R.	*O.O.*
(i) (*a*) **Si hoc putas, erras**	**Si illud putaret, eum errare**
(*b*) **Si putabis, errabis**	**Si putaret, eum erraturum esse**
(*c*) **Si putabas, errabas**	**Si putaret, eum errare**
(*d*) **Si putavisti, erravisti**	**Si putavisset, eum erravisse**
(*e*) **Si putaveris, errabis**	**Si putavisset, eum erraturum esse**
(ii) (*a*) **Si putes, erres**	**Si putaret, eum erraturum esse**
(*b*) **Si putavisses, erravisses**	**Si putavisset, eum erraturum fuisse**

Note.—(i) The Fut. Perf. Indic. in the Protasis of (i) (*e*) becomes Pluperf. Subjunct.

(ii) The Verb of the Protasis of (ii) (*a*), although referring to the **Remote Future** (see Chap. 21), now goes into the **Imperf. Subjunct.,** because it depends on a Historic Verb.

(iii) Conversion of thè Remote Present type, **si putares, errares**, seems to have been generally avoided by Latin authors.

The above scheme for conversion also holds good for the **Passive** Voice, except when there is an Apodosis of the (ii) (*b*) type; there is no Future Perfect Infinitive Passive in Latin, and to take its place Latin uses the **Future Perfect** Infinitive of **sum** impersonally, followed by **ut** and the Imperfect Subjunctive **Passive** of the required Verb; what would have been the Subject of an Infin. Clause now becomes the Subject of the Verb in the Subjunctive (unless, as in the second example below, the Verb is Intransitive):

> **Nisi auxilia subvenissent, futurum fuisse ut oppidani superarentur.**
> *If reserves had not arrived, the townspeople would have been defeated.*

> **Si auxilia celerius subvenissent, futurum fuisse ut hostibus diutius resisteretur.**
> *If reserves had arrived sooner, the enemy would have been resisted longer.*

Graphic use of Primary Tenses of Subjunctive in Oratio Obliqua

Even though they use a Historic Main Verb to introduce Oratio Obliqua, Caesar and Livy often revert to a Present instead of an Imperfect Subjunctive in a Subordinate Clause, and to a Perfect instead of a Pluperfect. Their purpose is to make the speech more vivid and to introduce variety. This practice should be noticed rather than imitated:

> **Esse nonnullos, quorum auctoritas apud plebem plurimum valeat.**
> *There were some whose authority had very great influence with the common people.*

> **Romani si casu intervenerint, fortunae habendam gratiam.**
> *If the Romans had appeared by chance, then thanks should be given to fortune.*

EXERCISE 118. (*Translate both into English O.O. and into English O.R.*)

1. Milites habere facultatem quam petivissent.
2. Tribus horis Aduatucam eos venire posse, ubi plus praedae esset.
3. Si regnum appeteret, se Vercingetorigem ex oppido expulsurum esse.
4. Galli obsides quos imperavisset statim ad se adducerent.
5. Tutos se esse, quod monte Cevenna ut muro muniti essent.
6. Num illos timere ut Caesar auxilium mitteret?
7. Tot esse hostes ut non sine magna difficultate repelli possent.
8. Si quis in senectute pristinum robur conservare vellet, naturae legibus ab eo parendum esse.
9. Si navem conscendisset, eum periturum esse.
10. Si consules exploratores emisissent, non futurum fuisse ut exercitus circumveniretur.
11. Etsi exigua pars aestatis superesset, se in Britanniam tunc profecturum esse.
12. Fore ut hostes, si in monte manerent, ab aqua intercluderentur.
13. Sulpicium, dum iter ad Galliam facit, multis in urbibus se reficere potuisse, non tamen esse moratum.
14. Si illi se iuvarent, onus statim levius sibi fore.
15. Simul atque ver esse coepisset, Verrem ita se dedisse itineribus, ut eum nemo in equo sedentem videret.
16. Non esse dubium quin novae copiae iam missae essent.
17. Nisi frumentum celavissent, Siculos morituros fuisse.
18. Utinam uxor adfuisset, ut se consolaretur.
19. Onera sibi imponi, quae non posse ferri.
20. Velle se reperire cur Fabius ita moraretur.

EXERCISE 119. (*Translate into Oratio Obliqua*)

1. Do not be upset by this disaster which you have suffered.
2. I have crossed the Rhine, because the Gauls invited me.

3. If you burn your towns, you will defend your country more easily.
4. Attack the Gauls while they are still waiting for the Germans.
5. Simonides returned home, because he had been warned in a dream.
6. If you had not defended Avaricum, fewer men would have been killed.
7. Troy was captured, after it had been besieged for ten years.
8. We are afraid that our goods will be plundered by Verres.
9. If we lead back the army, the enemy will plunder our territory.
10. Caesar reached Gaul before he was expected.
11. If Sulpicius had returned, we should have thanked him.
12. The Gauls have killed several Roman citizens who were living at Cenabum.
13. Shall we reject a poet who has celebrated the glory of the Roman people?
14. If you were to take away the column, you would lose your other eye.
15. The soldiers finished the work, although they were weary with the long march.
16. Those who reach old age should exercise their minds.
17. If I have you, I shall not seem to have died utterly!
18. Are we not to be moved by the voices of the poets?
19. Whatever ship came from Asia was at once detained by Verres.
20. Finish quickly the war which you have undertaken, and do not shirk the difficulties.

EXERCISE 120.

A SUGGESTION FOR DISARMAMENT AND PEACE

When he entered upon the last phase of his struggle with Pompey, Caesar landed in Ēpīrus, just south of Ōricum, early in

48 B.C., *while it was still winter. By this time Pompey was on the march from Thessalonica to Dyrrhachium. Caesar makes an offer of peace, but it was rejected by Pompey.*

Demonstravimus L. Vibullium Rufum, Pompei praefectum, bis in potestatem pervenisse Caesaris atque ab eo esse dimissum, semel ad Corfinium,[1] iterum in Hispania. Hunc pro suis beneficiis Caesar idoneum iudicaverat, quem cum mandatis ad Cn. Pompeium mitteret, eundemque apud Cn. Pompeium auctoritatem habere intellegebat. Erat autem haec summa mandatorum: debere utrumque pertinaciae finem facere et ab armis discedere neque amplius fortunam periclitari. Satis esse magna utrinque incommoda accepta, quae pro disciplina et praeceptis habere possent, ut reliquos casus timerent: illum Italia expulsum, amissa Sicilia et Sardinia[2] duabusque Hispaniis et cohortibus in Italia atque Hispania civium Romanorum cxxx; se morte Curionis et detrimento Africani exercitus tanto militumque deditione ad Curictam.[3] Proinde sibi ac reipublicae parcerent, cum, quantum in bello fortuna posset, iam ipsi incommodis suis satis essent documento. Hoc unum esse tempus de pace agendi, dum sibi uterque confideret[4] et pares ambo viderentur; si vero alteri paulum modo tribuisset fortuna, non esse usurum[5] condicionibus pacis eum, qui superior videretur, neque fore aequa parte contentum, qui se omnia habiturum confideret. Condiciones pacis, quoniam antea convenire non potuissent, Romae ab senatu et a populo peti debere. Id interesse reipublicae et ipsis placere oportere. Si uterque in contione statim iuravisset se triduo proximo exercitum dimissurum,

---

[1] A town in central east Italy, which had surrendered to Caesar after a siege in 48.

[2] Sicily and Sardinia were lost to Pompey in 48.

[3] Caesar had ordered Cūrio to gain control of Africa, but he was outwitted and overcome by the help of Juba, king of the Numidians, who supported the cause of Pompey. **magnum incommodum accepisse** must be supplied after **se**.

[4] The tense and mood should be studied, for the precise meaning of **dum**.

[5] *observe.*

depositis armis auxiliisque, quibus nunc confiderent, necessario populi senatusque iudicio fore utrumque contentum.

Caesar, *Civil War*, III, 10.

EXERCISE 121. (*Translate direct speech into Oratio Obliqua*)
Caesar sent Vibullius as ambassador to negotiate with Pompey. 'It is a sign of obstinacy to tempt fortune and continue the war. Warned by the setbacks we have already suffered, let us both fear future calamities; Italy, Sicily, Spain are witnesses, in all of which countries you lost so many men; Africa is a witness, in which Curio was killed and so many of my men surrendered. Ought we not now to spare not only ourselves but also the republic, while the opportunity is offered? We have both found out how great in war is the influence of fortune. Since today we appear to be equal, now is the time to seek peace. If we continue the war, he who shall seem to himself to be only a little superior to the other, will not be content with the terms of peace. It is not from us, but from the senate and Roman people that terms should be sought. I will swear to dismiss my army within three days, if you will swear to do the same; then, when we have laid down arms, we shall have to abide by[1] the decision of the senate and people.'

[1] **maneo in**, with Abl.

Chapter 29
Order of Words and Sentences

The main constructions in Latin have now been covered. It may, perhaps, be felt that not enough has been said about the word and sentence order that we find in Latin authors. This may be true, but to have emphasized this point, important as it is, at earlier stages, would probably have hindered progress. In any case, the reader has been continually studying original Latin throughout the book, and he will have unconsciously absorbed some of the main principles.

The following observations and examples may be useful. An understanding of them will help in more advanced translation and composition, and in their light the Latin extracts in the main body of the book may be studied afresh.

Word Order

(*a*) While it is true that the Verb is almost always the most important word in a Latin sentence and is placed at the end, sometimes for the sake of emphasis the end position is occupied by some other part of speech:

Iam vero videte hominis audaciam!
Now look at the fellow's impudence!

Sometimes for the sake of emphasis the last place in the sentence is taken by the Subject:

Facilius in morbos incidunt adulescentes.
The young fall ill more easily.

(*b*) Next in importance to the last place in the sentence is the first place:

Delenda est Carthago.
Carthage must be destroyed.

166

Conclamat omnis multitudo.
The whole crowd shouted together.

(*c*) Latin has a particular fondness for clauses which are parallel in construction, with the order of words carefully balanced:

Patriae deesse aliis turpe, Camillo etiam nefas est.
To fail one's country is to other men a disgrace, to Camillus a crime.

Often, for the sake of variety (sometimes for contrast), the order of the second clause is inverted; compare in English *I cannot dig, to beg I am ashamed*:

Vident sociorum calamitates, querimonias audiunt.
They see the disasters of their allies, they hear their complaints.

This inverted order is often found with two Nouns, each qualified by an Adjective, the two pairs being joined by **-que,** e.g. **viros fortes egregiosque cives,** with the two Nouns outside; **fortissimos viros civesque optimos,** with the two Adjectives outside.

(*d*) The Relative Clause frequently precedes the Clause which contains the Antecedent, as was noticed in Chap. 1:

Quod cuique temporis ad vivendum datur, eo debet esse contentus.
A man should be content with the length of life that is allotted to him.

Structure of Complex Sentence

In dealing with trivial subjects, in the writing of letters, and in graphic descriptions, Latin authors generally use short sentences with only few Subordinate Clauses, but orators like Cicero, and historians like Livy and Caesar, using a large canvas to describe grand subjects, frequently indulged in Complex Sentences which are connected together in such a way that the construction and meaning are not complete until we reach the last clause; as in the simple sentence, so in the longer sentence, the last clause generally contains the Main Verb.

In this way the mind of the reader or listener is kept in suspense; it is not so much that the Verb or Clause at the end provides the key for the Subordinate Clauses which precede them, as that the last clause contains the most important action or thought or statement in the narrative or speech.

The following is a rough guide to the order of Clauses, etc., which we find in a Complex Sentence:

(*a*) As a general rule, unless a new topic is introduced, some connexion with the previous sentence, e.g. a Conjunction or a connecting Relative or an Adverb or Adverbial expression of Time or Place; here are some beginnings:

> **Itaque Hannibal** . . .   **Litteras igitur nuntiosque** . . .
> **Nam quod ad hostes appropinquabat, Caesar** . . .
> **Qui omnibus rebus subito perterriti** . . . (**qui** referring to
> **Germani** in the previous sentence) **Qua re nuntiata** . . .
> **Inde ad rupem muniendam** . . .   **Eodem fere tempore** . . .

(*b*) The Subject, if expressed (it will often be in the Verb), together with words or Clauses closely connected with the Subject, e.g. words in Apposition or Participles in agreement or a Relative Clause:

> **Lucius Paulus consul iterum** . . .
> **At Caesar biduum in his locis moratus** . . .
> **Principes Britanniae, qui post proelium ad Caesarem convenerant** . . .

(*c*) Words or Adverbial Clauses which explain the Time, Place, Cause, Purpose, etc. of the Main Clause, i.e. Clauses which answer the questions *when, where, why?*, etc.

(*d*) Noun Clauses—Indirect Statement, Indirect Question, Indirect Command, i.e. Clauses which are the immediate Object of the Main Verb.

(*e*) The Main Clause, containing the Main Verb.

(1) Here is a short example which illustrates the order of (*a*), (*c*), and (*e*):

Hoc proelio facto reliquas copias Helvetiorum ut consequi posset, pontem in Arare faciendum curat atque ita exercitum traducit.

After this engagement he had a bridge built over the Saône and sent his army across it so that he might be able to pursue the rest of the Helvetian forces.

(2) Here the Latin contains (*b*) and (*c*), then two Main Clauses, the second enclosing two Noun Clauses (*d*), one of which in turn encloses another Noun Clause.

Hostes proelio superati, simul atque se ex fuga receperunt, statim ad Caesarem legatos de pace miserunt, obsides daturos quaeque imperasset sese facturos polliciti sunt.

As soon as the enemy, thus defeated, had recovered from their rout, they at once sent ambassadors to Caesar to treat for peace, promising to give hostages and carry out his orders.

(3) The following sentence contains a Subject and two Predicates, with four Adverbial Clauses enclosed, the last three qualifying the first:

Labienus, ut erat ei praeceptum a Caesare, ne proelium committeret, nisi ipsius copiae prope hostium castra visae essent, ut undique uno tempore in hostes impetus fieret, monte occupato nostros exspectabat proelioque abstinebat.

Labienus acted in accordance with Caesar's instruction: he was not to join battle unless Caesar's own forces were visible near the enemy's camp, so that there could be a simultaneous attack from all sides; he therefore seized the hill and waited for our troops without engaging the enemy.

(4) Here an Adverbial Clause qualifies the Participle referring to the Subject, and a Noun Clause is the Object of the Main Verb.

Crassus equitum praefectos cohortatus, ut magnis praemiis pollicitationibusque suos incitarent, quid fieri velit ostendit.

> *Crassus urged the commanders of cavalry to rouse their men*
> *by big rewards and promises and showed what he wanted*
> *to be done.*

There are many exceptions to the arrangement set out above, due to change of emphasis or for the sake of variety or rhythm. For instance, the Main Verb often precedes an Indirect Statement, Final Clauses or Indirect Commands, and naturally would precede Consecutive Clauses and Fearing Clauses and also the uses of such conjunctions as **quominus** and **quin.**

The underlying principle is that strict attention is paid to the logical sequence of thoughts and events; more often than not the Main Clause stands at the end to hammer home the most important part of the sentence; when the Main Clause occupies an earlier position than the end, it may happen that the important part of the sentence is contained in a Subordinate Clause, e.g. an Indirect Statement or a Consecutive.

Rhythm and sound are a matter of ear and of experience; Cicero himself brought the rhythm of his sentence endings to a fine art and his favourite cadences, as they are called, should be studied, if we wish to write good Latin prose. For the moment three observations may be made: (1) although the tendency should be to 'enclose' Subordinate Clauses, care should be taken by means of change in word order to avoid having several verbs piled up together at the end; (2) a sentence should never close with a verse-ending, particularly a hexameter ending; e.g. **cives iussit discedere** is to be preferred to **cīvēs dīscēdĕrĕ iŭssĭt;** (3) a sentence should end with a word of some weight, consisting of three or more syllables.

(5) Here is a passage describing Caesar's thoughts and actions after receiving a deputation from mutineers at Corfinium. In the English we have several Main Clauses corresponding to the sequence of 'events'; in Caesar's original Latin everything is gathered together with various Clauses subordinated to two Main Clauses at the end.

When he learnt the situation, Caesar considered it vital to get
possession of the town as soon as possible and to transfer the
cohorts to himself in the camp, so that no bribes or improvement

*in morale or false messages should bring about a change of heart,
for often in time of war, as he knew, important events intervene
through small occasions. At the same time he was afraid that
through the entrance of the soldiers and the lack of discipline by
night the town might be looted; accordingly he commended the
deputation that had arrived and sent them back into the town,
while ordering that the gates and walls should be carefully
watched.*

Quibus rebus cognitis Caesar, etsi magni interesse arbitrabatur quam primum oppido potiri cohortesque ad se in castra
traducere, ne qua aut largitionibus aut animi confirmatione
aut falsis nuntiis commutatio fieret voluntatis, quod saepe in
bello parvis momentis magni casus intercederent, tamen
veritus, ne militum introitu et nocturni temporis licentia
oppidum diriperetur, eos, qui venerant, collaudat atque in
oppidum dimittit, portas murosque asservari iubet.

From Caesar, *Civil War*, I, 21.

(6) It must not however be thought that the merit of a Latin
Prose consists in the length of its complex sentences. There are
many places where the short sentence is needed, and we must
always be on our guard against over-elaboration.

Here is a simple piece of narrative that does not require a
great deal of structural alteration; indeed, Livy's original is a
masterpiece of simplicity. A close study of it will bring to notice
some of the points that have been mentioned above about the
order of words and clauses, variety, and emphasis.

*After duly consulting the auspices, he set out at midnight in
order to seize his objective before the enemy got wind of his
scheme; he then led his men past the enemy's camp, and, as dawn
broke, drew up his line and despatched three cohorts right up to
their very rampart. The barbarians, surprised that the Romans
had appeared in their rear, rushed this way and that to take up
arms too. Meanwhile the consul spoke to his troops: 'You have no
hope anywhere except in courage, my men, and I have taken good
care that you should not. Between our camp and ourselves are the
enemy and in the rear is enemy territory. The noblest path is the
safest: to have your hope based on courage.' Therefore he bade*

the cohorts to be withdrawn with the idea of drawing the enemy out by a feigned retreat. It turned out as he had expected. Thinking that the Romans had panicked and were in flight, they made a sally from the gate and manned with armed men all the remaining ground between their camp and their enemy's line.

Nocte media, cum auspicio operam dedisset, profectus, ut locum quem vellet, priusquam hostes sentirent, caperet, praeter castra hostium circumducit et prima luce acie instructa sub ipsum vallum tres cohortes mittit. Mirantes barbari ab tergo apparuisse Romanum discurrere et ipsi ad arma. Interim consul apud suos 'Nusquam nisi in virtute spes est, milites' inquit, 'et ego sedulo, ne esset, feci. Inter castra nostra et nos medii hostes et ab tergo hostium ager est. Quod pulcherrimum, idem tutissimum: in virtute spem positam habere.' Sub haec cohortes recipi iubet, ut barbaros simulatione fugae eliceret. Id, quod crediderat, evenit. Pertimuisse et cedere rati Romanos porta erumpunt et, quantum inter castra sua et aciem hostium relictum erat loci, armatis complent.

From Livy, xxxiv, 14.

Every sentence in this piece is worthy of study, and the order of words in every sentence; in particular, the enclosing of clauses in the first sentence, the position of **mirantes** in l. 4, the placing of **spes** next to **in virtute** in l. 6 (see also l. 9), the placing of the Relative Clause before the Main Clause in ll. 8 and 12-13, and the Latin fondness for parallelism in **quod pulcherrimum, idem tutissimum,** which in its telling terseness has almost an epigrammatic force. Mention should be made too of the use of the dramatic Present Tense, varied in the second sentence by the use of the Historic Infinitive, often used instead of the Imperfect Indicative in vivid descriptions.

It is hoped that what has been written in this chapter will be useful as a guide both in translation work and in composition. Once we have grasped the principles of word order and structure of the Latin sentence and of the logical sequence of Subordinate Clauses, we are, even with a limited vocabulary, some way towards elucidating the meaning. The next step is to retain the meaning, but to give the Latin sentence its natural English form, remembering that we shall in many places substitute sentences that are short and detached, and that the idioms of the two languages often differ.

In composition we shall employ the reverse process. Once we have got the meaning of a passage clear in our heads, we shall ask ourselves which sentences should be fused into a single complex sentence and which sentences should be allowed to remain detached or coordinate. We must also remember that in addition to the logical connexion supplied by subordination, Latin often demands, by the use of Conjunctions, the Relative, etc., some connexion between the sentences themselves.

Epilogue

Haec studia adulescentiam alunt, senectutem oblectant, secundas res ornant, adversis perfugium ac solatium praebent, delectant domi, non impediunt foris, pernoctant nobiscum, peregrinantur, rusticantur.

From Cicero, *Pro Archia*, 16.

Latin-English Vocabulary

Verbs which are followed by 1 *or* 2 *or* 4, *to show the number of their Conjugation, are conjugated regularly.*
Proper Nouns are usually not given, if they are the same in English as in Latin.
Long quantities have been omitted from common terminations, but have been inserted where guidance may be helpful.

Ā, ab (Abl.), *from; by* (agent).

abdo, -ere, -didi, -ditum, *I remove, hide.*

abdūco, -ere, -duxi, -ductum, *I lead away.*

abeo, -īre, -ii, -itum, *I go away.*

abhinc, *ago.*

abicio, -icere, -iēci, -iectum, *I throw away, cast aside.*

abscēdo, -ere, -cessi, -cessum, *I withdraw.*

absum, -esse, -fui, *I am away, absent; am wanting.*

āc, *and.*

accēdo, -ere, -cessi, -cessum, ad, *I reach, am added to.*

accidit, *it happens, happened.*

accīdo, -ere, -cīdi, -cīsum, *I cut into.*

accipio, -cipere, -cēpi, -ceptum, *I receive, hear, suffer.*

accūso, 1, *I accuse.*

ācer, ācris, ācre, *keen, fierce.*

acerbus, -a, -um, *grievous.*

aciēs, aciēi (f.), *line of battle.*

acūtus, -a, -um, *shrewd.*

ad (Acc.), *to, towards, at, against, up to* (of number).

addo, -ere, -didi, -ditum, *I add.*

addūco, -ere, -duxi, -ductum (ad), *I bring* (to), *induce.*

adeo, -īre, -ii, -itum, *I approach.*

adeo (Advb.), *so much, to such an extent.*

adfero, -ferre, attuli, allātum (or adlātum), *I bring.*

adhibeo, 2, *I use, take* (*food*), *apply.*

adhūc, *still.*

adimo, -ere, -ēmi, -emptum, *take away, confiscate.*

adipiscor, -i, -eptus sum, *I obtain.*

aditus, -us (m.), *approach, entrance.*

adiungo, -ere, -iunxi, -iunctum, *I join to,* so *win over.*

adiuvo, -āre, -iūvi, -iūtum, *I help.*

adlevo, 1, *I lighten.*

administro, 1, rem, *I administer affairs.*

admoveo, -ēre, -mōvi, -mōtum, ad, *I apply to.*

adnoto, 1, *I notice.*

adorior, -orīri, -ortus sum, *I attack.*

adsequor, -i, -secūtus sum, *I obtain.*

adservo, 1, *I keep safe.*

adsto, -stāre, -stiti, ad, *I stand near.*

adsum, -esse, -fui, *I am present, near, at hand.*

adulescens, -entis (m.), *young man.*

adulescentia, -ae (f.), *youth.*

advenio, -īre, -vēni, -ventum (ad), *I arrive (at).*

adventus, -us (m.), *arrival.*

adversārius, -i (m.), *opponent.*

adversor, 1, Dep., *I am against.*

adversus, -a, -um, *unfavourable;* rēs adversae (f. pl.), *adversity.*

aedifico, 1, *I build.*

aeger, aegra, aegrum, *sick.*

aegrōto, 1, *I am ill.*

aequus, -a, -um, *level, fair.*

aestās, -tātis (f.), *summer.*

aestimo, 1, *I value.*

aetās, -tātis (f.), *age.*

aeternitās, -tātis (f.), *immortality.*

affero, see adfero.

afficio, -ficere, -fēci, -fectum, *I treat;* affectus, -a, -um, *weak, ill.*

affirmo, 1, *I declare.*

afflictus, -a, -um, *wretched.*

afflīgo, -ere, -flixi, -flictum, *I knock down.*

Afrāniāni, -orum (m.), *soldiers of Afranius.*

ager, agri (m.), *field, territory.*

agmen, agminis (n.), *column.*

ago, -ere, ēgi, actum, *I drive, do, act; fare, get on; play the part of;* ago dē (Abl.), *I negotiate about;* grātias ago, *I give* or *render thanks.*

alcēs, alcis (f.), *elk.*

Alexander, Alexandri (m.), *Alexander.*

aliēnus, -i (m.), *foreigner.*

aliquando, *sometimes, at some time;* (in command clauses), *now at last.*

aliqui, aliqua, aliquod (Adj.), *some.*

aliquis, aliquid (Pron.), *someone, something.*

alius, alia, aliud, *other, another;* alii . . . , alii, *some . . . , others;* alius āc (atque), *other than.*

allicio, -licere, -lexi, -lectum, *I attract.*

alo, -ere, alui, altum, *I nourish.*

Alpes, -ium (f.), *the Alps.*

alter, altera, alterum, *the one* or *the other (of two).*

altitūdo, -dinis (f.), *depth.*

altus, -a, -um, *high, deep.*

ambo, ambae, ambo, *both.*

amīcitia, -ae (f.), *friendship.*

amīcus, -i (m.), *friend.*

āmitto, -ere, -mīsi, -missum, *I lose.*

amplitūdo, -dinis (f.), *size, extent.*

amplius, *more, longer.*

amplus, -a, -um, *great, splendid, honourable.*

an (in indir. question), *or.*
angustus, -a, -um, *narrow.*
animadverto, -ere, -verti, -versum, *I notice.*
animus, -i (m.), *soul, mind, spirit;* **in animo habeo,** *I intend.*
annus, -i (m.), *year.*
annuus, -a, -um, *lasting a year.*
ante (Acc.), *before, in front of.*
ante (Advb.), *before.*
anteā (Advb.), *before.*
antecēdo, -ere, -cessi, -cessum, *I surpass.*
anteeo, -īre, -ii, *I surpass.*
antequam (Conj.), *before.*
anxius, -a, -um, *anxious.*
apertus, -a, -um, *open.*
appāret, *it is evident.*
apparo, 1, *I prepare.*
appello, 1, *I call.*
appeto, -ere, -petīvi or **-ii, -petī-tum,** *I strive after.*
applico, -āre, -plicāvi or **-plicui, -plicātum** or **-plicitum,** *I place near.*
approbo, 1, *I approve.*
appropinquo, 1 (intrans.), *I approach.*
aptus, -a, -um (ad), *suitable (for).*
apud (Acc.), *among, in the presence of, in the eyes of, with, at the house of.*
aqua, -ae (f.), *water.*
aquila, -ae (f.), *eagle, standard* (of legion).
aquor, 1, Dep., *I fetch water.*
arbitror, 1, Dep., *I think.*
arbor, arboris (f.), *tree.*

arcesso, -ere, arcessīvi, arces-sītum, *I send for.*
arcus, -us (m.), *bow.*
ārea, -ae (f.), *threshing-floor.*
argentum, -i (n.), *silver.*
argūmentum, -i (n.), *proof, evidence.*
arguo, -ere, -ui, -ūtum, *I prove, assert.*
arma, -orum (n.), *arms;* **arma moveo,** *I start a war, rising.*
armo, 1, *I arm.*
ars, artis (f.), *art.*
articulus, -i (m.), *joint.*
artificium, -i (n.), *cunning.*
Arvernus, -i (m.), *an Arvernian.*
ascendo, -ere, -scendi, -scensum, *I climb, mount;* **nāvem ascendo,** *I embark.*
Asiāticus, -a, -um, *Asiatic.*
aspectus, -us (m.), *appearance.*
asperitās, -tātis (f.), *roughness.*
assentātio, -ōnis (f.), *flattery.*
assequor, -i, -secūtus sum, *I obtain.*
assuesco, -ere, -suēvi, -suētum, ad, *I grow used to.*
astrum, -i (n.), *star.*
at, *but.*
Athēnae, -arum (f.), *Athens.*
atque, *and.*
attingo, -ere, -tigi, -tactum, *I reach, border upon.*
auctor, -tōris (c.), *instigator.*
auctōritās, -tātis (f.), *authority, influence.*
audācia, -ae (f.), *daring, boldness.*
audeo, -ēre, ausus sum, *I dare.*

audio, 4, *I hear.*
aufero, -ferre, abstuli, ablātum, *I take away, remove.*
augeo, -ēre, auxi, auctum (trans.), *I increase.*
aureus, -a, -um, *golden.*
aurum, -i (n.), *gold.*
ausim, archaic form of pres. subj. of audeo, *I would venture.*
aut, *or;* aut . . . aut, *either . . . or.*
autem, *but, moreover.*
auxilium, -i (n.), *help;* auxilia, -orum, *allied troops.*
Avāricum, -i (n.), *Avaricum,* now *Bourges.*
avāritia, -ae (f.), *greed.*
avia, -ae (f.), *grandmother.*
avidus, -a, -um, *greedy.*

Barbarus, -a, -um, *uncivilised;* barbarus, -i (m.), *barbarian, foreigner.*
Belgae, -arum (m.), *the Belgians.*
bellum, -i (n.), *war.*
bene, *well.*
beneficium, -i (n.), *good service, kindness.*
bestia, -ae (f.), *wild animal.*
biennium, -i (n.), *space of two years, two years.*
bis, *twice.*
bonum, -i (n.), *good, advantage;* bona, -orum, *goods, property.*
bonus, -a, -um, *good, fine.*
bōs, bovis (c.), *ox, cow.*
brevis, -e, *short.*
Britanni, -orum (m.), *the Britons.*
Britannia, -ae (f.), *Britain.*

Brundisium, -i (n.), *Brundisium,* now *Brindisi.*
būcula, -ae (f.), *heifer.*

Cado, -ere, cecidi, cāsum, *I fall.*
caecus, -a, -um, *blind.*
caedēs, caedis (f.), *slaughter, massacre.*
caedo, -ere, cecīdi, caesum, *I kill.*
caelum, -i (n.), *climate.*
Caesar, Caesaris (m.), *Caesar.*
calcio, 1, *I furnish with shoes.*
campus, -i (m.), *plain.*
canis, canis (c.), *dog.*
cano, -ere, cecini, cantum, *I sing;* receptui cano, *I sound the retreat.*
capillus, -i (m.), *hair.*
capio, capere, cēpi, captum, *I take, capture, take up* (*arms*), *adopt* (*plan*).
Capitōlium, -i (n.), *the Capitol.*
capra, -ae (f.), *she-goat.*
captīvus, -i (m.), *prisoner.*
caput, capitis (n.), *head, life;* capitis damno, 1, *I condemn to death.*
carbaseus, -a, -um, *of linen.*
carcer, carceris (m.), *prison.*
careo, 2 (Abl.), *I am free from.*
caro, carnis (f.), *flesh, meat.*
Carthāgo, -ginis (f.), *Carthage.*
cārus, -a, -um, *dear.*
cāseus, -i (m.), *cheese.*
castē, *piously.*
castellum, -i (n.), *fort.*
castra, -orum (n.), *camp.*
cāsus, -us (m.), *chance, calamity.*

causa, -ae (f.), *reason, cause;* (*law*) *case; commission;* **causā** (after Gen.), *for the sake of, for, because of.*

caveo, -ēre, cāvi, cautum, *I am on guard* (*against*).

cēdo, -ere, cessi, cessum, *I retire, withdraw, give in.*

celebro, 1, *I celebrate.*

celeritās, -tātis (f.), *speed.*

celeriter, *quickly.*

cēlo, 1 (trans.), *I hide.*

Cenabum, -i (n.), *Cenabum,* now *Orleans.*

censeo, -ēre, censui, censum, *I am of opinion, propose.*

centum, *a hundred.*

centurio, -ōnis (m.), *centurion.*

certātim, *eagerly,* properly *in rivalry.*

certē, *certainly.*

certus, -a, -um, *definite, certain;* **certiōrem facio,** *I inform.*

cervix, cervīcis (f.), gen. used in pl., *neck.*

cesso, 1, *I do nothing, slacken my efforts.*

cēteri, -ae, -a, *the rest, the others.*

Cevenna, -ae (f.), *the Cevennes,* mountain in s. of Gaul.

cibus, -i (m.), *food.*

Cicero, -ōnis (m.), *Cicero.*

cingo, -ere, cinxi, cinctum, *I surround; I man* (*a wall*).

circiter (Advb.), *about* (of number).

circumclūdo, -ere, -clūsi, -clūsum, *I surround.*

circumdo, -dare, -dedi, -datum, *I surround.*

circumfundo, -ere, fūdi, -fūsum (in Passive), *I crowd around.*

circummūnio, 4, *I blockade.*

circumsisto, -ere, -steti, *I stand round.*

circumvenio, -īre, -vēni, -ventum, *I surround.*

citrā (Acc.), *on this side of.*

cīvis, cīvis (c.), *citizen.*

cīvitās, -tātis (f.), *state; citizenship.*

clam, *secretly.*

clāmito, 1, *I cry aloud.*

clāmor, clāmōris (m.), *shout.*

clārus, -a, -um, *famous.*

classis, classis (f.), *fleet.*

cliens, -entis (m.), *retainer, follower.*

coepi, coepisse, coeperam, *I began.*

coerceo, 2, *I check, confine.*

cognitor, -tōris (m.), *one who vouches for identity, guarantor.*

cognosco, -ere, -nōvi, -nitum, *I find out, learn.*

cōgo, -ere, coēgi, coactum, *I collect, compel.*

cohibeo, 2, *I check, hold back.*

cohors, cohortis (f.), *cohort.*

cohortor, 1, Dep., *I encourage.*

colligo, -ere, -lēgi, -lectum, *I rally.*

collis, collis (m.), *hill.*

colloco, 1, *I place, station.*

colloquium, -i (n.), *conference.*

collum, -i (n.), *neck.*

colo, -ere, colui, cultum, *I cultivate, worship, honour.*

colōnus, -i (m.), *colonist.*

color, colōris (m.), *colour.*

columna, -ae (f.), *column.*

commeātus, -us (m.), *leave of absence, furlough.*

commemoro, 1, *I relate.*

commendo, 1, *I recommend, entrust.*

committo, -ere, -mīsi, -missum, *I join (battle).*

commodum, -i (n.), *advantage.*

commodus, -a, -um, *satisfactory, convenient;* commodior, *better (in health).*

commoneo, 2, *I forcibly remind.*

commoveo, -ēre, -mōvi, -mōtum, *I move, disturb.*

commūnis, -e, *common, shared in common.*

comparo, 1, *I make ready, provide.*

comperio, -īre, -peri, -pertum, *I discover.*

compleo, -ēre, -plēvi, -plētum, *I fill, man.*

complexus, -us (m.), *embrace.*

compōno, -ere, -posui, -positum, *I compose, smoothe.*

concēdo, -ere, -cessi, -cessum, *I allow, pardon.*

concido, -ere, -cidi, *I fall down.*

concilio, 1, *I win over.*

concilium, -i (n.), *meeting.*

conclāmo, 1, *I cry out together.*

concordia, -ae (f.), *harmony.*

concurro, -ere, -curri, -cursum, *I run together, charge.*

concurso, -āre, *I travel about.*

concursus, -us (m.), *onset, charge.*

condicio, -ōnis (f.), *term, condition.*

condūco, -ere, -duxi, -ductum, *I hire.*

confectus, -a, -um, *weakened, exhausted.*

confero, -ferre, -tuli, collātum, *I collect, gather, devote.*

confertus, -a, -um, *pressed close.*

conficio, -ficere, -fēci, -fectum, *I finish, end, accomplish, exhaust.*

confīdo, -ere, -fīsus sum (Dat.), *I trust, have confidence in; am confident.*

confirmo, 1, *I strengthen, encourage; declare.*

confligo, -ere, -flixi, -flictum (intrans.), *I fight.*

confugio, -fugere, -fūgi, *I flee for refuge.*

congrego, 1, *I gather together.*

congressus, -us (m.), *meeting.*

cōnicio, -icere, -iēci, -iectum, *I throw.*

coniungo, -ere, -iunxi, -iunctum, *I join.*

coniux, coniugis (c.), *wife, husband.*

cōnor, 1, Dep., *I try.*

conquīro, -ere, -quīsīvi, -quīsītum, *I seek out.*

conscendo, -ere, -scendi, -scensum, *I ascend;* nāvem c., *I embark.*

consensus, -us (m.), *agreement.*

consequor, -i, -secūtus sum, *I obtain.*

conservo, 1, *I preserve, save, leave unharmed.*

consīdo, -ere, -sēdi, -sessum, *I take up a position.*

consilium, -i (n.), *plan, policy.*

consisto, -ere, -stiti, -stitum, *I stand still, take up a position, stop, make a stay.*

consōlor, 1, Dep., *I comfort.*

conspectus, -us (m.), *sight.*

conspicio, -spicere, -spexi, -spectum, *I catch sight of.*

constantia, -ae (f.), *determination.*

constituo, -ere, -stitui, -stitūtum, *I station; determine, resolve, decide.*

consuesco, -ere, -suēvi, -suētum, *I am accustomed.*

consuētūdo, -dinis (f.), *custom.*

consul, consulis (m.), *consul.*

consulāris, -e, *of consular rank.*

consulo, -ere, -sului, -sultum (with Dat.), *I have regard for.*

consūmo, -ere, -sumpsi, -sumptum, *I spend.*

consurgo, -ere, -surrexi, -surrectum, *I rise up.*

contego, -ere, -texi, -tectum, *I cover.*

contendo, -ere, -tendi, -tentum, *I hasten, march, fight, struggle;* **contendo ab,** *I entreat.*

contentus, -a, -um, *satisfied.*

continens, Gen. continentis, *continuous.*

contineo, -ēre, -tinui, -tentum, *I restrain, bound.*

contingo, -ere, -tigi, -tactum, *I border upon.*

contio, -ōnis (f.), *public assembly.*

contrā (Acc.), *against, opposite.*

contrā (Advb.), *on the other hand;* **contrā atque,** *contrary to.*

convenio, -īre, -vēni, -ventum, *I come together, assemble; agree.*

convīvium, -i (n.), *banquet.*

convoco, 1, *I call together.*

coorior, -orīri, -ortus sum, *I rise.*

cōpia, -ae (f.), *abundance;* **cōpiae, -arum,** *forces;* **novae c.,** *reinforcements.*

cōram (Advb.), *in person.*

cornū, -us (n.), *horn.*

corōna, -ae (f.), *garland.*

corpus, corporis (n.), *body.*

cotīdiē, *daily.*

crās, *tomorrow.*

crēdo, -ere, crēdidi, crēditum (Dat.), *I believe.*

crūdēlis, -e, *cruel.*

crūdēlitās, -tātis (f.), *cruelty.*

crūs, crūris (n.), *leg.*

crux, crucis (f.), *cross.*

cubiculum, -i (n.), *bedroom.*

cubīle, cubīlis (n.), *lair.*

culpo, 1, *I blame.*

culta, -orum (n.), *cultivated lands.*

cum (Prep. with Abl.), *with.*

cum (Conj.), *since; when; whenever; although.*

cunctor, 1, Dep., *I delay.*

cuneātim, *in wedge formation.*

cupiditās, -tātis (f.), *greed.*

cupidus, -a, -um, *eager, fond, greedy.*

cupio, cupere, cupīvi, cupītum, *I desire.*

cūr? *why?*

cūra, -ae (f.), *care, diligence.*

Cūrio, -ōnis (m.), *Curio.*

cūro, 1, *I look after, refresh; see to, cause;* **cūro ut,** *I see to it that.*

custōdiae, -arum (f.), *used for sentinels, guards.*

Cȳzicus, -i (f.), *Cyzicus,* island city, s. of Sea of Marmora.

Damno, 1, *I condemn.*

dē (Abl.), *down from, about, concerning, for* (e.g. **dē vīta**).

dēbeo, 2, *I ought.*

dēbilito, 1, *I weaken.*

dēcēdo, -ere, -cessi, -cessum, *I come down; die.*

decem, *ten.*

dēdecus, dēdecoris (n.), *disgrace.*

dēdico, 1, *I dedicate.*

dēditio, -ōnis (f.), *surrender.*

dēdo, -ere, -didi, -ditum (trans.), *I surrender;* **mē dēdo,** *I surrender* (intrans.).

dēfatīgātio, -ōnis (f.), *exhaustion.*

dēfendo, -ere, -fendi, -fensum, *I defend, protect.*

dēfensio, -ōnis (f.), *defence.*

dēfensor, -sōris (m.), *defender.*

dēfero, -ferre, -tuli, -lātum, ad, *I convey to, I confer upon.*

dēfessus, -a, -um, *tired, exhausted.*

dēficio, -ficere, -fēci, -fectum, *I fail, flag, desert.*

dēfīnio, 4, *I limit, bound.*

dēicio, -icere, -iēci, -iectum, *I throw down.*

deīnceps, *in turn.*

deīnde, *then, next.*

dēlecto, 1, *I delight, please.*

dēlībero, 1, *I deliberate, consider.*

dēlūbrum, -i (n.), *shrine.*

dēmentia, -ae (f.), *madness.*

dēminuo, -ere, -minui, -minūtum, *I diminish.*

dēmitto, -ere, -mīsi, -missum, mē, *I descend.*

dēmonstro, 1, *I show, mention.*

dēnique, *finally, in fact.*

dēpereo, -īre, -perii, *I perish, am lost.*

dēpōno, -ere, -posui, -positum, *I lay aside, lay down.*

dēpopulor, 1, Dep., *I ravage.*

dēprecor, 1, Dep., *I avert by prayer;* **d. nē,** *I ask someone not to.*

dēprehendo, or **dēprendo, -ere, -di, -sum,** *I apprehend, detect.*

dēscendo, -ere, -scendi, -scensum, *I go down, descend.*

dēsero, -ere, -serui, -sertum, *I desert, abandon.*

dēsīdero, 1, *I miss, lose.*

dēsilio, -īre, -silui, -sultum, *I leap down.*

dēsipio, -ere, *I am silly, act foolishly.*

dēsisto, -ere, -stiti, -stitum, *I*

cease; with or without **ab**, *I cease from;* also with infin.

dēspēro, 1, *I despair.*

dēsum, -esse, -fui (often with Dat.), *I am wanting, lacking, fail.*

dēterreo, 2, *I prevent.*

dētrīmentum, -i (n.), *loss.*

dētrūdo, -ere, -trūsi, -trūsum, *I thrust down.*

deus, -i (m.), *god.*

dīco, -ere, dixi, dictum, *I say.*

dictum, -i (n.), *saying, word.*

diēs, -ēi (m.), *day.*

differo, -ferre, distuli, dīlātum, *I put off;* (intrans.), *I differ.*

difficilis, -e, *difficult.*

difficultās, -tātis (f.), *difficulty.*

diffīdo, -ere, -fīsus sum (Dat.), *I mistrust.*

dignitās, -tātis (f.), *prestige.*

dignus, -a, -um, *worthy.*

dīgredior, -gredi, -gressus sum, *I go aside.*

dīlātio, -ōnis (f.), *delay, procrastination.*

dīlectus, -us (m.), *levy.*

dīligenter, *carefully.*

dīligentia, -ae (f.), *care.*

dīligo, -ere, -lexi, -lectum, *I love.*

dīmico, 1, *I fight.*

dīmitto, -ere, -mīsi, -missum, *I send aside, send forth, disband, let go, let slip, pass over.*

dīreptio, -ōnis (f.), *plundering.*

dīrigo, -ere, -rexi, -rectum, *I draw up.*

dīripio, -ripere, -ripui, -reptum, *I plunder.*

discēdo, -ere, -cessi, -cessum, *I depart;* **ab armis discēdo**, *I give up fighting.*

disciplīna, -ae (f.), *instruction, lesson.*

disclūdo, -ere, -clūsi, -clūsum, *I shut off, separate.*

disco, -ere, didici, *I learn.*

discrīmen, discrīminis (n.), *crisis.*

discutio, -cutere, -cussi, -cussum, *I clear away.*

dispersus, -a, -um, *scattered.*

dispōno, -ere, -posui, -positum, *I arrange, station.*

dissentio, -īre, -sensi, -sensum, **ab**, *I disagree with.*

dissimilis, -e (with Gen.), *unlike.*

disto, -stāre, *I am distant.*

diū, *for a long time.*

dīvido, -ere, dīvīsi, dīvīsum, *I divide.*

dīvīnus, -a, -um, *divine.*

dīvitiae, -arum (f.), *riches.*

do, dare, dedi, datum, *I give, devote.*

documentum, -i (n.), *proof.*

doleo, 2, *I grieve.*

dolor, dolōris (m.), *grief.*

domicilium, -i (n.), *a home.*

domus, -us or **-i** (f.), *household;* **domum**, *homewards;* **domi**, *at home.*

dōnec, *until.*

dōnum, -i (n.), *gift.*

dormio, 4, *I sleep.*

dubito, 1, *I hesitate, doubt.*

dubius, -a, -um, *doubtful;* **sine dubio,** *without doubt.*

dūco, -ere, duxi, ductum, *I lead.*

dum, *while; as long as; until.*

dummodo, *provided that.*

duo, duae, duo, *two.*

duodecim, *twelve.*

duodēvīginti, *eighteen.*

dūro, 1, *I harden.*

dūrus, -a, -um, *hard, severe, hardy, adverse.*

dux, ducis (c.), *leader, guide, general.*

Ē, ex (Abl.), *out of, from, by reason of, of* (after a number).

effero, -ferre, extuli, ēlātum, *I carry out.*

efficio, -ficere, -fēci, -fectum, *I make, form.*

effugio, -fugere, -fūgi, *I escape.*

effugium, -i (n.), *means of escape.*

egens, Gen. **egentis,** *needy.*

egeo, -ēre, egui (Abl.), *I need.*

ego, *I.*

ēgredior, -gredi, -gressus sum, *I go out;* **ē nāvi ēg.,** *I disembark.*

ēicio, -icere, -iēci, -iectum, *I cast out;* **mē ēi.,** *I rush out.*

elephantus, -i (m.), *elephant.*

ēlicio, -licere, -licui, -licitum, *I entice.*

ēligo, -ere, -lēgi, -lectum, *I choose.*

ēmigro, 1, *I depart.*

ēmitto, -ere, -mīsi, -missum, *I send out.*

ēmorior, -mori, -mortuus sum, *I die.*

enim, *for.*

eo, īre, ii, itum, *I go, advance.*

eo (Advb.), *thither, to that place, to that extent; by that amount;* **eo magis,** *all the more.*

eodem, *to the same place.*

epistola, -ae (f.), *letter.*

epulae, -arum (f.), *feast, banquet.*

eques, equitis (m.), *cavalry-man;* **equites,** *cavalry.*

equidem, *indeed.*

equitātus, -us (m. collective Noun), *cavalry.*

equito, 1, *I ride.*

equus, -i (m.), *horse.*

ergo, *therefore.*

ērigo, -ere, -rexi, -rectum, *I raise.*

ēripio, -ripere, -ripui, -reptum, *I snatch away.*

erro, 1, *I make a mistake, am wrong.*

ēruptio, -ōnis (f.), *sally.*

esseda, -ae (f.), *war-chariot.*

essedum, -i, *war-chariot;* also used for *carriage.*

et, *and;* **et . . . et,** *both . . . and.*

etiam, *also, even.*

etiamsī, *even if.*

Etrusci, -orum (m.), *the Etruscans.*

etsī, *even if, although.*

ēvasto, 1, *I devastate.*

ēvenit, -vēnit, *it turns out.*

ēvoco, 1, *I summon.*

ēvolo, 1, *I fly out.*

ex, *see* **ē.**

excēdo, -ere, -cessi, -cessum, ē vītā, *I die.*

excipio, -cipere, -cēpi, -ceptum, *I catch, intercept, welcome.*

exemplum, -i (n.), *example.*

exerceo, 2, *I train, exercise.*

exercitātio, -ōnis (f.), *exercise.*

exercito, 1, *I exercise.*

exercitus, -us (m.), *army.*

exiguus, -a, -um, *small.*

eximius, -a, -um, *extraordinary, uncommon.*

existimātio, -ōnis (f.), *opinion, public opinion.*

existimo, 1, *I think, imagine.*

exitium, -i (n.), *destruction, ruin.*

exitus, -us (m.), *outlet, passage.*

exorior, -orīri, -ortus sum, *I spring up, rise.*

expedio, 4, *I make ready.*

expello, -ere, -puli, -pulsum, *I drive out.*

experior, -perīri, -pertus sum, *I try, make an attempt.*

expeto, -ere, -petīvi, -petītum, *I seek out.*

expleo, -ēre, -plēvi, -plētum, *I fill up, make good.*

explōrātor, -tōris (m.), *scout.*

explōro, 1, *I reconnoitre.*

expugno, 1, *I storm.*

exsequiae, -arum (f.), *funeral procession.*

exsequor, -i, -secūtus sum, *I carry out, perform.*

exsilium, -i (n.), *exile.*

exsisto, -ere, -stiti, -stitum, *I exist.*

exspecto, 1, *I wait, wait for, expect.*

exstinguo, -ere, -stinxi, -stinctum, *I put out, snuff out.*

exterebro, 1, *I bore out.*

exterus, -a, -um, *foreign.*

extrā (Acc.), *outside.*

extraho, -ere, -traxi, -tractum, *I draw out.*

extrēmus, -a, -um, *furthest, extreme, last, advanced.*

extrinsecus, *on the outside.*

Faber, fabri (m.), *workman.*

fābula, -ae (f.), *a play.*

facile, *easily.*

facilis, -e, *easy.*

facio, facere, fēci, factum, *I make, do;* facio ut, *I see that;* nōn possum facere quīn, *I cannot help.*

factum, -i (n.), *deed.*

facultās, -tātis (f.), *chance, opportunity.*

fallo, -ere, fefelli, falsum, *I deceive.*

falsus, -a, -um, *false.*

fāma, -ae (f.), *report, reputation, fame.*

famēs, famis (f.), *hunger.*

familia, -ae (f.), *household.*

familiāris, -is (m.), *intimate friend.*

fānum, -i (n.), *temple.*

farcio, -īre, farsi, fartum, *I stuff.*

fatīgo, 1 (trans.), *I tire.*

Favōnius, -i (m.), *west wind.*

fēmina, -ae (f.), *woman.*

fera, -ae (f.), *wild beast.*

ferē, *almost.*

fero, ferre, tuli, lātum, *I carry, bear, bring, win, endure, propose* (*law*); **ferunt,** *they say.*

ferrum, -i (n.), *iron, iron head* (*of spear*), *sword.*

festīno, 1, *I hasten, hurry.*

fidēlis, -e, *faithful.*

fidēs, fidēi (f.), *faith, good faith, trust, protection.*

fidūcia, -ae (f.), *trust, confidence.*

fīdus, -a, -um, *faithful.*

figūra, -ae (f.), *shape.*

fīlia, -ae (f.), *daughter.*

fīliola, -ae (f.), *little daughter.*

fīlius, -i (m.), *son.*

fīnis, fīnis (m.), *end, crowningpoint;* **fīnes** (pl.), *boundaries, territory.*

fīnitimus, -a, -um, *neighbouring.*

fīo, fieri, factus sum, *I am done;* **nōn potest fieri quīn,** *it is impossible that . . . not.*

fixus, -a, -um, *fixed, ordained.*

flāgito, 1, *I demand.*

flecto, -ere, flexi, flexum, *I bend, sway.*

fleo, flēre, flēvi, flētum, *I weep.*

fluctus, -us (m.), *wave.*

flūmen, flūminis (n.), *river.*

forīs, *outside, abroad.*

fortis, -e, *brave.*

fortitūdo, -dinis (f.), *bravery.*

fortūna, -ae (f.), *fortune, chance.*

fortūnātus, -a, -um, *lucky, prosperous.*

forum, -i (n.), *forum, marketplace.*

fossa, -ae (f.), *ditch.*

fovea, -ae (f.), *pit.*

fragor, fragōris (m.), *crash.*

frango, -ere, frēgi, fractum, *I break.*

frāter, frātris (m.), *brother.*

frētus, -a, -um, *with* Abl., *relying upon.*

frīgus, frīgoris (n.), *cold, frost.*

fructus, -us (m.), *fruit, harvest.*

frūmentārius, -a, -um, *of corn;* **rēs frūm.,** *corn-supply.*

frūmentātio, -ōnis (f.), *cornsupply.*

frūmentor, 1, Dep., *I fetch corn, forage.*

frūmentum, -i (n.), *corn;* (pl.), *probably corn-crops.*

fruor, -i, fructus sum (Abl.), *I enjoy.*

fuga, -ae (f.), *flight, rout.*

fugio, fugere, fūgi (fugitūrus), *I flee; escape from, escape the notice of.*

fūnus, fūneris (n.), *funeral.*

Gallia, -ae (f.), *Gaul.*

Gallicus, -a, -um, *Gallic.*

Gallus, -i (m.), *a Gaul.*

gaudeo, -ēre, gāvīsus sum, *I rejoice.*

gemma, -ae (f.), *jewel.*

gener, generi (m.), *son-in-law.*

gens, gentis (f.), *race, tribe.*

genus, generis (n.), *kind.*

Germāni, -orum (m.), *the Germans.*

gero, -ere, gessi, gestum, *I carry, accomplish, do, wage* (*war*);

mē gero, *I behave myself;* **negōtium gero,** *I finish an operation;* **rem gero,** *I fight an action.*

gladius, -i (m.), *sword.*

glōria, -ae (f.), *glory, renown.*

Graecia, -ae (f.), *Greece.*

Graecus, -a, -um, *Greek;* **Graecus, -i** (m.), a *Greek.*

grātia, -ae (f.), *thanks;* **grātiam refero,** *I return thanks;* **grātias ago,** *I give thanks.*

grātulor, 1, Dep. (Dat.), *I congratulate.*

grātus, -a, -um, *pleasing, welcome.*

gravis, -e, *heavy, serious.*

gravitās, -tātis (f.), *weight.*

Habeo, 2, *I have, hold, keep, consider, count;* **honōrem habeo** with Dat., *I give honour to.*

Hannibal, -balis (m.), *Hannibal.*

haud, *not.*

Helvētii, -orum (m.), *the Helvetians.*

herculēs, *by Hercules!*

herī, *yesterday.*

hesternus, -a, -um, *of yesterday.*

hīberna, -orum (n.), *winter-quarters.*

hībernus, -a, -um, *of winter, wintry.*

hīc, haec, hōc (Pron. and Adj.), *he, she, it; this; the latter.*

bīc (Advb.), *here.*

hiems, hiemis (f.), *winter.*

Hispānia, -ae (f.), *Spain.*

hodiē, *today.*

Homērus, -i (m.), *Homer.*

homo, hominis (m.), *man.*

honōs, honōris (m.), *honour.*

hōra, -ae (f.), *hour.*

horridus, -a, -um, *terrible, awe-inspiring.*

hortātio, -ōnis (f.), *exhortation.*

hortor, 1, Dep., *I encourage, exhort.*

hostis, hostis (c.), *enemy (of country).*

hūc, *hither.*

humo, 1, *I bury.*

Iam, *already, now.*

ibi, *there.*

īdem, eadem, idem (Pron. and Adj.), *the same;* **īdem āc** **(atque),** *the same as.*

idōneus, -a, -um, *suitable.*

igitur, *therefore.*

ignārus, -a, -um, *ignorant.*

ignōminia, -ʒe (f.), *disgrace.*

ignōro, 1, *I do not know;* **nōn ignōro,** *I am well aware.*

ignosco, -ere, -nōvi, -nōtum (Dat.), *I pardon, forgive.*

ignōtus, -a, -um, *unknown.*

Ilias, Īliadis (f.), *the Iliad.*

ille, illa, illud (Pron. and Adj.), *he, she, it; that (yonder); the famous.*

illūcescit, -ere, illuxit, *it dawns.*

illustris, -e, *notable, distinguished.*

Illyricum, -i (n.), *Illyricum,* Roman province to the east of the Adriatic.

imber, imbris (m.), *rain-storm.*

immānis, -e, *huge.*

immitto, -ere, -mīsi, -missum, *I discharge;* mē immitto, *I hurl myself.*

immortālis, -e, *immortal.*

impedīmenta, -orum (n.), *baggage.*

impedio, 4, *I hinder, prevent.*

impedītus, -a, -um, *encumbered, embarrassed.*

imperātor, -tōris (m.), *commander, general.*

imperītus, -a, -um, *unskilled.*

imperium, -i (n.), *order, command, dominion.*

impero, 1 (Dat.), *I command;* with object in Acc., *I requisition, give orders for.*

impertio, 4, *I bestow;* mē impertio, *I show myself.*

impetro, 1, *I gain* (*by request*)*; gain a request.*

impetus, -us (m.), *attack, rush.*

impiger, impigra, impigrum, *energetic.*

impius, -a, -um, *wicked.*

implōrātio, -ōnis (f.), *supplication.*

impōno, -ere, -posui, -positum, aliquid alicui, *I set* or *lay something upon someone; I put on board.*

impūne, *without punishment, safely.*

impūnītus, -a, -um, *unpunished.*

in (Acc.), *into, on to, with regard to, against.*

in (Abl.), *in, on, in the time of.*

inauro, 1, *I gild.*

incautus, -a, -um, *unwary.*

incendo, -ere, -cendi, -censum, *I set on fire, burn, inflame, rouse.*

incertus, -a, -um, *uncertain.*

incido, -ere, -cidi, in with Acc., *I fall into; happen.*

incipio, -cipere, -cēpi, -ceptum, *begin.*

incitāmentum, -i (n.), *incentive, spur.*

incito, 1, *I rouse.*

incolumis, -e, *safe.*

incommodum, -i (n.), *setback, disaster.*

incursio, -ōnis (f.), *raid.*

incursus, -us (m.), *attack.*

inde, *thence.*

indicium, -i (n.), *information.*

indignitās, -tātis (f.), *loss of dignity.*

indignus, -a, -um, *unworthy; intolerable, shameful.*

industria, -ae, (f.), *diligence.*

ineo, -īre, -ii, -itum, *I enter, begin.*

infāmia, -ae (f.), *bad reputation.*

infans, -fantis (c.), *little child.*

infero, -ferre, -tuli, illātum or inlātum, bellum with Dat., *I make war upon;* terrōrem inf., *I strike terror into.*

inficio, -ficere, -fēci, -fectum, *I stain.*

infīnītus, -a, -um, *countless.*

infirmitās, -tātis (f.), *weakness.*

infirmus, -a, -um, *weak.*

infrā (Acc.), *below, smaller than.*

ingenium, -i (n.), *talents, ability.*

ingens, Gen. **ingentis,** *huge, big.*

ingrātus, -a, -um, *displeasing.*

ingravesco, -ere, *I grow heavy* or *worse.*

inīquitās, -tātis (f.), *unfavourableness.*

inīquus, -a, -um, *unfavourable.*

initium, -i (n.), *beginning.*

iniūria, -ae (f.), *wrongdoing, wrong.*

iniūriā, *unjustly.*

iniussu, *without command.*

iniustus, -a, -um, *unjust.*

inlustris, see **illustris.**

inopia, -ae (f.), *scarcity.*

inopīnans, Gen., **inopīnantis,** *unaware.*

inquam (defective verb), **inquit,** *say I, says he.*

insequor, -i, -secūtus sum, *I follow up, pursue.*

insidiae, -arum (f.), *ambush.*

insinuo, 1, **mē,** *I wind my way.*

instillo, 1, with Acc. and Dat., *I pour something into something.*

instituo, -ere, -stitui, -stitūtum, *I educate;* also intrans., *I begin.*

institūtum, -i (n.), *practice.*

insto, -stāre, -stiti, -stātum, *I draw nigh.*

instruo, -ere, -struxi, -structum, *I draw up.*

insuētus, -a, -um, with Gen., *unaccustomed to.*

insula, -ae (f.), *island.*

insuperābilis, -e, *impassable.*

intellego, -ere, -lexi, -lectum, *I understand, realize, perceive.*

intentus, -a, -um, *taut.*

inter (Acc.), *between, among;* **inter sē,** *each other.*

interclūdo, -ere, -clūsi, -clūsum, *I shut off, cut off, block.*

interdum, *sometimes.*

intereā, *meanwhile.*

interest, -esse, -fuit, *it matters, is of importance.*

interficio, -ficere, -fēci, -fectum, *I kill.*

interim, *meanwhile.*

interrogo, 1, *I question.*

intersum, -esse, -fui (Dat.), *I take part in.*

intrā (Acc.), *within, inside.*

intro, 1, *I enter.*

inultus, -a, -um, *unavenged.*

inūtilis, -e, *useless.*

invādo, -ere, -vāsi, -vāsum, *I invade.*

invenio, -īre, -vēni, -ventum, *I find.*

inviso, -ere, -vīsi, -vīsum, *I visit.*

invītātio, -ōnis (f.), *invitation.*

invīto, 1, *I invite.*

invītus, -a, -um, *unwilling.*

ipse, ipsa, ipsum, *self, very.*

is, ea, id (Pron. and Adj.), *he, she, it; this* or *that* (unemphatic).

iste, ista, istud (Pron. and Adj.), *he, she, it; that* (*near you* or *of yours*); used for *the defendant.*

ita, *thus, in this way;* **ita . . . ut,** *in such a way that.*

Ītalia, -ae (f.), *Italy.*

itaque, *therefore.*

iter, itineris (n.), *way, journey, march.*

iterum, *again, a second time, once more.*

iubeo, -ēre, iussi, iussum, *I order, command.*

iūcundus, -a, -um, *pleasant.*

iūdex, -dicis (c.), *judge, juror.*

iūdicium, -i (n.), *trial, decision.*

iūdico, 1, *I judge, think.*

iugum, -i (n.), *ridge.*

iunctus, -a, -um, *united.*

Iuppiter, Iovis (m.), *Jupiter.*

iūro, 1, *I swear.*

iūs, iūris (n.), *right, justice.*

iustus, -a, -um, *just.*

iuvenis, Gen. iuvenis, *young.*

iuvo, -āre, iūvi, iūtum, *I help; iuvat, it delights.*

Labor, labōris (m.), *work, toil, labour, exertion.*

labōro, 1, *I work.*

labrum, -i (n.), *rim.*

lāc, lactis (n.), *milk.*

lacrima, -ae (f.), *tear.*

languesco, -ere, langui, *I grow weak.*

languidus, -a, -um, *slack, sluggish.*

lapis, lapidis (m.), *stone, milestone.*

lateo, -ēre, latui, *I lie hid, lurk.*

Latīnus, -a, -um, *Latin.*

latrōcinium, -i (n.), *robbery.*

latus, lateris (n.), *flank.*

lātus, -a, -um, *wide.*

laudo, 1, *I praise.*

laus, laudis (f.), *praise, renown.*

lautumiae, -arum (f.), *a stone-quarry.*

laxo, 1, *I extend, open.*

lectīca, -ae (f.), *litter.*

lectus, -i (m.), *bed.*

lectus, -a, -um, *select.*

lēgātio, -ōnis (f.), *embassy, mission.*

lēgātus, -i (m.), *ambassador, lieutenant, lieutenant-general.*

legio, -ōnis (f.), *legion.*

legiōnārius, -a, -um, *of a legion.*

lego, -ere, lēgi, lectum, *I read.*

lēnitās, -tātis (f.), *gentleness, mercifulness.*

levis, -e, *light, slight.*

levo, 1, *I refresh.*

lex, lēgis (f.), *law.*

libenter, *willingly; with good appetite.*

liber, libri (m.), *book.*

līber, lībera, līberum, *free.*

līberālis, -e, *generous.*

līberi, -orum (m.), *children.*

lībero, 1, *I free, set free.*

lībertās, -tātis (f.), *freedom.*

licet, licēre, licuit, *it is allowed, lawful; although.*

Liger, Ligeris (m.), *the Loire.*

lingua, -ae (f.), *tongue, language.*

linteus, -a, -um, *linen.*

litterae, -arum (f.), *a letter, despatch.*

lītus, lītoris (n.), *shore.*

locus, -i (Nom. and Acc. pl. also loca) (m.), *place, position, ground.*

longē, *far.*
longinquus, -a, -um, *distant.*
longitūdo, -dinis (f.), *length.*
longus, -a, -um, *long, tedious.*
loquor, -i, locūtus sum, *I speak.*
luctus, -us (m.), *grief, mourning.*
lūmen, lūminis (m.), *lamp,* properly *light.*
lux, lūcis (f.), *light, dawn;* **prīma lux,** *daybreak.*

Maeror, maerōris (m.), *grief.*
magis, *more* (of degree).
magister, magistri (m.), *schoolmaster.*
magistrātus, -us (m.), *magistrate.*
magnitūdo, -dinis (f.), *size, intensity.*
magno opere, *greatly, fervently.*
magnus, -a, -um, *great, large, important;* **magni,** *at a great price, highly; much* (with **refert**).
māior, māius, *greater, more important.*
māiōres, -um (m.), *ancestors.*
male, *badly.*
mālo, malle, mālui, *I prefer.*
malum, -i (n.), *trouble, calamity.*
mancipium, -i (n.), *slave.*
mandātum, -i (n.), *commission.*
maneo, -ēre, mansi, mansum, *I remain.*
manus, -us (f.), *hand, band (of men), body (of troops).*
mare, maris (n.), *sea.*
margarīta, -ae (f.), *pearl.*
marītus, -i (m.), *husband.*

māter familiae, mātris fam. (f.), *mistress of household.*
mātrōna, -ae (f.), *wife.*
mātūrē, *early.*
maximē, *especially, exceedingly.*
maximus, -a, -um, *very great, greatest;* **maximi,** *very highly; very much* (with **interest**).
medicīna, -ae (f.), *medicine.*
meditātio, -ōnis (f.), *preparation.*
medius, -a, -um, *middle.*
Melitensis, -e, *Maltese.*
memor, Gen. **memoris,** *mindful, remembering.*
mens, mentis (f.), *mind.*
mensis, mensis (m.), *month.*
mentio, -ōnis (f.), *mention.*
mercātor, -tōris (m.), *merchant.*
mereor, 2, Dep., *I deserve;* **bene mereor dē,** *I deserve well of.*
merx, mercis (f.), *merchandise.*
meto, -ere, messui, messum, *I reap.*
metuo, -ere, -ui, -ūtum, *I fear.*
metus, -us (m.), *fear.*
mīles, mīlitis (c.), *soldier.*
mīliēs, *a thousand times.*
mīlitāris, *of a soldier* or *of war;* **rēs m.,** *the art of war, campaigning.*
mīlitia, -ae (f.), *warfare, campaigning.*
mille, *a thousand;* **mīlia, -ium** (n. pl. followed by Gen.), *thousands;* **mille passūs,** *one mile;* **mīlia passuum,** *miles.*
minimo, *at a very short distance.*
minor, 1, Dep., *I threaten.*

minor, minus, *less.*

minus (Advb.), *less.*

mīrābilis, -e, *wonderful.*

mīror, 1, Dep., *I wonder, am surprised.*

miser, misera, miserum, *wretched, poor.*

miseret, -ēre, miseruit, *it pities.*

miseria, -ae (f.), *wretchedness.*

misericordia, -ae (f.), *pity.*

mitto, -ere, mīsi, missum, *I send.*

modicus, -a, -um, *moderate.*

modo, *only.*

modus, -i (m.), *kind.*

molestē, *with difficulty;* molestē fero, *I am annoyed.*

molestus, -a, -um, *troublesome.*

molliter, *gently.*

moneo, 2, *I advise, warn.*

monimentum, -i (n.), *monument.*

mons, montis (m.), *mountain.*

monstrum, -i (n.), *monster.*

mora, -ae (f.), *delay.*

morbus, -i (m.), *disease, illness.*

morior, mori, mortuus sum, *I die.*

moror, 1, Dep. (trans. and intrans.), *I delay; I stay.*

mors, mortis (f.), *death.*

mortiferē, *fatally.*

mortuus, -a, -um, *dead.*

mōs, mōris (m.), *custom.*

moveo, -ēre, mōvi, mōtum, *I move, stir;* arma m., *I start a war, rising;* castra m., *I strike camp.*

mox, *soon.*

muliebris, -e, *effeminate.*

mulier, mulieris (f.), *woman.*

multitūdo, -dinis (f.), *large number, crowd.*

multo, *by much, far.*

multum, *much.*

multus, -a, -um, *much;* multā nocte, *late at night.*

mūnio, 4, *I fortify, defend.*

mūnītio, -ōnis (f.), *fortification.*

mūnus, mūneris (n.), *service.*

mūrus, -i (m.), *wall.*

mutilus, -a, -um, with Abl., *bereft of, without.*

Nam, *for.*

nanciscor, -i, nactus sum, *I obtain.*

Narbo, -bōnis (m.), *Narbo, now Narbonne.*

nāris, nāris (f.), *nostril.*

narro, 1, *I relate, tell.*

nātio, -ōnis (f.), *people.*

nato, 1, *I swim.*

nātūra, -ae (f.), *nature.*

nātus, -us (m.), *birth.*

nātus, -a, -um, with Abl. *son of;* (with years) *aged.*

naufragium, -i (n.), *shipwreck.*

nāvicula, -ae (f.), *small boat.*

nāviculārius, -i (m.), *ship-master.*

nāvigium, -i (n.), *boat.*

nāvigo, 1, *I sail.*

nāvis, nāvis (f.), *ship.*

-ne, interrogative particle.

nē (Advb. with subj.), *not;* (Conj.), *in order that . . . not, that . . . not;* (after verbs of fearing) *that, lest.*

nē . . . quidem, *not even.*

nec, *and not;* nec . . . nec, *neither
. . . nor.*

necessārio, *necessarily.*

necessārius, -a, -um, *necessary,
essential.*

necne (in indir. question), *or not.*

neco, 1, *I kill.*

nefārius, -a, -um, *abominable.*

neglego, -ere, -lexi, -lectum, *I
neglect.*

negōtium, -i (n.), *business, operation, trouble.*

nēmo, Acc. nēminem (no Gen. or
Abl.), *no one.*

nempe, *of course.*

neptis, neptis (f.), *grand-daughter.*

nēquāquam, *by no means.*

neque, *and not;* neque . . . neque,
neither . . . nor.

nescio, 4, *I do not know.*

nēve (in indir. command and
petition), *and not.*

nihil, *nothing;* with Gen., *no.*

nihilōminus, *nevertheless.*

nimium, *too much.*

nimius, -a, -um, *excessive.*

ningit, ninxit, *it snows.*

nisi, *unless, if not.*

nix, nivis (f.), *snow.*

no, nāre, nāvi, *I swim.*

nōbilis, -e, *noble.*

noceo, 2 (Dat.), *I harm, injure.*

noctu, *by night.*

nocturnus, -a, -um, *of the night.*

nōlo, nolle, nōlui, *I am unwilling.*

nōmen, nōminis (n.), *name.*

nōn, *not.*

nōnāgintā, *ninety.*

nōndum, *not yet.*

nonne? *not in question of which
the expected answer is* yes.

nonnulli, -ae, -a, *some.*

nōs, *we.*

noster, nostra, nostrum, *our.*

noto, 1, *I observe.*

nōtus, -a, -um, *known, well-
known.*

novus, -a, -um, *new, strange,
singular;* agmen novissimum,
rearguard; novae cōpiae, *reinforcements;* rēs novae, *revolu-
tion.*

nox, noctis (f.), *night.*

nūbo, -ere, nupsi, nuptum (Dat.),
I marry (a man).

nūdo, 1, *I strip.*

nullus, -a, -um, *no, none.*

num? *surely . . . not* in direct
questions of which the answer
is already felt to be *no;
whether, if,* in indir. question.

numerus, -i (m.), *number, quantity.*

nunc, *now.*

nunquam, *never.*

nuntio, 1, *I announce, report.*

nuntius, -i (m.), *messenger; message, news.*

Ō (exclamation used with Voc.
or Acc.), *O.*

ob (Acc.), *on account of.*

obeo, -īre, -ii, -itum, *I go to;*
mortem ob., *I meet death;*
mūnus ob., *I perform a service;*
prōvinciam ob., *I inspect a
province.*

oblecto, 1, *I entertain.*

obruo, -ere, -rui, -rutum, *I bury.*

obscūrus, -a, -um, *obscure, lowly, unknown.*

obsecro, 1, *I beseech.*

obses, obsidis (c.), *hostage.*

obsideo, -ēre, -sēdi, -sessum, *I besiege.*

obtineo, -ēre, -tinui, -tentum, *I hold (office, province); I gain; rem ob., I gain purpose, victory.*

occāsio, -ōnis (f.), *opportunity.*

occīdo, -ere, -cīdi, -cīsum, *I kill.*

occultus, -a, -um, *secret.*

occupātus, -a, -um, *busied.*

occurro, -ere, -curri, -cursum (Dat.), *I meet, go to meet.*

Ōceanus, -i (m.), *the ocean, Atlantic.*

octaphorus (Adj. with fem. form as masc.), *carried by eight bearers.*

oculus, -i (m.), *eye.*

odium, -i (n.), *hatred.*

odor, odōris (m.), *spices.*

offendo, -ere, -fendi, -fensum, *I strike the eye of; I displease.*

offero, -ferre, obtuli, oblātum, *I offer.*

officium, -i (n.), *duty.*

oleum, -i (n.), *oil.*

ōlim, *once, formerly.*

Olympia, -ae (f.), *Olympia,* sacred region in Elis in s. Greece.

omnīno, *altogether.*

omnis, -e, *all, every, whole.*

onerārius, -a, -um, *of burden, freight-carrying.*

onus, oneris (n.), *burden, cargo.*

opem (Acc. s.), opis (f.), *help*

operio, -īre, operui, opertum, *I conceal.*

opertus, -a, -um, *covered.*

oportet, -ēre, oportuit, *it behoves.*

oppidum, -i (n.), *stronghold, town.*

opportūnitās, -tātis (f.), *favourable opportunity.*

opprimo, -ere, -pressi, -pressum, *I overwhelm, overpower.*

oppugnātio, -ōnis, *besieging.*

oppugno, 1, *I attack, besiege.*

optimus, -a, -um, *very good, excellent.*

opus, operis (n.), *work; siegework;* opus est alicui with Abl., *someone has need of.*

ōrātio, -ōnis (f.), *speech.*

ōrātor, -tōris (m.), *orator.*

orbis, orbis (m.), *circle;* orbis terrarum, *the world.*

orbitās, -tātis (f.), *bereavement.*

orbus, -a, -um, *bereaved.*

ordo, -dinis (m.), *rank, order.*

orior, orīri, ortus sum, *I rise.*

orno, 1, *I adorn, embellish, honour.*

ōro, 1, *I beg, beseech.*

ostendo, -ere, -tendi, -tensum or -tentum, *I show.*

ōtium, -i (n.), *leisure.*

Pābulor, 1, Dep., *I forage.*

pābulum, -i (n.), *fodder.*

paene, *almost.*

paenitet, -ēre, paenituit, *it repents.*

pallium, -i (n.), *cloak.*
palma, -ae (f.), *palm of hand.*
palūs, palūdis (f.), *marsh.*
pār, Gen. **paris,** *equal, to match.*
parātus, -a, -um, *ready.*
parco, -ere, peperci, parsum (Dat.), *I spare.*
parens, -entis (c.), *parent.*
pāreo, 2 (Dat.), *I obey.*
paro, 1, *I prepare, get ready.*
pars, partis (f.), *part, share, some, direction;* **aliquā ex parte,** *in some degree.*
parum (with Gen.), *too little.*
parvulus, -a, -um, *very small.*
passus, -us (m.), *pace, yard;* **mille passūs,** *a mile.*
passus, -a, -um, *outstretched.*
patefacio, -facere, -fēci, -factum, *I open up.*
pateo, -ēre, patui, *I am open, lie open;* hence **patens,** *open.*
pater, patris (m.), *father.*
patiens, Gen. **patientis,** *full of endurance.*
patior, pati, passus sum, *I suffer, endure, allow.*
patria, -ae (f.), *native land, country.*
patruus, -i (m.), *uncle* (on father's side).
pauci, -ae, -a, *few.*
paulo, *by a little, a little.*
paulum, *a little, little.*
pax, pācis (f.), *peace.*
pectus, pectoris (n.), *breast.*
pecūnia, -ae (f.), *money.*

pecus, pecoris (n. Collective Noun), *cattle.*
penetro, 1 (intrans.), *I penetrate.*
per (Acc.), *through, throughout, by means of.*
percipio, -cipere, -cēpi, -ceptum, *I perceive;* **fructum per.,** *I reap the fruit.*
percrepo, -āre, -crepui, -crepitum, *I resound.*
perditus, -a, -um, *ruined; abandoned, criminal.*
perdūco, -ere, -duxi, -ductum, *I win over.*
peregrīnor, 1, Dep., *I travel abroad.*
pereo, -īre, -ii, -itum, *I perish, die.*
perfacilis, -e, *very easy.*
perfero, -ferre, -tuli, -lātum, *I bear, carry, bring, convey, endure, carry out.*
perficio, -ficere, -fēci, -fectum, *I finish, complete, bring to an end;* **perficio ut,** *I see to it that.*
perfidia, -ae (f.), *faithlessness.*
perfodio, -fodere, -fōdi, -fossum, *I pierce.*
perfuga, -ae (m.), *deserter.*
perfugium, -i (n.), *refuge.*
pergo, -ere, perrexi, perrectum, *I proceed.*
perīclitor, 1, Dep. (trans.), *I put to the test, tempt;* (intrans.), *I am exposed to danger.*
perīculōsus, -a, -um, *dangerous.*
perīculum, -i (n.), *danger, peril.*
perītus, -a, -um, *skilled.*
perlūcidus, -a, -um, *transparent.*

permagnus, -a, -um, *very large.*
permaneo, -ēre, -mansi, -mansum,
I remain.
permoveo, -ēre, -mōvi, -mōtum, *I
stir, move deeply.*
permulti, -ae, -a, *very many.*
pernocto, 1, *I pass the night.*
Persae, -arum (m.), *the Persians.*
persaepe, *very often.*
persequor, -i, -secūtus sum, *I pursue.*
persevērantia, -ae (f.), *steadfast-
ness.*
persevēro, 1, *I continue stead-
fastly.*
perspicio, -spicere, -spexi, -spec-
tum, *I look closely at, explore,
see clearly.*
persto, -stāre, -stiti, -stātum, *I
stand firm.*
persuādeo, -ēre, -suāsi, -suāsum
(Dat.), *I persuade.*
perterebro, 1, *I bore through.*
perterreo, 2, *I thoroughly
frighten.*
pertinācia, -ae (f.), *obstinacy.*
perturbo, 1, *I disturb, upset.*
pervenio, -ire, -vēni, -ventum, *I
arrive;* pervenio ad, *I reach,
come to.*
pēs, pedis (m.), *foot.*
peto, -ere, petīvi, petītum, *I
attack, seek, make for, entreat.*
piget, -ēre, piguit, *it displeases,
vexes, irks.*
pīlum, -i (n.), *javelin.*
pīrāta, -ae (m.), *pirate.*

piscātōrius, -a, -um, *fishing-.*
placeo, 2 (Dat.), *I please;* placet,
it pleases, is agreeable; mihi
placet, *I agree (that), am
resolved.*
placidē, *quietly.*
plānē, *utterly.*
plānities, -ēi (f.), *plain.*
plēnus, -a, -um, *full.*
plūrimi, -ae, -a, *most.*
plūs (Noun in s.), Gen. plūris,
more; pl. plūres, plūra.
pōculum, -i (n.), *cup.*
poena, -ae (f.), *punishment.*
Poeni, -orum (m.), *the Carthaginians.*
poēta, -ae (m.), *poet.*
polliceor, 2, Dep., *I promise.*
pollicitātio, -ōnis (f.), *promise.*
pondus, ponderis (n.), *weight.*
pōno, -ere, posui, positum, *I place,
set.*
pons, pontis (m.), *bridge.*
populus, -i (m.), *people, tribe.*
porrigo, -ere, -rexi, -rectum, *I
stretch, hand.*
porta, -ae (f.), *gate.*
porto, 1, *I carry.*
portus, -us (m.), *harbour.*
posco, -ere, poposci, *I demand.*
possum, posse, potui, *I am able,
can, have power.*
post (Acc.), *after.*
post (Advb.), *after, afterwards.*
posteā, *afterwards.*
posterus, -a, -um, *next.*
postquam (Conj.), *after.*
postrīdiē, *on the next day.*

potentia, -ae (f.), *power*.
potestās, -tātis (f.), *power, opportunity*.
pōtio, -ōnis (f.), *drink*.
potior, potīri, potītus sum (Abl.) *I get possession of, obtain*.
potius, *rather*.
prae (Abl.), *in comparison with*.
praebeo, 2, *I offer, afford;* **mē p.,** *I show myself*.
praeceps, Gen. **praecipitis,** *headlong*.
praeceptum, -i (n.), *injunction, warning*.
praeclārus, -a, -um, *distinguished, brilliant, glorious*.
praeclūdo, -ere, -clūsi, -clūsum, *I close (something to someone), shut off*.
praeco, -ōnis (m.), *herald, publisher*.
praeda, -ae (f.), *booty*.
praedīco, -ere, -dixi, -dictum, *I warn*.
praedor, 1, Dep. (trans. and intrans.), *I plunder*.
praefectus, -i (m.), *commander*.
praemitto, -ere, -mīsi, -missum, *I send forward*.
praemium, -i (n.), *reward*.
praeoccupo, 1, *I seize beforehand*.
praesertim, *especially*.
praesidium, -i (n.), *protection, garrison*.
praestans, Gen. **praestantis,** *outstanding*.
praesto, -stāre, -stiti, -stātum or

-stitum, *I fulfil, discharge; show*.
praesum, -esse, -fui (Dat.), *I am in command of*.
praeter (Acc.), *except, contrary to, beyond*.
praetereā, *besides*.
praetor, -tōris, *praetor, governor*.
praetōrius, -a, -um, *of a praetor* or *governor*.
prandeo, -ēre, prandi, pransum, *I have breakfast;* participle, **pransus** with Act. meaning.
preces, -um (f.), *prayers*.
premo, -ere, pressi, pressum, *I press, crowd, overwhelm*.
prīdiē, *on the day before*.
prīmo, *at first*.
prīmum, *first, for the first time;* **quam prīmum,** *as soon as possible*.
prīmus, -a, -um, *first;* **in prīmis,** *especially*.
princeps, principis (c.), *chief*.
principātus, -us (m.), *office of chieftain*.
prior, prius, *former*.
pristinus, -a, -um, *former*.
prius, *before*.
priusquam (Conj.), *before*.
prō (Abl.), *in front of, on behalf of, in place of, as, in return for, in accordance with*.
probo, 1, *I approve of*.
prōcēdo, -ere, -cessi, -cessum, *I go forward, advance*.
procul, *far*.

prōcumbo, -ere, -cubui, -cubitum, *I sink down.*

prōcurro, -ere, -curri, -cursum, *I run forward.*

prōditio, -ōnis (f.), *treachery, treason.*

prōdo, -ere, -didi, -ditum, *I betray.*

proelium, -i (n.), *battle.*

prōfero, -ferre, -tuli, -lātum, *I bring forth.*

prōficio, -ficere, -fēci, -fectum, *I make progress.*

proficiscor, -i, profectus sum, *I set out, start.*

prōgredior, -gredi, -gressus sum, *I advance.*

prohibeo, 2, *I keep off, cut off, prevent.*

prōicio, -icere, -iēci, -iectum, *I fling forward, throw down, cast forth;* so prōiectus, -a, -um, *falling forward, throwing oneself forward.*

prōinde, *therefore.*

prōinde āc sī, *just as if.*

prōmissus, -a, -um, *hanging down, long.*

prōmitto, -ere, -mīsi, -missum, *I promise.*

prōmoveo, -ēre, -mōvi, -mōtum, *I move forward.*

prope (Acc.), *near.*

prope (Advb.), *nearly, almost.*

propero, 1, *I hasten, hurry.*

propter (Acc.), *on account of.*

proptereā quod, *on account of the fact that.*

prōrumpo, -ere, -rūpi, -ruptum, *I burst forth.*

prōsequor, -i, -secutūs sum, *I pursue, proceed against.*

prospectus, -us (m.), *sight, view.*

prōsum, prōdesse, prōfui (Dat.), *I am of advantage (to), avail.*

prōvideo, -ēre, -vīdi, -vīsum, *I foresee.*

prōvincia, -ae (f.), *province.*

proximus, -a, -um, *nearest, next.*

prūdens, Gen. prūdentis, *sensible, wise.*

publicē, *on behalf of the state.*

publicum, -i (n.), *public place;* in publicum, *into the open, out of doors.*

publicus, -a, -um, *public.*

pudet, -ēre, puduit, *it shames.*

puer, pueri (m.), *boy.*

pugio, -ōnis (m.), *dagger.*

pugna, -ae (f.), *fight, battle, combat.*

pugno, 1, *I fight.*

pulcher, pulchra, pulchrum, *beautiful.*

pulchritūdo, -dinis (f.), *beauty, good looks.*

pulvīnus, -i (m.), *cushion.*

pūnio, 4, *I punish.*

purpura, -ae (f.), *purple,* so *purple cloth.*

puto, 1, *I think.*

Quadrāgintā, *forty.*

quaero, -ere, quaesīvi, quaesītum, *I seek;* q. ex, *I ask someone.*

quaeso, -ere, -īvi or -ii, *I beseech.*

quaestio, -ōnis (f.), *inquiry,* so *court.*

quālis, -e? *of what sort?; as,* corresponding to **tālis.**

quam (Advb.), (in questions, with Adj. and Advb.), *how;* corresponding to **tam,** *as;* (after comparative), *than;* (before superlative), *as . . . as possible.*

quamdiū, *as long as.*

quamvīs, *however much, although.*

quando? *when?;* **quando** is also used causally, *since.*

quanquam, *although.*

quantum? *how much?*

quantus, -a, -um? *how big? as,* corresponding to **tantus;** so also **quantum,** *as,* corresponding to **tantum.**

quā rē, *wherefore.*

quartus decimus, *fourteenth.*

quasi, *as if.*

quattuor, *four.*

-que, *and.*

queo, quīre, quīvi or **quii, quitum,** *I am able.*

queror, -i, questus sum, *I complain.*

qui, quae, quod (rel. Pron.), *who, which.*

qui, quae or **qua, quod** (indef. Adj. after **sī, nisi, num, nē, cum**) *any.*

quia, *because.*

quicumque, quaecumque, quodcumque (Pron. and Adj.), *whoever, whatever.*

quid? *why?*

quīdam, quaedam, quiddam (quoddam) (indef. Pron. and Adj.), *a certain person, a certain, some.*

quidem, *indeed.*

quiēs, quiētis (f.), *rest, sleep.*

quiesco, -ere, quiēvi, quiētum, *I rest, sleep.*

quīn, *that not, but that;* **quīn immo, quīn etiam,** *may even, what is more.*

quindecim, *fifteen.*

quinque, *five.*

quis? quid? (interrog. Pron.), *who? what?*

quis, quid (indef. Pron. after **sī, nisi, num, nē, cum**), *anyone, anything.*

quispiam, *anyone.*

quisquam (indef. Pron. after neg.), *anyone.*

quisque (indef. Pron.), *each;* **ut quisque,** *whenever anyone;* **optimus quisque,** *all the best men.*

quisquis, *whoever.*

quo (Advb.), *whither.*

quo, *by what amount, how much;* **quo** with comparative, followed by **eo** with comparative, *the more . . . , the more.*

quo (used as Conj.) with comparative in final clause, *in order that;* after **nōn,** in causal clause, *because.*

quoad, *until, as far as.*

quōcumque, *whithersoever.*

quod, *because; the fact that;* **quod sī,** *but if.*

quōminus, *that not, from,* after verbs of *hindering* and *preventing.*

quōmodo? *how?*

quondam, *once (upon a time).*

quoniam, *since.*

quoque, *also.*

quot? *how many? as,* corresponding to **tot.**

quotiēs, *as often as, whenever; as,* corresponding to **totiēs.**

Rādix, -dīcis (f.), *root.*

rapio, rapere, rapui, raptum (trans.), *I hurry away.*

ratio, -ōnis (f.), *method.*

ratis, ratis (f.), *raft.*

rebello, 1, *I revolt.*

recens, Gen. **recentis,** *recent.*

receptus, -us (m.), *retreat.*

recipero, 1, *I recover.*

recipio, -cipere, -cēpi, -ceptum, mē, *I retreat, retire, bring myself back.*

reclīno, 1 (trans.), *I lean back.*

recurro, -ere, -curri, *I hurry back.*

recūsātio, -ōnis (f.), *refusal, objection.*

recūso, 1, *I refuse.*

reddo, -ere, reddidi, redditum, *I render, make.*

redeo, -īre, -ii, -itum, *I return.*

redintegro, 1, *I renew, recruit.*

reditus, -us (m.), *return.*

redūco, -ere, -duxi, -ductum, *I lead back.*

refero, -ferre, rettuli, relātum, *I carry back, relate;* **grātiam r.,** *I return thanks.*

rēfert, rēferre, *it concerns, matters to.*

reficio, -ficere, -fēci, -fectum, *I restore, repair, refresh.*

refugio, -fugere, -fūgi, *I escape.*

regio, -ōnis (f.), *district;* **regiōnes,** *boundaries, confines.*

regnum, -i (n.), *kingly power, kingdom.*

rego, -ere, rexi, rectum, *I control.*

regredior, -gredi, -gressus sum, *I go back, return.*

relinquo, -ere, -līqui, -lictum, *I leave, leave behind, abandon.*

reliquus, -a, -um, *remaining, rest, future.*

remaneo, -ēre, -mansi, *I stay behind.*

remedium, -i (n.), *remedy.*

renuntio, 1, *I give an account of.*

repello, -ere, reppuli, repulsum, *I drive back.*

repente, *suddenly.*

repentīnus, -a, -um, *sudden.*

reperio, -īre, repperi, repertum, *I find, discover.*

repeto, -ere, -petīvi, –petītum, *I demand.*

reprimo, -ere, -pressi, -pressum, *I curb, check.*

repudio, 1, *I reject.*

requiesco, -ere, -quiēvi, -quiētum, *I rest.*

rēs, rei (f.), *thing, matter, affair,*

event, exploit; rēs mīlitaris, *the art of war.*

rescrībo, -ere, -scripsi, -scriptum, *I write back* or *in answer.*

resisto, -ere, restiti (Dat.), *I resist.*

respondeo, -ēre, -spondi, -sponsum, *I reply, answer.*

rēspublica, reīpublicae (f.), *state, commonwealth.*

retardo, 1, *I keep back, delay.*

rēticulum, -i (n.), *net-work bag.*

retineo, -ēre, -tinui, -tentum, *I keep back, detain.*

rēvērā, *really, in fact.*

revertor, -i, -reversus sum, *I turn back.*

revoco, 1, *I recall.*

rex, rēgis (m.), *king.*

Rhēnus, -i (m.), *the Rhine.*

rīdeo, -ēre, rīsi, rīsum, *I laugh, smile.*

rōbur, rōboris (n.), *strength.*

rōbustus, -a, -um, *strong.*

rogo, 1, *I ask, ask for.*

Rōma, -ae (f.), *Rome.*

Rōmānus, -a, -um, *Roman;* Rōmānus, -i (m.), *a Roman.*

rosa, -ae (f.), *rose.*

rumpo, -ere, rūpi, ruptum, *I break.*

ruo, -ere, rui, (ruiturus), *I rush.*

rursus, *again.*

rūs, rūris (n.), *country* (opp. to *town*).

rusticor, 1, Dep., *I live in the country.*

Saepe, *often.*

saepio, -īre, saepsi, saeptum, *I enclose.*

sagittārius, -i (m.), *archer.*

salūs, salūtis (f.), *safety.*

salūtāris, -e, *advantageous.*

salvus, -a, -um, *safe, unharmed.*

Samnītes, -ium (m.), *the Samnites.*

sānē, *in truth, to be sure.*

sāno, 1, *I cure, remedy.*

sapiens, Gen. sapientis, *wise.*

sapientia, -ae (f.), *wisdom.*

satio, 1, *I sate;* satiātus, *having had enough of.*

satis, with Gen., *enough.*

satis (Advb.), *enough, sufficiently.*

saxum, -i (n.), *stone, rock.*

scālae, -arum (f.), *ladder.*

scientia, -ae (f.), *knowledge.*

scīlicet, *doubtless.*

scio, 4, *I know.*

Scīpio, -ōnis (m.), *Scipio.*

scrībo, -ere, scripsi, scriptum, *I write.*

scriptor, -tōris (m.), *writer.*

Scythae, -arum (m.), *the Scythians.*

sē or sēsē (reflexive Pron.), *himself, herself, itself, themselves.*

sēclūdo, -ere, -clūsi, -clūsum, *I shut off.*

sector, 1, Dep., *I pursue.*

secundum (Acc.), *after.*

secundus, -a, -um, *second; favourable;* rēs secundae, *prosperity.*

sed, *but.*

sedeo, -ēre, sēdi, sessum, *I sit.*

sēditio, -ōnis (f.), *mutiny.*
semel, *once.*
sēmita, -ae (f.), *path.*
semper, *always.*
senātor, -tōris (m.), *senator.*
senātōrius, -a, -um, *senatorial.*
senātus, -us (m.), *senate.*
senectūs, -tūtis (f.), *old age.*
senex, Gen. senis (Adj.), *old;* (Noun), *old man.*
sententia, -ae (f.), *opinion, way of thinking, purpose.*
sentio, -īre, sensi, sensum, *I feel, perceive.*
septiēs, *seven times.*
sepultūra, -ae (f.), *burial.*
sequor, -i, secūtus sum, *I follow.*
sermo, sermōnis (m.), *language, conversation.*
servio, 4 (Dat.), *I serve, am devoted to.*
servitium, -i (n. collective Noun), *slaves.*
servo, 1, *I save, keep.*
servulus, -i (m.), *wretched slave.*
servus, -i (m.), *slave.*
sescenti, -ae, -a, *six hundred.*
sevērus, -a, -um, *harsh, stern.*
sex, *six.*
sī, *if.*
sīc, *thus, in such a manner.*
siccus, -a, -um, *dry.*
Sicilia, -ae (f.), *Sicily.*
Siculi, -orum (m.), *the Sicilians.*
sīcut, *just as.*
significo, 1, *I make known, make signs.*

signum, -i (n.), *sign, standard, signal.*
silentium, -i (n.), *silence.*
sileo, -ēre, silui, *I am silent.*
silva, -ae (f.), *wood, forest.*
simul, *at the same time.*
simul āc (atque), *as soon as.*
simulātio, -ōnis (f.), *pretence.*
simulo, 1, *I pretend.*
sīn, *but if.*
sine (Abl.), *without.*
singulāris, -e, *single, solitary, remarkable.*
sinus, -us (m.), *bosom.*
sitis, sitis (f.), *thirst.*
situs, situs (m.), *position.*
sīve . . . sīve, *whether . . . or.*
societās, -tātis (f.), *association.*
socius, -i (m.), *ally.*
sōl, sōlis (m.), *sun.*
sōlātium, -i (n.), *comfort.*
soleo, -ēre, solitus sum, *I am accustomed, wont.*
solidus, -a, -um, *solid.*
sōlitūdo, -dinis (f.), *desert, wilderness.*
solitus, -a, -um, *usual.*
sōlum, *only.*
sōlus, -a, -um, *alone.*
somnium, -i (n.), *dream.*
spatium, -i (n.), *space, distance.*
speciēs, -ēi (f.), *appearance.*
spēro, 1, *I hope, hope for.*
spēs, spei (f.), *hope, expectation.*
spīritus, -us (m.), *breath.*
spolio, 1, *I rob.*
sponte (f. Abl.), *of one's own accord.*

statim, *at once, immediately.*
statīvus, -a, -um, *stationary.*
statua, -ae (f.), *statue.*
statuo, -ere, statui, statūtum, *I determine.*
status, -us (m.), *state, condition.*
sto, stāre, steti, statum, *I stand;* per mē stat, *it is due to me.*
strepitus, -us (m.), *noise.*
stringo, -ere, strinxi, strictum, *I unsheathe.*
studeo, -ēre, studui (Dat.), *I devote my attention to.*
studiōsē, *enthusiastically.*
studium, -i (n.), *keenness, enthusiasm, pursuit, application.*
stultitia, -ae (f.), *folly.*
stultus, -a, -um, *foolish.*
suādeo, -ēre, suāsi, suāsum (Dat.), *I advise, urge.*
sub (Abl.), *under.*
subicio, -icere, -iēci, -iectum, *I allege.*
subito, *suddenly.*
sublevo, 1, *I lift up.*
subluo, -ere, -lūtum, *I wash the foot of* (used of *a river*).
subruo, -ere, -rui, -rutum, *I undermine.*
subsidium, -i (n.), *support, help.*
subsum, -esse, *I am near, approach.*
subvenio, -īre, -vēni, -ventum (Dat.), *I come to the help of, aid.*
succumbo, -ere, -cubui, -cubitum, *I give in.*
succurro, -ere, -curri, -cursum (Dat.), *I help.*

sūdor, sūdōris (m.), lit. *sweat, so toil, effort.*
suffero, -ferre, sustuli, sublātum, *I take upon myself.*
sum, esse, fui, *I am.*
summa, -ae (f.), *the chief points.*
summus, -a, -um, *highest, utmost, distinguished;* s. columna, *the top of the column.*
sūmo, -ere, sumpsi, sumptum, *I take.*
superior, -ius, *higher, superior, stronger.*
supero, 1, *I overcome, conquer; win.*
supersum, -esse, -fui (Dat.), *I survive; am left.*
supplēmentum, -i (n.), *reinforcements.*
supplicium, -i (n.), *punishment, torture.*
suscipio, -cipere, -cēpi, -ceptum, *I undertake.*
suspīcio, -ōnis (f.), *suspicion.*
suspicor, 1, Dep., *I suspect.*
sustineo, -ēre, -tinui, -tentum, *I check, withstand, resist.*
suus, -a, -um (reflexive Adj.), *his, her, its, their, own.*
symphōnia, -ae (f.), *music.*
Syrācūsae, -arum (f.), *Syracuse.*
Syrācūsāni, -orum (m.), *the Syracusans.*

Tabernāculum, -i (n.), *tent.*
taedet, -ēre, taeduit, *it wearies.*
tālāris, -e, *reaching to the ankles.*
tālis, -e, *such.*

tam (with Adj. and Advb.), *so.*
tamen, *yet, however.*
tandem, *at length.*
tanquam, *as if, as though.*
tantum, *so much, so little, just enough.*
tantus, -a, -um, *so big, so great, so large.*
taurus, -i (m.), *bull.*
tectum, -i (n.), *house.*
telum, -i (n.), *weapon.*
temperantia, -ae (f.), *self-control.*
tempestas, -tatis (f.), *weather, storm.*
templum, -i (n.), *temple.*
tempto, 1, *I try, attempt.*
tempus, temporis (n.), *time, season.*
teneo, -ere, tenui, tentum, *I hold, detain.*
tenuis, -e, *slight, meagre, weak, insignificant.*
tergum, -i (n.), *back, rear;* a tergo, *in the rear.*
terra, -ae (f.), *land.*
terror, terroris (f.), *dread, terror.*
testimonium, -i (n.), *evidence.*
testudo, -dinis (f.), *tortoise* (formed of shields held over soldiers' heads).
timeo, -ere, timui, *I fear, am afraid.*
timor, timoris (m.), *fear.*
tollo, -ere, sustuli, sublatum, *I raise, remove, take away.*
tot, *so many.*
toties, *so often.*
totus, -a, -um, *whole.*

trado, -ere, -didi, -ditum, *I hand on.*
traho, -ere, traxi, tractum, *I drag.*
trans (Acc.), *across.*
Transalpinus, -a, -um, *Transalpine.*
transeo, -ire, -ii, -itum, *I cross.*
transfero, -ferre, -tuli, -latum, *I direct.*
transporto, 1, *I transport, carry across.*
tres, tria, *three.*
tribunus, -i (m.), *tribune.*
tribuo, -ere, -ui, -utum, *I assign, give.*
triduum, -i (n.), *space of three days.*
tu, *you* (s.).
tum, *then.*
tumultus, -us (m.), *confusion.*
tumulus, -i (m.), *barrow, tomb.*
tunc, *then.*
tunica, -ae (f.), *tunic.*
turma, -ae (f.), *squadron.*
turpis, -e, *disgraceful.*
turris, turris (f.), *tower.*
tus, turis (n.), *incense.*
tutus, -a, -um, *safe.*
tuus, -a, -um, *your* (s.).
tyrannus, -i (m.), *tyrant.*
Tyrius, -a, -um, *Tyrian.*
Tyrus, -i (f.), *Tyre,* city of the Phoenicians.

Ubi, *where, when, as soon as.*
ubicumque, *wherever.*
ullus, -a, -um (after neg.), *any.*
ultimus, -a, -um, *furthest, remotest.*

ūnā, *together, at the same time.*

unde, *whence, from which.*

undique, *from all sides, on all sides.*

ūniversus, -a, -um, *whole;* **ūniversī**, *in a body.*

unquam (after neg.), *ever.*

ūnus, -a, -um, *one, single.*

urbānus, -a, -um, *of the city.*

urbs, urbis (f.), *city.*

urgeo, -ēre, ursi, *I bear hard upon.*

ūrus, -i (m.), *bison.*

usque, *all the way;* **usque ad**, *right up to.*

ūsurpātio, -ōnis (f.), *a making use.*

ūsus, -us (m.), *use, benefit.*

ut (with indic.), *as, whenever;* (with subj.), *that, so that, in order that;* (after a verb of fearing), *that . . . not.*

uterque, utraque, utrumque, *each of two.*

utinam! *would that!*

ūtor, -i, ūsus sum (Abl.), *I use, make use of.*

utrinque, *on both sides.*

utrum (in double indir. question), *whether.*

uxor, uxōris (f.), *wife.*

Vagor, 1, Dep., *I wander.*

valeo, 2, *I am well;* **valē**, *farewell.*

valētūdo, -dinis (f.), *health, good or bad.*

vasto, 1, *I ravage, lay waste.*

vector, -tōris (n.), *passenger.*

vehementer, *strongly, exceedingly.*

veho, -ere, vexi, vectum, *I carry;* **vehor**, *I ride.*

vel (with superlative), *the very; even.*

vēlōcitās, -tātis (f.), *speed.*

vēlum, -i (n.), *awning.*

velut sī, *as if, as though.*

vēnālis, vēnālis (m.), *young slave (for sale).*

vēnātio, -ōnis (f.), *hunting.*

vēnātor, -tōris (m.), *hunter.*

venio, -īre, vēni, ventum, *I come.*

ventus, -i (m.), *wind.*

vēr, vēris (n.), *spring.*

verbum, -i (n.), *word.*

Vercingetorix, -rigis (m.), *Vercingetorix.*

vērē, *truly, true enough.*

verēcundia, -ae (f.), *modesty.*

vereor, 2, Dep., *I fear.*

vēro, *indeed, but indeed, however.*

Verrēs, Verris (m.), *Verres.*

versor, 1, Dep., *in* with Abl., *I am engaged in, take part in.*

versus (Advb.) after place-names, *towards.*

vērus, -a, -um, *true.*

vescor, -i (Abl.), *I feed on.*

vesperascit, -ere, *it becomes evening.*

vester, vestra, vestrum, *your (pl.).*

vestigium, -i (n.), *track.*

vestio, 4, *I clothe.*

vestis, vestis (f.), *clothing.*

vestītus, -us (m.), *clothing.*

veto, -āre, vetui, vetitum, *I forbid, order . . . not.*

via, -ae (f.), *way, road.*

vicem, in, *in turn.*

vīcēsimus, -a, -um, *twentieth.*

victōria, -ae (f.), *victory.*

video, -ēre, vīdi, vīsum, *I see;* videor, *I seem.*

vigeo, -ēre, *I am strong, vigorous.*

vigilia, -ae (f.), *watch.*

vīginti, *twenty.*

vinco, -ere, vīci, victum, *I conquer;* (intrans.), *win a victory.*

vinculum, or vinclum, -i (n.), *chain,* so in pl. *prison.*

vindico, 1, *I lay claim to, take vengeance on.*

vīnea, -ae (f.), *mantlet.*

vīnum, -i (n.), *wine.*

violo, 1, *I harm.*

vir, viri (m.), *man.*

virgo, -ginis (f.), *maiden.*

virtūs, -tūtis (f.), *courage, merits, ability.*

vīs, Acc. vim, Abl. vī (f.), *might, strength, violence;* pl. vīres, vīrium, *strength.*

vīso, -ere, vīsi, vīsum, *I visit.*

vīta, -ae (f.), *life* (used also as term of endearment).

vīto, 1, *I avoid.*

vitrum, -i (n.), *woad.*

vīvo, -ere, vixi, victum, *I live.*

vīvus, -a, -um, *living, alive.*

vix, *hardly, scarcely, with difficulty.*

vixdum, *scarcely yet.*

voco, 1, *I call, invite, summon.*

volo, velle, volui, *I wish, am willing.*

voluntās, -tātis (f.), *wish, will.*

vōs, *you* (pl.).

vox, vōcis (f.), *voice, cry, words.*

vulgus, -i (m. or n.), *mob.*

vulnero, 1, *I wound.*

vulnus, vulneris (n.), *wound, loss.*

vultus, -us (m.), *countenance.*

English-Latin Vocabulary

Verbs which are followed by 1 or 2 or 4, to show the number of their Conjugation, are conjugated regularly.

Proper Nouns are usually not given, if they are the same in Latin as in English.

Long quantities have been omitted from common terminations, but have been inserted where guidance may be helpful.

A (*certain*), **quidam, quaedam, quoddam.**

able, I am, **possum, posse, potui.**

about (*concerning*), **dē** (Abl.).

about to. Future Participle.

absent, **absens, -sentis.**

accomplish, I, **conficio, -ficere, -fēci, -fectum.**

accord, of my own, **sponte meā.**

accuse, I, **accūso,** 1.

Achilles, **Achillēs, -is** (m.).

acquit, I, **absolvo, -ere, -solvi, -solūtum.**

across, **trans** (Acc.).

act, I, **ago, -ere, ēgi, actum.**

admire, I, **admīror,** 1, Dep.

adopt a plan, I, **consilium capio, capere, cēpi, captum.**

advance, I, **prōcēdo, incēdo, -ere, -cessi, -cessum; prōgredior, -gredi, -gressus sum.**

advantage, **commodum, -i** (n.).

advantageous, it is, **bono est** (Ch. 7).

advice, **consilium, -i** (n.).

advise, I, **moneo,** 2.

afraid, I am, also *afraid of,* **timeo,** 2.

Afranius, soldiers of, **Afrāniāni, -orum** (m.).

after (Conj.), **postquam;** (Prep.), **post** (Acc.).

again, **rursus.**

against (*enemy*), **adversus** (Acc.); (*disease*), **contrā** (Acc.).

age of, at the, aged, **nātus, -a, -um.**

ago, **abhinc** (Acc.).

agreed, it is, **constat** (Ch. 13).

aim at, I, **appeto, -ere, -petīvi** or **-ii, -petītum.**

Alexander, **Alexander, Alexandri** (m.).

Alexandria, **Alexandrīa, -ae** (f.).

alive, **vīvus, -a, -um.**

alive, I am, **vīvo, -ere, vixi, victum.**

all, **omnis, omne.**

all the more, **eo magis** (eo **plūs,** for *quantity*).

alliance, **societās, -tātis** (f.).

allow, I, **sino, -ere, sīvi, situm; patior, pati, passus sum.**

allowed, I am, **mihi licet** (Ch. 13).

206

almost, **ferē.**

alone, **sōlus, -a, -um;** (*only*), **sōlum.**

Alps, the, **Alpes, -ium** (f.).

already, **iam.**

also, **etiam, quoque.**

although, **quanquam; etsī; cum; quamvīs** (Ch. 23).

always, **semper.**

am I, **sum, esse, fui;** (*distant*), **absum, -esse, -fui.**

ambassador, **lēgātus, -i** (m.).

ambush, **insidiae, -arum** (f.).

among, **inter** (Acc.); (*in the eyes of, in the presence of*), **apud** (Acc.).

ancestors, **māiōres, -um** (m.).

and, **et; āc** (before consonant), **atque; -que.**

and . . . not (in indir. command), **nēve.**

anger, **īra, -ae** (f.).

annoyed that, I am, **mē piget** or **molestē fero** (both followed by Acc. and Infin.).

another, **alius, alia, aliud.**

any (after negative), **ullus, -a, -um,** but **sī, nisi, num, nē, cum,** are followed by **quis, quae** or **qua, quod.**

anyhow, **certē.**

anyone (after **sī, nisi, num, nē, cum**), **quis.**

appear to, I, **videor, -ēri, vīsus sum,** with Infin.

appearance, **speciēs, speciēi** (f.); **forma, -ae** (f.).

approach, I, **appropinquo,** 1 (intrans.), **ad.**

approve of, I, **probo,** 1.

archer, **sagittārius, -i** (m.).

Archimedes, **Archimēdēs, -is** (m.).

arise, I, **orior, orīri, ortus sum; coorior.**

arm, I, **armo,** 1.

arm (*of body*), **bracchium, -i** (n.).

arms, **arma, -orum** (n.); *in arms*, **armātus, -ā, -um.**

army, **exercitus, -us** (m.).

arouse, I, **excito,** 1.

arrival, **adventus, -us** (m.).

arrive, I, **pervenio, -īre, -vēni, -ventum.**

art, **ars, artis** (f.).

as . . . as (correlatives), **tam . . . quam.**

as . . . as possible, **quam** with superlative; *as soon as possible*, **quam prīmum.**

as if, **quasi, velut sī.**

as long as, **dum** (Ch. 17).

as many . . . as, **tot . . . quot.**

as much . . . as, **tantum . . . quantum** (with Gen.).

as soon as, **simul āc** (atque).

as though, **tanquam.**

ashamed, I am, **mē pudet, pudēre, puduit** (Ch. 13).

ask, I (*question*), **rogo,** 1.

ask, I (*request*), **rogo,** 1; (*someone for something*), **ōro,** 1, with two Acc.

assemble, I, **convenio, -īre, -vēni, ventum.**

associate, **socius, -i** (m.).

at (*because of*), **propter** (Acc.), or

Abl. of Cause; (*place where*), sometimes in (Abl.).

Athenian, Athēniensis, -e (m.).

Athens, Athēnae, -arum (f.).

attack, I, oppugno, 1; impetum facio in (Acc.).

attack, impetus, -us (m.).

attention to, I pay, studeo, -ēre, studui (Dat.).

attention, with, attentē.

autumn, auctumnus, -i (m.).

avenge, I, vindico, 1; ulciscor, -i, ultus sum.

avoid, I, vīto, 1.

aware, I am well, haud ignōro, 1.

away (*distant*), *I am,* absum, -esse, abfui or āfui.

Back, retro.

baggage, impedīmenta, -orum (n.).

band, manus, -us (f.).

banish, I, expello, -ere, -puli, -pulsum.

banquet, convīvium, -i (n.).

battle, proelium, -i (n.).

bear, I, fero, ferre, tuli, lātum.

beauty, pulchritūdo, -dinis (f.).

because, quia, quod; *not because,* nōn quod or nōn quō (Ch. 24).

because of, propter (Acc.); sometimes Abl. of Cause.

become, I, fīo, fieri, factus sum; *become of,* see note on Ex. 82.

bed, lectus, -i (m.).

bedroom, cubiculum, -i (n.).

before (Conj.), antequam; (Prep.), ante (Acc.); (Advb.), anteā.

beg, I, ōro, 1.

begin, I, incipio, -cipere, -cēpi, -ceptum; also, *I began,* coepi, coepisse, coeperam.

behalf of, on, prō (Abl.).

behave myself, I, mē gero, -ere, gessi, gestum.

behind, ā tergo.

believe, I, crēdo, -ere, crēdidi, crēditum; *I could believe* (Ch. 19).

below, infrā (Acc.).

besides, praishereā.

besiege, I, obsideo, -ēre, -sēdi, -sessum.

betake myself, I, mē confero, -ferre, -tuli, collātum.

betray, I, prōdo, -ere, -didi, -ditum.

better, melior, melius; (*in health*), commodior.

beware, to, cavēre, cāvi, cautum.

big, magnus, -a, -um; *biggest,* maximus.

bitter (*of punishment*), acerbus, -a, -um.

Bituriges, the, Bituriges, -um (m.).

bivouac, I, consīdo, -ere, -sēdi, -sessum.

blame, I, culpo, 1.

blame, culpa, -ae (f.).

blind, caecus, -a, um.

block, I, obstruo, -ere, -struxi, -structum.

body, corpus, corporis (n.).

boldness, audācia, -ae (f.).

book, liber, libri (m.).

booty, praeda, -ae (f.).

bore, I, perterebro, 1; *I bore out,*
exterebro, 1.

both (Adj.), ambo, ambae, ambo.

both . . . and, et . . . et.

bow, arcus, -us (m.).

boy, puer, pueri (m.).

brave, fortis, forte.

bravery, fortitūdo, -dinis (f.).

break, I, frango, -ere, frēgi,
fractum.

breakfast, I have, prandeo, -ēre,
prandi, pransum.

breast, pectus, pectoris (n.).

breathe, I, spīro, 1.

bridge, pons, pontis (m.).

bright, nitidus, -a, -um.

bring, I, fero, ferre, tuli, lātum;
(to), affero, -ferre, attuli, allātum (with Dat.).

Britain, Britannia, -ae (f.).

Britons, the, Britanni, -orum (m.).

bronze, āes, āeris (n.).

build, I, aedifico, 1.

building, aedificium, -i (n.).

burden, onus, oneris (n.); *I am a
burden to,* oneri sum, with Dat.

burn, I (trans.), incendo, -ere,
-cendi, -censum.

bury, I, sepelio, -īre, -īvi, sepul-
tum.

business, the, rēs, rei (f.); *(com-
merce),* negōtium, -i (n.).

business of, it is the, interest (Ch.
13).

busy, occupātus, -a, -um.

but, sed; tamen (2nd word);
autem (2nd word).

but if, sīn.

by (agent), ā, ab before vowel
(Abl.).

by means of, per (Acc.).

by now, iam.

Caesar, Caesar, Caesaris (m.).

calamity, cāsus, -us (m.).

call, I (*summon*), voco, 1; (*out*),
ēvoco; (*by name*), appello, 1;
voco, 1.

camp, castra, -orum (n.).

can, I, possum, posse, potui.

capture, I, capio, capere, cēpi,
captum.

care, dīligentia, -ae (f.).

carefully, dīligenter.

cargo, onus, oneris (n.).

carry, I, fero, ferre, tuli, lātum.

carry out, I (*funeral*), dūco, -ere,
duxi, ductum.

Carthage, Carthāgo, -ginis (f.).

Carthaginian, Carthāginiensis, -e;

Carthaginians, the, Poeni,
-orum (m.).

case, in this, see *circumstances.*

cast out, I, ēicio, ēicere, ēiēci,
ēiectum.

catch, I, see *capture.*

catch sight of, I, conspicio,
-spicere, -spexi, -spectum; con-
spicor, 1, Dep.

Cato, Cato, -ōnis (m.).

cattle, pecus, pecoris (n. collective Noun).

cause, I, cūro, 1 (Ch. 10).

cavalry, equites, -um (m.); equitātus, -us (m. collective Noun).

celebrate, I, celebro, 1.

Cevennes, the, Cevenna, -ae (f.).
chain, vinculum, -i (n.).
chance (*opportunity*), facultās, -tātis (f.).
chance, by, cāsu.
characteristic of, see Ch. 3.
charge, I, impetum facio in (Acc.).
charge of, I am in, praesum, -esse, -fui (Dat.); *I put someone in charge of,* praeficio aliquem, followed by Dat.
chariot (*war*), esseda, -ae (f.).
chief, chieftain, princeps, principis (c.).
children, līberi, -orum (m.).
Cicero, Cicero, -ōnis (m.).
circumstances, in these, quae cum ita sint, essent.
citizen, cīvis, cīvis (c.).
citizenship, cīvitās, -tātis (f.).
city, urbs, urbis (f.).
civilian dress, in, togātus, -a, -um.
claim, I, vindico, 1.
clear away, I, discutio, -cutere, -cussi, -cussum.
clemency, lēnitās, -tātis (f.).
cleverness, ingenium, -i (n.).
client, my, use hīc.
climb, I, supero, 1; ascendo, -ere, -scendi, -scensum.
clothe, I, vestio, 4.
cohort, cohors, cohortis (f.).
cold (Noun), frīgus, frīgoris (n.).
colleague, collēga, -ae (m.).
collect, I (*corn*), comporto, 1; (*troops*), cōgo, -ere, coēgi, coactum.
colonist, colōnus, -i (m.).

column (*pillar*), columna, -ae (f.).
combat, pugna, -ae (f.).
come, I, venio, -īre, vēni, ventum; (*back*), redeo, -īre, -ii, -itum; (*down*), dēscendo, -ere, -scendi, -scensum; (*out*), ēgredior, -gredi, -gressus sum.
comfort, I, consōlor, 1, Dep.
command, I, impero, 1 (Dat.).
command, imperium, -i (n.).
commander, praefectus, -i (m.).
commission, mandāta, -orum (pl.).
commit, I (*crime*), admitto, -ere, -mīsi, -missum; (*entrust*), mando, 1.
complain, I, queror, -i, questus sum.
complete, I, perficio, conficio, -ficere, -fēci, -fectum.
completely defeat, I, dēvinco, -ere, -vīci, -victum.
conceal, I, cēlo, 1.
concerns, it, interest (Ch.13).
condemn, I, damno, 1.
conduct, I, dēdūco, -ere, -duxi, -ductum.
conquer, I, supero, 1; vinco, -ere, vīci, victum.
consecrate, I, consecro, 1.
consider my own interests, I, mihi consulo, -ere, -sului, -sultum.
construct, I, facio, facere, fēci, factum.
consul, consul, consulis (m.).
consult, I, consulo, -ere, -sului, -sultum (Acc.); *I consult my own interests,* mihi consulo.

content, contentus, -a, -um.
continue, I (make continuous), continuo, 1; (*prolong*), dūco, -ere, duxi, ductum.
contrary to, contrā āc (atque) (Ch. 26).
convey, I, dēfero, -ferre, -tuli, -lātum.
corn, frūmentum, -i (n.).
corn-supply, rēs frūmentāria, rei frūmentāriae (f.).
corrupt, I, corrumpo, -ere, -rūpi, -ruptum.
council, concilium, -i (n.).
country, terra, -ae (f.); (*ground*), locus, -i (m.); (*native land,* patria, -ae (f.); (opp. *to town*), rūs, rūris (n.).
courage, virtūs, -tūtis (f.).
courageously, fortiter.
course, cursus, -us (m.).
court (law), quaestio, -ōnis (f.), properly *inquiry.*
covet, I, concupisco, -ere, -cupīvi or -ii, -cupītum.
crime, scelus, sceleris (n.).
crisis, discrīmen, -minis (n.).
cross, I (mountain), supero, 1; *mountain* or *river,* transeo, -īre, -ii, -itum (trans.); transgredior, -gredi, -gressus sum.
crowd, multitūdo, -dinis (f.).
cruelty, crūdēlitās, -tātis (f.).
crush, I, opprimo, -ere, -pressi, -pressum.
cry, vox, vōcis (f.).
Curio, Cūrio, -ōnis (m.).
cushion, pulvīnus, -i (m.).

custom, mōs, mōris (m.).
cut off from, I, interclūdo, -ere, -clūsi, -clūsum, ab.

Dagger, pugio, -ōnis (m.).
daily, cotīdiē, in dies.
damage, I, laedo, -ere, laesi, laesum.
danger, perīculum, -i (n.).
dare, I, audeo, -ēre, ausus sum.
daring, audācia, -ae (f.).
darling, vīta, -ae (f.).
daughter, fīlia, -ae (f.).
dawn, prīma lux, prīmae lūcis (f.).
dawns, it, lūcescit, -ere.
day, diēs, diēi (m.); *every day,* cotīdiē.
dead, mortuus, -a, -um.
dear, cārus, -a, -um.
death, mors, mortis (f.).
decide, I, constituo, -ere, -stitui, -stitūtum.
decision, iūdicium, -i (n.).
deed, factum, -i (n.).
deep, altus, -a, -um.
defeat, I, see *conquer; I completely defeat,* dēvinco, -ere, -vīci, -victum.
defend, I, dēfendo, -ere, -fendi, -fensum.
defendant, the, use iste.
definite, certus, -a, -um.
delay, I (intr.), moror, cunctor, both 1, Dep.
delay, mora, -ae (f.).
delight, I, dēlecto, 1; *I am delighted to,* mē dēlectat (Ch. 13).

212 English-Latin Vocabulary

demand, *I*, **postulo**, 1; **posco,
-ere, poposci.**
deny, *I*, **nego**, 1; with neg., see
Ch. 25.
dependent, **cliens, -entis** (m.).
desert, *I*, **dēsero, -ere, -serui,
-sertum.**
deserve, *I*, **mereor**, 2, Dep.; *I
deserve to*, **mereor qui** with
subjunct.; *I deserve well of*,
bene mereor dē (Abl.).
desire, *I* or *am desirous of*, **cupio,
cupere, cupīvi** (or **-ii**), **cupītum.**
desire, **cupiditās, -tātis** (f.);
studium, -i (n.).
despair, *I*, **dēspēro**, 1.
despatch, **litterae, -arum** (f.).
despise, *I*, **contemno, -ere,
-tempsi, -temptum.**
detain, *I*, **teneo, -ēre, tenui,
tentum.**
determine, *I*, see *decide*.
devote myself, *I*, **mē do, dare,
dedi, datum.**
die, *I*, **morior, mori, mortuus sum.**
different from, **alius, alia, aliud,
āc (atque).**
difficult, **difficilis, -e.**
difficulty, **difficultās, -tātis** (f.);
with difficulty, **aegrē.**
dig, *I*, **fodio, fodere, fōdi, fossum.**
diligence, **industria, -ae** (f.).
diminish, *I*, **dēminuo, -ere, -minui,
-minūtum.**
dinner, *I have*, **cēno**, 1.
direct, *I*, **rego, -ere, rexi, rectum.**
disadvantage (*of ground*), **inīquitās, -tātis** (f.).

disagree with, *I*, **dissentio, -īre,
-sensi, -sensum, ab.**
disaster, **clādēs, clādis** (f.); in-
commodum, -i (n.).
disband, *I*, **dīmitto, -ere, -mīsi,
-missum.**
discover, *I*, **reperio, -īre, repperi,
repertum.**
disease, **morbus, -i** (m.).
disembark, *I* (trans.), **expōno,
-ere, -posui, -positum;** (intr.),
**ex nāvi ēgredior, -gredi, -gres-
sus sum.**
dishonour, **ignōminia, -ae** (f.).
dislodge, *I*, **dēicio, -icere, -iēci,
-iectum.**
dismiss, *I*, **dīmitto, -ere, -mīsi,
-missum.**
distinction, **dignitās, -tātis** (f.).
distinguished, **conspicuus, -a, -um.**
distrust, *I*, **diffīdo, -ere, -fīsus sum**
(Dat.).
ditch, **fossa, -ae** (f.).
divide someone from, *I*, **disclūdo,
-ere,-clūsi,-clūsum, aliquem ab.**
do, *I*, **facio, facere, fēci, factum.**
do not, **nōlī, nōlīte** (with infin.).
doctor, **medicus, -i** (m.).
dog, **canis, canis** (c.).
doubt, *I*, **dubito**, 1.
doubt, there is no, use Adj., **nōn
dubium est.**
dream, **somnium, -i** (n.).
drink, *I*, **bibo, -ere, bibi.**
drive out, *I*, **expello, -ere, -puli,
-pulsum.**
due to me that . . . not, it is, **per
me stat quōminus** (Ch. 25).

duty, officium, -i (n.); *it is the duty of*, see Ch. 3.

Each, quisque, quaeque, quidque (quodque).
eager for, I am, studeo, -ēre, studui (Dat.).
eager for, cupidus, -a, -um, with Gen.
easily, facile.
easy, facilis, -e.
Eburones, the, Eburōnes, -um.
effeminate, effēminātus.
eight hundred, octingenti, -ae, -a.
eighty, octōgintā.
either ... *or*, aut ... aut.
elect, I, creo, 1.
elephant, elephantus, -i (m.).
elk, alcēs, alcis (f.).
embassy, lēgātio, -ōnis (f.).
embellish, I, orno, 1.
empty, vacuus, -a, -um.
encourage, I, confirmo, 1; hortor or cohortor, 1, Dep.
end, fīnis, fīnis (m.).
endowed, praeditus, -a, -um.
endure, I, fero, ferre, tuli, lātum.
enemy, hostis, hostis (c.), mostly used in pl. for *the enemy*.
engaged in, occupātus, -a, -um, in with Abl.
engine of war, tormentum bellicum, tormenti bellici (n.).
enough, satis; *enough of*, satis with Gen.
enter, I, intro, 1; ineo, -īre, -ii, -itum (both trans.).
enthusiasm, studium, -i (n.).

entice, I, ēlicio, -licere, -licui, -licitum.
entrenchment, mūnītio, -ōnis (f.).
entrust, I, mando, 1.
envoy, lēgātus, -i (m.).
envy, I, invideo, -ēre, -vīdi, -vīsum (Dat.).
Ephesus, Ephesus, -i (f.).
equal, pār, Gen. paris; *on equal terms*, aequo Marte.
equally ... *as*, aequē āc (atque).
escape, I, effugio, -fugere, -fūgi.
especially, maximē.
even, etiam; et.
even if, etiamsī (Ch. 23).
even though, quamvīs (Ch. 23).
event, rēs, rei (f.).
ever, if, sī quando.
every, omnis, omne.
everyone knows, see Ch. 25.
everywhere, ubīque.
excel, I, supero, 1.
except (after neg. clause), nisi.
excite, I, excito, 1.
exercise, I, exerceo, 2.
exhort, I, hortor or cohortor, 1, Dep.
exile, exsilium, -i (n.).
expect, I (trans.), exspecto, 1; (intrans. of *things desired*) use spēro, 1.
extraordinary, singulāris, -e.
extreme, extrēmus, -a, -um.
eye, oculus, -i (m.).

Face, I, obviam eo, īre, ii, itum, with Dat.

fail, I (*a person*), dēsum, dēesse, dēfui (Dat.).

fall into or *on to, I*, incido, -ere, -cidi, -cāsum, with in and Acc.; (*down*), concido, -ere, concidi.

fame, fāma, -ae (f.).

famous, illustris, -e; clārus, -a, -um; sometimes ille.

far and wide, longē lātēque.

far away, I am, longē or multum absum.

far, by, multo.

farmer, agricola, -ae (m.).

father, pater, patris (m.).

favourable (*of ground*), aequus, -a, -um; (*of wind*), secundus, -a, -um.

fear, I, timeo, -ēre, timui; vereor, 2, Dep.

feign, I, simulo, 1.

fetch, I, peto, -ere, petīvi, petītum.

few, pauci, -ae, -a.

field, ager, agri (m.).

fight, I, pugno, 1.

find, I, invenio, -īre, -vēni, -ventum.

find out (*from*), *I,* cognosco, -ere, -nōvi, -nitum (ex).

finish (*complete*), *I,* conficio, perficio, -ficere, -fēci, -fectum.

first, prīmus, -a, -um.

first (Advb.), prīmo.

five, quinque.

flee, I, fugio, fugere, fūgi (fugitūrus).

fleet, classis, classis (f.).

flight, fuga, -ae (f.).

flourish, I, flōreo, -ēre, flōrui.

fly out, I, ēvolo, 1.

following, the (*words, speech*), hīc, haec, hōc.

food, cibus, -i (m.).

foot, pēs, pedis (m.); *on foot,* pedibus.

for (Conj.), nam; enim (2nd word).

for (*on behalf of*), prō (Abl.), but often, Dat. of Advantage.

for (*the purpose of*), ad (Acc.).

for, in return, prō (Abl.).

forage, I, pābulor, 1, Dep.

forage, pābulum, -i (n.).

foraging, pābulātio, -ōnis (f.).

force (*of men*), manus, -us (f.).

force of arms, by, vi et armis.

forced march, magnum iter, magni itineris (n.).

forces, cōpiae, -arum (f.).

foreign, barbarus, -a, -um.

foreigners, barbari, -orum (m.).

foresee, I, prōvideo, -ēre, -vīdi, -vīsum.

foresight, prōvidentia, -ae (f.).

forest, silva, -ae (f.).

former, pristinus, -a, -um.

formerly, anteā.

fortification, mūnītio, -ōnis (f.).

fortify, I, mūnio, 4.

fortune, fortūna, -ae (f.).

forum, forum, -i (n.).

four, quattuor.

free (*from*), *I,* lībero (ab).

free from, I am, vaco, 1 (Abl.).

freedom, lībertās, -tātis (f.).

friend, amīcus, -i (m.).

friendship, amīcitia, -ae (f.).

frightened, I am, timeo, -ēre, timui.

from, ā, ab before vowel (Abl.); (*out of*), ē, ex before vowel.

from where, unde.

front, in, ā fronte.

fruits, fructus, -us (m.) (used in sing.).

fugitive, use pres. participle of fugio.

funeral, fūnus, fūneris (n.).

furthermore, praetereā.

furthest, ultimus, -a, -um.

future (Adj.), reliquus, -a, -um.

Garland, corōna, -ae.

garrison, praesidium, -i (n.).

gate, porta, -ae (f.).

Gaul, Gallia, -ae (f.); *of Gaul,* Gallicus, -a, -um.

Gaul, a, Gallus, -i (m.).

general, imperātor, -tōris (m.); dux, ducis (c.).

gentlemen of the jury, iūdices, -um (m.).

Germans, the, Germāni, -orum (m.).

get ready, I, paro, 1.

give, I, do, dare, dedi, datum.

give way, I, cēdo, -ere, cessi, cessum.

glory, glōria, -ae (f.).

go, I, eo, īre, ii, itum; (*away*), abeo; (*back*), redeo; regredior, -gredi, -gressus sum.

goes on, this, haec aguntur.

god, deus, -i (m.).

goddess, dea, -ae (f.).

gold, aurum, -i (n.).

golden, aureus, -a, -um.

good, bonus, -a, -um.

goods, bona, -orum (n.).

goose, anser, anseris (m.).

governor, praetor, -tōris (m.).

grandmother, avia, -ae (f.).

grateful, I am, grātiam habeo, 2.

great, magnus, -a, -um; *so great,* tantus, -a, -um.

greatest, maximus, -a, -um.

greed, avāritia, -ae (f.).

greedy for, avidus, -a, -um, with Gen.

Greek (*language*), lingua Graeca, linguae Graecae (f.).

Greek (Adj.), Graecus, -a, -um.

Greeks, the, Graeci, -orum (m.).

ground, often locus, -i (m.).

ground, I hold my, in loco persto, -stāre, -stiti, stātum.

grow old, I, senesco, -ere, senui.

grows light, it, see *it dawns.*

guard, I am on my, caveo, -ēre, cāvi, cautum.

guard, I, custōdio, 4.

guard, a, custōs, -tōdis (c.).

guard (*protection*), praesidium, -i (n.).

guide, dux, ducis (c.).

Hand, I, porrigo, -ere, -rexi, -rectum; (*over*), trādo, -ere, -didi, -ditum.

hand, I am at, adsum, -esse, -fui.

hand, manus, -us (f.).

Hannibal, Hannibal, -balis (m.).

happens, it, accidit, perf. accidit.

216 English-Latin Vocabulary

happy, **beātus, -a, -um.**

harbour, **portus, -us** (m.).

harm, I, **laedo, -ere, laesi, laesum** (Acc.); **noceo,** 2 (Dat.).

Hasdrubal, **Hasdrubal, -balis** (m.).

hasten, I, **propero,** 1; **contendo, -ere, -tendi, -tentum.**

hate, I, **ōdi, ōdisse, ōderam;** *I am hated by,* **odio sum** with Dat.

have, I, **habeo,** 2; often expressed by **sum** with Dat. of Possessor; *I have in mind,* **in animo habeo.**

he, is; **ille.**

hear, I, **audio,** 4.

heavy, **gravis, -e.**

heifer, **būcula, -ae** (f.).

Helen, **Helena, -ae** (f.).

help, **iuvo, -āre, iūvi, iūtum;** so also **adiuvo** (both with Acc.); **subvenio, -īre, -vēni, -ventum** (Dat.). *I cannot help . . . ,* **nōn possum facere quīn** (Ch. 25).

help, **auxilium, -i** (n.).

Hercules, **Herculēs, Herculis** (m.).

here, **hīc.**

hide, I, **cēlo,** 1.

highly (of value), **magni.**

hill, **collis, collis** (m.).

himself (reflexive Pron.), **sē.**

hinder, I, **impedio,** 4.

hindrance, **impedīmentum, -i** (n.).

his, **ēius;** *his own* (reflexive), **suus, -a, -um.**

historian, **rērum scriptor, -tōris** (m.).

hither, **hūc.**

hold, I, **teneo, -ēre, tenui, tentum;** *I hold my ground, see* ground.

home, **domus, -us** or **-i** (f.); *homewards,* **domum;** *at home,* **domi;** *from home,* **domo.**

Homer, **Homērus, -i** (m.).

honour, I, **colo, -ere, colui, cultum.**

honour, **honōs, honōris** (m.).

hope, hope for, I, **spēro,** 1.

hope, **spēs, spei** (f.).

horse, **equus, -i** (m.).

horseman, **eques, equitis** (m.); *horsemen,* **equitātus, -us** (m. collective Noun).

hospitality, **hospitium, -i** (n.).

hostage, **obses, obsidis** (c.).

house (country house), **villa, -ae** (f.).

household, **domus, -us** or **-i** (f.).

how (in what way)? **quemadmodum?**

how? (with Adj. and Advb.), **quam?**

how many? **quot?**

how much? **quantum?**

how often? **quotiēs?**

however, **tamen** (2nd word).

however (much), **quamvīs** (Ch. 23).

hundred, **centum.**

hurl, I, **cōnicio, -icere, -iēci, -iectum.**

hurry, I, **propero,** 1.

hurt, I, **violo,** 1.

husband, **vir, viri** (m.); **marītus, -i** (m.).

I, **ego.**

idle, **ignāvus, -a, -um.**

if (conditional), **sī**; *if* . . . *not*,
nisi; *if ever*, **sī quando**; *but if*,
sīn; *if only*, **dummodo** (Ch.
17).
ignorance, **ignōrantia, -ae** (f.).
ignorant of, I am, **ignōro**, 1.
ill, I am, **aegrōto**, 1.
ill-health, **gravis valētūdo, -dinis**
(f.).
illness, **morbus, -i** (m.).
import, I, **importo**, 1.
important, it is, **interest** (Ch. 13);
it is of great importance,
magni interest.
impossible not to, it is, see Ch. 25.
imprison, I, **in vincula cōnicio,
-icere, -iēci, -iectum**.
in, **in** (Abl.).
incautiously, **incautē**.
increase, I (trans.), **augeo, -ēre,
auxi, auctum**; (intrans., of
illness), **ingravesco, -ere**.
indeed, **certē**.
indulgence, **venia, -ae** (f.).
influence, **auctōritās, -tātis** (f.).
influence, I have, **possum, posse,
potui**.
ingenuity, **sollertia, -ae** (f.).
inhabitant, **incola, -ae** (c.).
injure, I, **laedo, -ere, laesi, laesum**.
inside, **intrā** (Acc.).
instigation of, at the, use **auctor,
-tōris** (c.). (Ch. 12).
interests of, I consider the, see
under *consider*.
into, **in** (Acc.).
invade, I, **invādo, -ere, -vāsi,
-vāsum**.

invent, I, **invenio, -īre, -vēni,
-ventum**.
invite to, I, **invīto**, 1, ut.
irked, I am, **mē piget, -ēre, piguit**.
island, **insula, -ae** (f.).
Italy, **Ītalia, -ae** (f.).

Journey, I, **iter facio, facere,
fēci, factum**.
journey, **iter, itineris** (n.); *I make
a journey*, **iter facio**.
judge, **iūdex, iūdicis** (m.).
Juno, **Iūno, -nōnis** (f.).
Jupiter, **Iuppiter, Iovis** (m.).
just, **iustus, -a, -um**.
just as, **sīcut**; *just as though*,
proinde āc sī (Ch. 26).

Keep, I, **teneo, -ēre, tenui,
tentum**; (in the sense of *retain*),
retineo, -ēre, -tinui, -tentum;
(*in*), **contineo**.
keep off, I, **arceo, -ēre, arcui**.
keep ranks, to, see under *ranks*.
keep someone from, I, **prohibeo
aliquem ab**.
keep well, I, **valeo**, 2.
kill, I, **neco**, 1; **occīdo, -ere,
-cīdi, -cīsum**; **interficio, -ficere,
-fēci, -fectum**.
kind of man to, is **qui** with subjunct.
kind (of indulgence), **bonus, -a,
-um**.
king, **rex, rēgis** (m.).
kingly power, **regnum, -i** (n.).
kingship, **regnum**.
knight, **eques, equitis** (m.).

218 English-Latin Vocabulary

know, I, scio, 4; *I know well*, prō certo habeo, haud ignōro.
know, I do not, ignōro, 1; nescio, 4.
knowing, not, ignārus with Gen.
knowledge, scientia, -ae (f.).
knowledge, having, conscius, -a, -um.
knowledge of, without, clam (Acc.).

Land, I (trans.), expōno, -ere, -posui, -positum.
land, terra, -ae (f.).
landing, ēgressus, -us (m.).
large, magnus, -a, -um.
Larissa, Lārisa, -ae (f.).
last, at (in commands), aliquando.
Latin, lingua Latīna, linguae Latīnae (f.).
Latin (Adj.), Latīnus, -a, -um.
Latium, Latium, -i (n.).
latter, the, hīc, haec, hōc.
law, lex, lēgis (f.).
lay down, I, dēpōno, -ere, -posui, -positum.
lay something upon someone, I, impōno aliquid alicui.
lazy, ignāvus, -a, -um.
lead, I, dūco, -ere, duxi, ductum; (*back*), redūco; (*down*), dēdūco; (*on*), indūco; (*out*), ēdūco.
leader, dux, ducis (c.).
lean, I (intrans.), *against*, mē reclīno, 1, ad.
learn (a subject), I, disco, -ere, didici.

least, at, certē.
leave (depart from), I, discēdo, -ere, -cessi, cessum, ab; exeo, -īre, -ii, -itum, ex.
leave (behind), I, relinquo, -ere, -līqui, -lictum.
left, I am, supersum, -esse, -fui.
leg, crūs, crūris (n.).
legion, legio, -ōnis (f.).
less, minus.
let slip, I, dīmitto, -ere, -mīsi, -missum.
letter, epistola, -ae (f.); litterae, -arum (f.).
level, aequus, -a, -um.
levy something from someone, I, impero, 1, aliquid alicui.
lieutenant, lieutenant-general, lēgātus, -i (m.).
life, vīta, -ae (f.).
light, levis, -e.
light, it grows, lūcescit, -ere.
like, tanquam (Ch. 26).
like, as much as you, quantumlibet.
like, I should, see Ch. 19.
listen, listen to, I, audio, 4.
literature, litterae, -arum (f.).
litter, lectīca, -ae (f.).
little, a, paulum; *a little distance*, paulum.
little, a (with compar.), paulo.
live, I, vīvo, -ere, vixi, victum; (*dwell*), incolo, -ere, -colui; habito, 1.
locality, locus, -i (m.).
Loire, the, Liger, Ligeris (m.).
long for, I, dēsīdero, 1.

long, **longus, -a, -um.**

long as, as, **dum** (Ch. 17).

long time, for a, **diū.**

longer (Advb.), **diūtius;** *no longer,* **nōn iam.**

look after, I, **tueor, -ēri, tuitus sum; cūro,** 1.

lose, I, **āmitto, -ere, -mīsi, -missum;** *I lose hope,* **spem dēpōno, -ere, -posui, -positum.**

loss, **dētrīmentum, -i** (n.); *cause* or *source of loss* (Ch. 7).

love, **amor, amōris** (m.).

luxury, **luxuria, -ae** (f.).

Made of, **factus, -a, -um, ex.**

magistrate, **magistrātus, -us** (m.).

make, I, **facio, facere, fēci, factum;** *(road),* **mūnio,** 4; *(speech),* **ōrātiōnem habeo;** *I make war against,* **bellum infero, -ferre, -tuli, illātum** or **inlātum,** with Dat.

make for, I, **peto, -ere, petīvi, petītum.**

Maltese, **Melitensis, -e.**

man, I, **compleo, -ēre, -plēvi, -plētum.**

man (opposed to *woman*), **vir, viri** (m.); (opposed to *animal*), **homo, hominis** (m.); *the man who,* **is qui** or **qui.**

mantlet, **vīnea, -ae** (f.).

many, **multi, -ae, -a.**

many times, **saepe.**

march, I, **contendo, -ere, -tendi, -tentum; iter facio.**

march, **iter, itineris** (n.).

mark of, see Ch. 3.

market-place, **forum, -i** (n.).

marry (*a man*), *I,* **nūbo, -ere, nupsi, nuptum.**

marry (*a woman*), *I,* **in mātrimōnium dūco.**

marsh, **palūs, palūdis** (f.).

master (*of household*), **dominus, -i** (m.).

matter, **rēs, rei** (f.).

may (*am allowed*), *I,* **mihi licet** (Ch. 13).

meanwhile, **interim.**

meet, I, **obviam eo, īre, ii, itum,** with Dat.

merchant, **mercātor, -tōris** (m.).

Mercury, **Mercurius, -i** (m.).

message, **nuntius, -i** (m.).

messenger, **nuntius, -i** (m.).

method, **genus, generis** (n.).

might have, I, **potui** with pres. infin.

mile, **mille passus;** pl. **mīlia passuum.**

mind, **animus, -i** (m.); *I have in mind,* **in animo habeo.**

more (degree), **magis;** *all the more,* **eo magis;** (quantity), **plūs,** Gen. **plūris** (Noun in sing.); pl. **plūres, plūra** (Adj.); *the more . . . , the more . . . ,* **quo** with comparative, **eo** with compar.

most, **plūrimi, -ae, -a.**

mother, **māter, mātris** (f.).

mountain, **mons, montis** (m.).

mouth, **ōs, ōris** (n.).

move (*camp*), *I*, moveo, -ēre, mōvi, mōtum; (*of feeling*), commoveo.

much, multum; *too much*, nimium, nimis.

music, symphōnia, -ae (f.).

my, meus, -a, -um.

Name, nōmen, nōminis (n.).

Narbo, Narbo, -bōnis (m.).

narrate, *I*, narro, 1.

nature, nātūra, -ae (f.).

nay, immo.

near, prope (Acc.); *so near to*, tam prope (Advb.) ab.

nearer, propius.

nearest, proximus, -a, -um.

nearly, *very* (with Verb), see Ch. 25.

neck, cervix, -vīcis (f.), gen. used in pl.

need of, *I have*, opus est mihi with Abl.

neglect, *I*, neglego, -ere, -lexi, -lectum.

negotiate, *I*, ago, -ere, ēgi, actum.

neighbouring, proximus, -a, -um.

neither . . . *nor*, neque . . . neque; nec . . . nec.

never, nunquam.

new, novus, -a, -um.

news, nuntius, -i (m.).

next day, *on the*, postrīdiē.

night, nox, noctis (f.).

ninety, nōnāgintā.

no, *none*, nullus, -a, -um.

no longer, nōn iam.

no one, nēmo, Acc. nēminem (no Gen. or Abl.).

noble (*action*), pulcher, pulchra, pulchrum.

nor, neque; nec.

not, nōn; (with jussive subj. and in ind. command and petition), nē; *in order that* . . . *not*, nē; *that* . . . *not*, after Verb of *fearing*, nē . . . nōn.

not?, in dir. question, expecting answer *yes*, nonne?; expecting answer *no*, num?

not because, nōn quō.

not only . . . *but also*, nōn modo . . . sed etiam.

not yet, nōndum.

nothing, nihil.

now, nunc; iam.

number, numerus, -i (m.); *small numbers*, paucitās, -tātis (f.).

Numidians, Numidae, -arum (m.).

O (exclamation), O with Voc. or Acc.

obey, *I*, pāreo, 2 (Dat.).

obstinacy, pertinācia, -ae (f.).

obtain, *I*, comparo, 1; (*weather*), nanciscor, -i, nactus sum.

obvious, manifestus, -a, -um.

occupied in, occupātus, -a, -um, in (Abl.).

off to, *I am setting*, proficiscor, -i, profectus sum, in (Acc.).

offer, *I*, offero, -ferre, obtuli, oblātum.

officer, praefectus, -i (m.).

often, saepe; *more often*, saepius.

old (of persons), senex, Gen. senis; compar. senior.

old age, senectūs, -tūtis (f.).

old man, senex, senis (m.).

old-time, priscus, -a, -um.

on, in (Abl.).

once (one time), semel.

once upon a time, quondam, ōlim.

once, at, statim.

one, ūnus, -a, -um.

one opposed to another, alius ... alius.

one (of two), alter, altera, alterum.

only, sōlum, modo.

open up, I, patefacio, -ere, -fēci, -factum.

opportunity, occāsio, -ōnis (f.); facultās, -tātis (f.); opportūnitās, -tātis (f.).

or, aut.

or not (in indir. questions), necne.

orator, ōrātor, -tōris (m.).

order I, iubeo, -ēre, iussi, iussum (infin.); impero, 1 (Dat. and ut with Subj.).

order (command), imperium, -i (n.); *by order*, iussu.

order that, in, ut (quo with comparative); *in order that . . . not*, nē.

other, alius, alia, aliud; *the other* (pl.), reliqui, -ae, -a.

other (of two), the, alter, altera, alterum.

ought, I, dēbeo, 2; mē oportet (Ch. 13); see also Ch. 9 and 10.

our, our own, noster, nostra, nostrum.

out of, ē, ex before vowel (Abl.).

outlive, I, supersum, -esse, -fui (Dat.).

outside (Prep.), extrā (Acc.).

outstanding, praestans, Gen. praestantis.

over (bridge *over* river), in (Abl.); *concerning*, dē (Abl.).

overcome, I, supero, 1; (used of troubles), opprimo, -ere, -pressi, -pressum.

overwhelm, I, obruo, -ere, -rui, -rutum.

owe, I, dēbeo, 2.

owing to, ob, propter (Acc.).

Panic, pavor, -ōris (m.).

panic-stricken, perterritus, -a, -um.

part, pars, partis (f.).

part in, I take, intersum, -esse, -fui (Dat.).

part of, it is the (see Ch. 3).

pass on, I (trans.), trādo, -ere, -didi, -ditum.

pass over the fact that, I, praetereo, -īre, -ii, -itum, quod.

passenger, vector, -tōris (m.).

pay, stīpendium, -i (n.).

peace, pax, pācis (f.).

pearl, margarīta, -ae (f.).

penalty, supplicium, -i (n.).

penetrate, I (intrans.), penetro, 1.

people, populus, -i (m.).

perceive, I, sentio, -īre, sensi, sensum.

222　English-Latin Vocabulary

perform, I, **fungor, -i, functus sum** (Abl.).
persevere, I, **persevēro, 1.**
persuade, I, **persuādeo, -ēre, -suāsi, -suāsum** (Dat.).
pierce, I, **perfodio, -fodere, -fōdi, -fossum.**
pirate, **pīrāta, -ae** (m.).
pity, **misericordia, -ae** (f.).
place, **locus, -i** (m.).
plague, **pestilentia, -ae** (f.).
plan, **consilium, -i** (n.).
play, a, **fābula, -ae** (f.).
pleasant, **iūcundus, -a, -um; grātus, -a, -um.**
pleasure, **voluptās, -tātis** (f.); *with pleasure,* **libenter.**
plenty of, I have, **abundo,** 1 (Abl.).
plunder, I (*person*), **spolio,** 1; **dīripio, -ripere, -ripui, -reptum;** (*goods*), **spolio,** 1; (*land*), **vasto,** 1.
plunder, **praeda, -ae** (f.).
poet, **poēta, -ae** (m.).
poetry, **versūs** (pl.), **versuum** (m.).
Pompey, **Pompēius, -i** (m.); *the Pompeians,* **Pompēiāni, -orum** (m.); *of Pompey,* **Pompēiānus, -a, -um.**
poor (*wretched*), **miser, misera, miserum.**
possible, as many as, see under *as.*
post, I, **constituo, -ere, -stitui, -stitūtum; dispōno, -ere, -posui, -positum.**
posterity, **posteri, -orum** (m.).

power (*ability*), **potestās, -tātis** (f.); (*of state*), **imperium, -i** (n.); (*authority*), **potestās.**
praetor, **praetor, -tōris** (m.).
praise, I, **laudo,** 1.
praise, **laus, laudis** (f.); *I win praise,* **laudem habeo.**
prayers, **preces, -um** (f.).
prefer, I, **mālo, malle, mālui;** *I prefer one thing to another,* **antepōno, -ere, -posui, -positum,** with Acc. followed by Dat.
prepare, I, **paro,** 1.
present, I am, **adsum, -esse, -fui.**
pretend, I, **simulo,** 1.
pretext, **causa, -ae** (f.).
prevent, I, **impedio,** 4; **prohibeo,** 2.
prison, **carcer, carceris** (m.).
prisoner, **captīvus -i** (m.).
private, **prīvātus, -a, -um.**
promise, I, **prōmitto, -ere, -mīsi, -missum; polliceor, -ēri, pollicitus sum.**
proof, **documentum, -i** (n.) (Ch. 7).
provided that, **dummodo** (Ch. 17).
province, **prōvincia, -ae** (f.).
prudent, **prūdens,** Gen. **prūdentis.**
punish, I, **pūnio,** 4; (*judicially*), **multo,** 1.
punishment, **supplicium, -i** (n.).
purple, **purpura, -ae** (f.).
pursue, I, **persequor, -i, -secūtus sum.**
put in charge, I, see under *charge.*

put to death, I, see *kill.*

Quantity, numerus, -i (m.).

quickly, celeriter.

Rains, it, pluit, pluere, pluit or plūvit.

rampart, vallum, -i (n.).

rank, ordo, -dinis (m.); *to keep ranks,* ordines servāre.

rather, I would, mālo, malle, mālui.

rather, potius.

ravage, I, dīripio, -ripere, -ripui, -reptum; (*land*), populor, 1, Dep.

reach, I, pervenio, -īre, -vēni, -ventum, ad.

read, I, lego, -ere, lēgi, lectum.

ready, I get, paro, 1.

ready, parātus, -a, -um.

realize, I, intellego, -ere, -lexi, -lectum; sentio, -īre, sensi, sensum.

really, rēvērā.

reap (*fruits*), *I,* percipio, -cipere, -cēpi, -ceptum.

rearguard, novissimum agmen, novissimi agminis (n.).

reason, causa, -ae (f.); *reason why,* causa propter quam.

rebellion, sēditio, -ōnis (f.).

recall, I, revoco, 1.

receive, I, accipio, -cipere, -cēpi, -ceptum.

reconnoitre, I, explōro, 1.

recover, I (trans.), recipero, 1; (intrans.), mē recipio ex.

reflect, I, cōgito, 1.

refuse (*to*), *I,* nōlo, nolle, nōlui; *after a neg.,* recūso, 1; (*something to someone*), recūso, 1.

reinforcements, novae cōpiae (f.).

reject, I, repudio, 1.

rejoice, I, gaudeo, -ēre, gāvīsus sum.

relations, propinqui, -orum (m.).

remain (*stay*), maneo, -ēre, mansi, (mansūrus).

remaining, reliquus, -a, -um.

remarkable, singulāris, -e.

remedy, I, sāno, 1.

remove, I (trans.), aufero, -ferre, abstuli, ablātum; removeo, -ēre, -mōvi, -mōtum.

render thanks, I, grātias ago, -ere, ēgi, actum.

renew, I, redintegro, 1.

renown, glōria, -ae (f.).

repair, I, reficio, -ficere, -fēci, -fectum.

reply, I, respondeo, -ēre, -spondi, -sponsum.

republic, rēspublica, reīpublicae (f.).

resist, I, resisto, -ere, restiti (Dat.).

resolve, I, constituo, -ere, -stitui, -stitūtum.

resolved, I am, mihi placuit.

rest, I, requiesco, -ere, -quiēvi, -quiētum.

rest, the, reliqui, -ae, -a; cēteri, -ae, -a.

retire, I, mē recipio, -cipere, -cēpi, -ceptum.

retreat, I, pedem refero, -ferre, rettuli, relātum; mē recipio; regredior, -gredi, -gressus sum.

return, I (intrans.), regredior; redeo, -īre, -ii, -itum.

return for, in, prō (Abl.).

revolt, I, deficio, -ficere, -fēci, -fectum.

reward, praemium, -i (n.).

Rhine, the, Rhēnus, -i (m.).

rich, dīves, Gen. dīvitis.

ride, I, equito, 1; in equo vehor, vehi, vectus sum: (*in a litter*), vehor.

ring (*with sound*), *I,* percrepo, -āre, -crepui, -crepitum.

river, flūmen, flūminis (n.).

road, via, -ae (f.).

rob, I, spolio, 1.

rogue, use participle perditus.

Roman (Adj.), Rōmānus, -a, -um; *a Roman,* Rōmānus, -i (m.).

Rome, Rōma, -ae (f.).

roof, tectum, -i (n.).

rose-petals, use rosa, -ae (f.).

round (Prep.), circum (Acc.).

rouse, I, excito, 1.

rout, I, fugo, 1.

rout, fuga, -ae (f.).

row, I, rēmigo, -āre.

rule, I, rego, -ere, rexi, rectum.

rush, I, ruo, -ere, rui, (ruitūrus).

Safe, tūtus, -a, -um.

safety, salūs, salūtis (f.); *in safety,* use Adj.

said he (with actual words of speech), inquit.

sail, I, nāvigo, 1.

sail, I set, nāvem solvo, -ere, solvi, solūtum.

salvation of, I am the, salūti sum, with Dat.

same, īdem, eadem, idem; *the same as,* īdem qui or īdem āc (atque).

same time, at the, simul.

save, I, conservo, 1; *I save life,* vītam servo, 1.

say, I, dīco, -ere, dixi, dictum; (*report*), nuntio, 1; *I say that . . . not,* nego, 1; *they say* (*relate*), ferunt; *said he,* see *said.*

scale, I, ascendo, -ere, -scendi, -scensum.

scarcely, vix.

Scipio, Scīpio, -ōnis (m.).

scout, explōrātor, -tōris (m.); so also speculātor.

Scythians, the, Scythae, -arum (m.).

sea, mare, maris (n.).

second (*of two*), alter, altera, alterum.

secretly, clam.

see, I, video, -ēre, vīdi, vīsum; (*catch sight of*), conspicio, -spicere, -spexi, -spectum.

see to, I, cūro, 1 (Ch. 10).

see that (imperative), fac (Ch. 19).

seek, seek for, I, peto, -ere, petīvi, petītum; quaero, -ere, quaesīvi, quaesītum; *I seek out,* conquīro, -ere, -quīsīvi, -quīsītum.

seem, I, videor, -ēri, vīsus sum.
seize, I, occupo, 1; (*booty*), corripio, -ripere, -ripui, -reptum.
self, ipse, ipsa, ipsum.
senate, senātus, -us (m.).
senator, senātor, -tōris (m.).
send, I, mitto, -ere, mīsi, missum; (*back*), remitto; (*forward*), praemitto; (*out*), ēmitto.
send for, I, arcesso, -ere, arcessīvi, arcessītum.
sentry, vigil, vigilis (m.).
set free, I, lībero, 1.
set off, I, see *set out.*
set out (*for*), *I,* proficiscor, -i, profectus sum, in (Acc.).
set sail, I, nāvem solvo, -ere, solvi, solūtum.
set up (*tent*), *I,* colloco, 1.
setback, incommodum, -i (n.).
settler, colōnus, -i (m.).
seven, septem.
seventy, septuāgintā.
several, complūres, -ium.
severe, gravis, -e.
shamelessness, impudentia, -ae (f.).
ship, nāvis, nāvis (f.).
shirk, I, dētrecto, 1.
shoot forth, I, ēmitto, -ere, -mīsi, -missum.
shore, lītus, lītoris (n.).
short, brevis, -e.
short time before, a, paulo ante.
shout, I, clāmo, 1.
shout, shouting, clāmor, clāmōris (m.).
show (*demonstrate*), *I,* ostendo,

-ere, -tendi, -tensum or -tentum; (*a quality*), praesto, -stāre, -stiti, -stātum or -stitum.
show thanks, I, grātiam referre, -ferre, rettuli, relātum.
show, spectāculum, -i (n.).
shrink from, I, dētrecto, 1 (trans.).
shut off from, I, interclūdo, -ere, -clūsi, -clūsum, ab.
Sicilians, the, Siculi, -ōrum (m.).
side of, on this, cis, citrā (Acc.).
siege, obsidio, -ōnis (f.).
sight of, I catch, see under *catch.*
sign of, it is a, see Ch. 3.
signal, make signals, I, significo, 1.
signal, signum, -i (n.).
silent, I am, taceo, 2; sileo, -ēre, silui.
Simonides, Simōnidēs, -is (m.).
since (*because*), cum.
sink, I (trans.), submergo, -ere, -mersi, -mersum.
six, sex.
sixty, sexāgintā.
skill, sollertia, -ae (f.); *skill* (*in*), perītia, -ae (f.) (with Gen.).
skilled in, perītus, -a, -um, with Gen.
slaughter, caedēs, caedis (f.).
slave, servus, -i (m.).
sleep, I, dormio, 4.
slight, tenuis, -e.
small, exiguus, -a, -um.
small numbers, paucitās, -tātis (f.).

226   English-Latin Vocabulary

snow, nix, nivis (f.).
snows, it, ningit, ninxit.
so (thus), ita.
so (with Adj. and Advb.), tam;
(with Verbs), adeo.
so great, tantus, -a, -um.
so many, tot; so many . . . as,
tot . . . quot.
so much (of) . . . as, tantum with
Gen. . . . quantum.
so much (degree), tantum.
so often, toties.
so that (in final clauses), ut; so
that . . . not, nē.
Socrates, Sōcratēs, Sōcratis (m.).
solid, solidus, -a, -um.
soldier, mīles, mīlitis (c.).
Solon, Solōn, -ōnis (m.).
some, aliqui, aliqua, aliquod;
(amount), aliquid; some . . . ,
others . . . , alii . . . , alii . . . ;
there are some who, sunt qui
(Ch. 5).
someone (after nē), quis; (in
potential clause), quispiam.
sometimes, interdum.
son, fīlius, -i (m.); son of, sometimes nātus with Abl.
song, carmen, carminis (n.).
soon, mox; as soon as possible,
quam prīmum.
soon as, as, simul āc (atque).
Sophocles, Sophoclēs, Sophoclis
(m.).
sorry, I am (regret), mē paenitet,
-ēre, paenituit (Ch. 13).
sorry for, I am (pity), mē
miseret, -ēre, miseruit (Ch. 13).

sow, I, sero, -ere, sēvi, satum.
space, spatium, -i (n.).
Spain, Hispānia, -ae (f.).
spare, I, parco, -ere, peperci,
parsum (Dat.).
speak, loquor, -i, locūtus sum.
speech, ōrātio, -ōnis (f.); contio,
-ōnis (f.); I make a speech, ōr.
habeo, 2.
speed, celeritās, -tātis (f.).
spend time (in), I, tempus ago,
-ere, ēgi, actum, in (Abl.).
spirit, animus, -i (m.).
spite of, in, use concessive clause
(Ch. 23).
spring, vēr, vēris (n.).
stand in the way of, I, obsto,
-stāre, -stiti, -stātum (Dat.).
start (for), I, see set out (for).
state, cīvitās, -tātis (f.); the
Roman commonwealth, rēs-
publica, reīpublicae (f.).
statue, statua, -ae (f.); signum,
-i (n.).
stature, statūra, -ae (f.).
stay, I, maneo, -ēre, mansi,
mansum; I make a stay at a
place, commoror, 1, Dep.
still (of time), adhūc; (nevertheless), nihilōminus; tamen.
stone, saxum, -i (n.).
stone-quarries, lautumiae, -arum
(f.).
stop, I (trans.), dēterreo, 2;
impedio, 4.
stop, I (intrans.), dēsisto, -ere,
-stiti, -stitum (with infin.).
storm, I take by, expugno, 1.

storm, tempestās, -tātis (f.).

strength, vīres, vīrium (f.).

strictness, sevēritās, -tātis (f.).

strike camp, I, castra moveo, -ēre, mōvi, mōtum.

strike terror into, I, terrōrem infero, -ferre, -tuli, illātum or inlātum, with Dat.

stronghold, oppidum, -i (n.).

stuff, I, farcio, -īre, farsi, fartum.

successful, I am, rem bene gero, -ere, gessi, gestum.

such, tālis, -e; (so great), tantus, -a, -um.

such . . . as (so great . . . as), tantus . . . quantus.

sudden, subitus, -a, -um.

sue for, I, peto, -ere, petīvi, petītum.

suffer (disaster), I, accipio, -cipere, -cēpi, -ceptum.

sufficient, satis.

suggest, I, subicio, -icere, -iēci, -iectum.

suitable (for), idōneus, -a, -um (ad).

summer, aestās, -tātis (f.).

summon, I, arcesso, -ere, arcessīvi, arcessītum; (a council), convoco, 1.

sunset, sōlis occāsus, -us (m.).

superior, I am, supero, 1.

superior, superior, -ius.

surely . . . not? num?

surpass, I, supero, 1; anteeo, -īre, -ii.

surrender, I (intrans.), mē dēdo, -ere, -didi, -ditum.

survive, I, supersum, -esse, -fui (Dat.).

swear, I, iūro, 1.

sweet, dulcis, -e.

swim, I, no, nāre, nāvi; nato, 1.

Syracusans, the, Syrācūsāni, -orum (m.).

Syracuse, Syrācūsae, -arum (f.).

Table, mensa, -ae (f.).

take across, I, transporto, 1.

take away, I, aufero, -ferre, abstuli, ablātum.

take by storm, I, expugno, 1.

take part in, I, see under part.

take up (arms), I, capio, capere, cēpi, captum.

task, opus, operis (n.).

taut, intentus, -a, -um.

tear, lacrima, -ae (f.).

tell (inform), I, certiōrem facio.

tell (order), I, see order.

tell (narrate), I, narro, 1.

temple, templum, -i (n.).

tempt (fortune), I, perīclitor, 1, Dep.

ten, decem.

tent, tabernāculum, -i (n.).

term, condicio, -ōnis (f.).

terrify, I, terreo, 2.

territory, ager, agri (m.); fīnes, fīnium (also territories).

Thames, the, Tamesis, Tamesis (m.).

than, quam.

thank, I, grātias ago, -ere, ēgi, actum.

thanks, grātiae, -ārum (f.); *I show thanks*, grātiam refero, -ferre, rettuli, relātum.

that (demonstr. Pron. and Adj.), is, ea, id (unemphatic); *that* (*over there*), ille, illa, illud.

that (in consecutive clauses), ut; *that* . . . *not*, ut nōn; *in order that, so that* (in final clauses), ut; *in order that, so that* . . . *not*, nē; *that* (in indir. commands and petitions), ut; *that* . . . *not*, nē; *that* (after verb of *fearing*), nē; *that not*, nē nōn.

theft, furtum, -i (n.).

their, eorum, earum, eorum; *their own* (reflexive), suus, -a, -um.

Themistocles, Themistoclēs, Themistoclis (m.).

themselves (reflexive Pron.), sē.

then (*next*), deīnde; tum.

thence, inde.

there, ibi.

therefore, itaque (1st word); igitur (2nd word).

thing, rēs, reī (f.); *a thing which*, id quod.

think, I, puto, 1; existimo, 1; used parenthetically, ut mihi vidētur.

this, hīc, haec, hōc; (unemphatic), is, ea, id.

thither, eo, illūc.

though, quanquam; etsī; cum; quamvīs (Ch. 23).

three, trēs, tria.

threshing-floor, ārea, -ae (f.).

through, throughout, per (Acc.); (*on account of*), propter (Acc.).

throw, I, cōnicio, -icere, -iēci, -iectum; (*away*), abicio.

thus, ita.

till, I, colo, -ere, colui, cultum.

till (Conj.), dum (Ch. 15).

time, tempus, temporis (n.); *at the same time*, simul.

tired of, I am, mē taedet, -ēre, taeduit (Ch. 13).

tired, fessus, -a, -um.

title, nōmen, nōminis (n.).

to, ad (Acc.).

today, hodiē.

together, ūnā; *together with*, cum (Abl.).

toil, I, labōro, 1.

toil, labor, labōris (m.).

tomorrow, crās.

tongue, lingua, -ae (f.).

too (with Adj. or Advb.), use comparative.

too much (*of*), nimium or nimis (with Gen.).

torture, supplicium, -i (n.).

towards (*place*), ad (Acc.); sometimes Advb. versus is used after a place-name, e.g. Narbōnem versus.

town, oppidum, -i (n.).

track, vestīgium, -i (n.).

train, I, exerceo, 2.

Transalpine, Transalpīnus, -a, -um.

transport, I, transporto, 1.

travel about, I, concurso, -āre.

treachery, perfidia, -ae (f.).

treason, māiestās, -tātis (f.).

tree, arbor, arboris (f.).

trench, fossa, -ae (f.).

tribe, populus, -i (m.); gens, gentis (f.).

tribune, tribūnus, -i (m.).

trick, dolus, -i (m.).

Trinobantes, the, Trinobantes, -um (m.).

triumph, triumphus, -i (m.).

troops, cōpiae, -arum (f.); often, mīlites, -um (c.).

trophy, tropaeum, -i (n.).

trouble, malum, -i (n.); incommodum, -i (n.).

Troy, Trōia, -ae (f.).

true, vērus, -a, -um.

trust, fidēs, fidēi (f.).

try, I, cōnor, 1, Dep.

turns out that, it, ēvenit ut.

twelve, duodecim.

twenty, vīginti.

two, duo, duae, duo.

Tyre, Tyrus, -i (f.).

Unbecoming to, it is, dēdecet, -ēre, dēdecuit, with Acc.

uncle (on father's side), patruus, -i (m.).

under (rest), sub (Abl.).

undergo, I, subeo, -īre, -ii, -itum; patior, pati, passus sum.

understand, I, intellego, -ere, -lexi, -lectum.

undertake, I, suscipio, -cipere, -cēpi, -ceptum.

unknown, ignōtus, -a, -um.

unless, nisi.

unpunished, impūnītus, -a, -um.

until, dum (Ch. 15); with Noun, usque ad.

unwilling, I am, nōlo, nolle, nōlui.

unwilling, invītus, -a, -um.

upset, I, perturbo, 1.

urge, I, hortor, 1, Dep.

use, I, ūtor, -i, ūsus sum (Abl.).

use to, I am of, prōsum, prōdesse, prōfui, with Dat.

used to, I, use imperfect of soleo, -ēre, solitus sum, with infin.

useful, ūtilis, -e; *I am useful for,* ūsui sum, with Dat.

useless, inūtilis, -e.

utmost, summus, -a, -um.

utter, I, ēmitto, -ere, -mīsi, -missum.

utterly, omnīno.

Valour, virtūs, -tūtis (f.).

value, I, aestimo, 1.

Veientines, the, Vēientes, -ium (m.).

Veii, Vēii, -orum (m.).

vengeance, I take, ulciscor, -i, ultus sum.

Vercingetorix, Vercingetorix, -rigis (m.).

Verres, Verrēs, Verris (m.).

verse, versus, -uum (m. pl.).

very (Adj.), ipse, ipsa, ipsum.

victory, victōria, -ae (f.); *I win a victory,* vinco, -ere, vīci, victum.

village, vīcus, -i (m.).

voice, vox, vōcis (f.).

vote that, I, mīhi placet with Acc. and infin.

voyage, nāvigātio, -ōnis (f.); *I go on a voyage,* nāvigo, 1.

Wage war, I, bellum gero, -ere, gessi, gestum.

wait, I, maneo, -ēre, mansi, mansum.

wait for, I, exspecto, 1.

wall, mūrus, -i (m.).

wander, I, vagor, 1, Dep.

want, I, volo, velle, volui.

war, bellum, -i (n.); *I make war upon,* see under *make.*

warn, I, moneo, 2.

waste time, I, tempus tero, -ere, trīvi, trītum.

water, aqua, -ae (f.).

water-supply, aquātio, -ōnis (f.).

way (method), modus, -i (m.).

we, nōs.

weakness, infirmitās, -tātis (f.).

wealth, dīvitiae, -arum (f.); opes, -um (f.).

weapons, arma, -orum (n.).

weary (of), I am, mē taedet (Ch. 13).

weary, fessus, -a, -um.

weather, tempestās, -tātis (f.).

weight, pondus, ponderis (n.).

weight, I have, valeo, 2.

well, bene.

well, I keep, valeo, 2.

what (a thing which), id quod.

what? (interrog. Pron.), see under *who?*

what? (interrog. Adj.), qui, quae, quod?

whatever, see under *whoever.*

wheel, I, signa converto, -ere, -verti, -versum.

when, ubi; cum; *at the time when,* quo tempore.

when? quando?

whence, unde.

whenever, cum (Ch. 16).

where, ubi.

where? ubi?

where, from, unde.

whether . . . or not (in double indir. question), utrum . . . necne.

whether . . . or (in double conditional clause), sīve (seu) . . . sīve (seu); neg. nōn.

while, dum (Ch. 17).

who, which (rel. Pron.), qui, quae, quod.

who? what? (interrog. Pron.), quis? quid?

whoever, whatever, quicumque, quaecumque, quodcumque.

whole, tōtus, -a, -um.

why? cūr?

wide, lātus, -a, -um.

wife, coniux, -iugis (f.).

win, win a victory, I, vinco, -ere, vīci, victum; *I win praise,* laudem habeo, 2.

win over, I, concilio, 1.

wind, ventus, -i (m.).

wine, vīnum, -i (n.).

winter, hiems, hiemis (f.).

wisdom, sapientia, -ae (f.).

wise, sapiens, Gen. sapientis;
(sensible), prūdens, Gen. prūdentis.
wish, I, volo, velle, volui; *I do not
wish,* nōlo, nolle, nōlui.
with (in company), cum (Abl.).
within (time), Abl.
without, sine (Abl.) (see also Ch.
25).
witness, testis, testis (c.).
woman, fēmina, -ae (f.); mulier,
mulieris (f.).
wonderful, mīrus, -a, -um.
wont, I am, soleo, -ēre, solitus
sum.
wood, silva, -ae (f.).
word, verbum, -i (n.).
work (toil, labor, labōris (m.);
(task), opus, operis (n.).
world, orbis (Gen. orbis) terrarum (m.); *all the world knows*
(see Ch. 25).
worship, I, colo, -ere, colui,
cultum.

worst (extreme), extrēmus, -a,
-um.
worthy of, dignus, -a, -um, with
Abl.
would that, utinam (Ch. 19).
wound, I, vulnero, 1.
wretched, miser, misera, miserum.
write (to), I, scrībo, -ere, scripsi,
scriptum, (ad).
wrong, iniūria, -ae (f.).

Year, annus, -i (m.).
year's, annuus, -a, -um.
yesterday, herī.
yet, tamen (2nd word); nihilōminus.
yet, not, nōndum.
you (s.), tū; (pl.), vōs.
young man, iuvenis, iuvenis
(m.).
younger, nātu minor.
your (s.), tuus, -a, -um; (pl.),
vester, vestra, vestrum.
youth, iuventūs, -tūtis (f.).